LANGUAGE FROM THE BODY

Iconicity and Metaphor in American Sign Language

What is the role of meaning in linguistic theory? Generative linguists have severely limited the influence of meaning, claiming that language is not affected by other cognitive processes and that semantics does not influence linguistic form. Conversely, cognitivist and functionalist linguists believe that meaning pervades and motivates all levels of linguistic structure. This dispute can now be resolved conclusively by evidence from signed languages. Signed languages are full of iconic linguistic items: words, inflections, and even syntactic constructions with structural similarities between their physical form and their referents' form. Iconic items can have concrete meanings and also abstract meanings through conceptual metaphors. *Language from the Body* relates iconicity and metaphor in a cognitivist framework, shows how iconic and metaphorical items are central to normal language use, and demonstrates that these items can only be understood properly through a cognitivist or related approach in which meaning can influence form.

Sarah F. Taub is Assistant Professor in the Department of ASL, Linguistics, and Interpretation at Gallaudet University.

LANGUAGE FROM THE BODY

Iconicity and Metaphor in American Sign Language

SARAH F. TAUB

Gallaudet University

CAMBRIDGE
UNIVERSITY PRESS

MW

PUBLISHED BY THE PRESS SYNDICATE OF THE UNIVERSITY OF CAMBRIDGE
The Pitt Building, Trumpington Street, Cambridge, United Kingdom

CAMBRIDGE UNIVERSITY PRESS
The Edinburgh Building, Cambridge CB2 2RU, UK
40 West 20th Street, New York, NY 10011-4211, USA
10 Stamford Road, Oakleigh, Melbourne 3166, Australia
Ruiz de Alarcón 13, 28014 Madrid, Spain
Dock House, The Waterfront, Cape Town 8001, South Africa

http://www.cambridge.org

First published 2001

Printed in the United States of America

Typeface Sabon 10/12.5 pt   *System* QuarkXPress™   [HT]

A catalog record for this book is available from the British Library

Library of Congress Cataloging-in-Publication Data
Taub, Sarah F., 1968–
Language from the body: iconicity and metaphor in American Sign Language /
Sarah F. Taub. p. cm.
Includes bibliographical references.
ISBN 0 521 77062 9
1. American Sign Language. 2. Iconicity (Linguistics) 3. Metaphor.
HV2474.T38   2001
419–dc21
00-040345

ISBN 0 521 77062 9 hardback

8 \18\03

If your mind
is not projected
into your hands
even 10,000 techniques
will be useless.

– Yamaoka Tesshu

Contents

List of Figures

Acknowledgments

Just as it takes a village to raise a child, it also takes a village to bring a book to completion. I thank those who have supported me both during the writing of this book in Berkeley, California, and during its revision in Washington, DC.

I am deeply grateful to Eve Sweetser for reading and commenting on many drafts and providing crucial academic and professional guidance. George Lakoff introduced me to cognitive linguistics and during the writing process gave me many invaluable theoretical and stylistic suggestions. Dan Slobin also read drafts and worked with me to rebuild the San Francisco Bay Area sign linguistics community.

Many of my colleagues have generously given their time in discussing these ideas with me. I would like to thank Jean Ann, Norine Berenz, Alan Cienki, Linda Coleman, Karen Emmorey, Gilles Fauconnier, Susan Fischer, Nancy Frishberg, Dedre Gentner, Ron Langacker, David McNeill, Susan Rutherford, Mark Turner, Ronnie Wilbur, Phyllis Wilcox, Sherman Wilcox, and three anonymous reviewers for Cambridge University Press. A special thanks goes to my fellow graduate students at Berkeley, the University of California, for hours of theoretical and personal discussions: Joe Grady, Chris Johnson, Pamela Morgan, and Kevin Moore in Linguistics and Reyna Lindert in Psychology. Likewise, I thank my colleagues at Gallaudet University for collegial and theoretical support, particularly Dennis Galvan, Scott Liddell, Ceil Lucas, and Mike Kemp, and my students Paul Dudis and Yuko Ogawa for their excitement and new ideas.

I am especially grateful to Tim Gough, who spent many hours answering my questions about American Sign Language (ASL) metaphors and who modeled signs in literally hundreds of photographs for the illustrations in this book; and to Sherry Hicks, who also modeled signs for my illustrations. Words cannot express my gratitude to Ella Mae Lentz, who taught me ASL, introduced me to the Deaf community, and supported my work on metaphor in many ways, not least by letting me analyze, quote, and translate her poetry. I also thank Cheri Smith and Ken Mikos, Ella's coworkers at Vista Community College and In Motion Press, for first-rate ASL instruction and for permission to work with Ella's poetry.

My friends and family have provided crucial support through the ups and downs of research and writing. I wish to thank Paul Rogers, who first showed me ASL, and Sharon Minsuk, Tim Salisbury, Andrew Hoerner, Loraine Hutchins, Liz Emmett-Mattox, and Greg Grass. Finally, deep thanks to my parents, Sonia and Lewis Taub, who taught me that there are no limits on what I can achieve, and whose love and generosity have never failed me.

CHAPTER ONE

A Glimpse of the Material

THE ABUNDANCE OF VISUAL IMAGERY IN AMERICAN SIGN LANGUAGE

Imagine that you are taking part in a conversation using American Sign Language (ASL), the language of the American Deaf community.[1] You are about to see an integration of visual imagery with linguistic structure on a scale that no spoken language can equal.

The signer is telling you about her kitchen. She sketches the four walls in space, then quickly identifies the appliances and furnishings. As she names each one – refrigerator, sink, cabinets, and so on – she places it within the sketched outline of the kitchen, punctuating each placement with a special head nod. Before long, a virtual map of the room floats in the space between you.

Now the signer is describing a conversation she had with her six-year-old son. She names her son and points to a spot on her right. Her body shifts to face rightward and her signing angles down toward where a six-year-old's face and body would be, as she reports how she asked her son to get her a towel; then her body shifts to face upward to the left as she gives his assent. The relative heights and locations of the signer and her son are clear to your mind's eye.

The woman goes on to describe how her son ran about the house to find the towel. Her index finger is extended upward from her fist, and she traces a complex path through the air with that handshape. The

---

[1] I follow the usual convention of using *Deaf* as a cultural label and *deaf* as an audiological label; that is, *Deaf* people participate in the community and culture of Deafness (which has its own folklore, customs, and language; cf. Lane et al. 1996), whereas *deaf* people are those with a severe hearing loss, regardless of whether they participate in mainstream or Deaf culture.

twists and turns of her hand sketch out for you the path her son took around the house: rapid and somewhat random.

Later, she is explaining to you how hard it can be to get the child to understand what she wants. Once again she uses the straight index-finger handshape; it moves from her temple toward her son's "spot" on her right, hits the palm of her other hand, and bounces off. (An English speaker might have said, "I can't get through to him.") Eventually, the son understands; now the finger moves from temple to hand and penetrates between the index and middle fingers. You can see the woman's thoughts metaphorically portrayed as objects traveling from her head to her son through a barrier.

All of these features of the conversation are perfectly normal, conventional features of ASL. They are not mime or playacting; you will find each one in standard ASL textbooks and dictionaries. But like mime, they contain vivid visual representations of physical forms. These signs and grammatical features bear a striking resemblance to the things they represent: they are *iconic* forms. (The fourth example is more complex; as we shall see, it is metaphorical as well as iconic, a fact with interesting implications.) This book investigates the impressive variety of iconic and metaphorical forms in signed languages, compares them to their tamer counterparts in spoken languages, and explores the implications for linguistic theory.

THE SIGN IS NOT ALWAYS ARBITRARY

Why should we care about iconic and metaphorical types of signing – other than their intrinsic beauty, of course? One answer is because they tell us a great deal about the nature of language itself.

For a long time, the doctrine of the "arbitrariness of the sign," attributed to de Saussure (1983 [1915]), has held sway in linguistics. A *lack* of connection between a word's form and its meaning has been seen as the highest property of language, the thing that raises humans above beasts. Any creature, this reasoning goes, could imitate a dog's bark and use that sound to mean *dog*; any creature can growl when angry and yip when frightened; humans alone have detached these sounds from immediate, intuitive associations and fashioned an elegant system of symbols from them. These symbolic forms, no longer restricted by the need to physically resemble their referents, are what allow us to talk about everything from amnesia to ethics.

According to this view, iconic forms are limited to playacting, imitations, and the rare onomatopoeic word, and their meanings can never be sophisticated or abstract in any way. As Liddell (1992) noted, and as we shall see in the next sections, this view is completely mistaken. Unfortunately, the intense prejudice against iconic forms led to prejudice against signed languages. People claimed for many years (some still do) on the basis of the iconic aspects of signed languages that they were merely mime, playacting, imitations – not true languages at all, and incapable of expressing abstract concepts (e.g., Greene 1975, cited in Lane 1992). This is wholly untrue, as linguists from Stokoe (1960) onward have shown. Nevertheless, part of the enterprise of proving ASL to be a language has focused on minimizing and discounting its iconicity to make it seem more like "true" languages – that is, supposedly arbitrary spoken languages (e.g., Hoemann 1975, Klima & Bellugi 1979; cf. McDonald 1982).

This enterprise, though understandable, is misguided. The relative scarceness of iconicity in spoken language is not a virtue – it is merely a consequence of the fact that most phenomena do not have a characteristic noise to be used in motivating a linguistic form (cf. Armstrong 1983, Stokoe 1986, Liddell 1992). In particular, three-dimensional spatial relationships, so crucial to language in many ways (e.g., Johnson 1987; Lakoff 1987; Langacker 1987; Regier 1996; Talmy 1985a, 1985b) cannot be represented iconically using the one-dimensional sequential medium of sound.[2] Even so, researchers are now finding (Haiman 1985a; Hinton, Nichols, & Ohala 1994) that iconicity is common enough to be of serious interest in the spoken languages of the world; if sound were not so limited in what it can iconically represent, they would no doubt have even more iconicity. Signed languages, created in space with the signer's body and perceived visually, have incredible potential for iconic expression of a broad range of basic conceptual structures (e.g., shapes, movements, locations, human actions), and this potential is fully realized.

METAPHOR LETS ICONIC SIGNS HAVE ABSTRACT MEANINGS

An exciting development in signed language research is the emerging recognition (e.g., Brennan 1990; Grushkin 1998; Holtemann 1990; Moy 1988; Taub 1997, 1998; Wilbur 1987; Wilcox 1993, 2000) of signs that combine metaphor and iconicity. *Conceptual metaphor* is the consistent use of one basic conceptual area to describe another, perhaps less self-evident area. For example, English consistently uses language about

---

[2] We can speculate on what spoken language might be like if, like dolphins, we had highly developed abilities to localize objects in space using sound, and if we could create sound patterns that appeared to be coming from specific locations. In such a species, sound-based language might be highly iconic in unexpected ways.

throwing and catching objects to describe communication of ideas (e.g., "I couldn't catch what you said"; "We were tossing ideas back and forth"; "It went over my head").

It has been argued (e.g., Lakoff 1992, Lakoff & Johnson 1980, Lakoff & Turner 1989) that these patterns of metaphorical language reflect how we think about abstract concepts: Because we have no direct sensory contact with ideas and their communication, we reason and talk about them on the basis of what we know about throwing and catching objects – a directly perceived activity that is easily accessible to other people. It is easy to believe that we share knowledge, and can thus share language, about an event like catching a ball, but it is harder to develop similar shared terminology about a communicated and understood idea. Because the two activities are analogous in certain ways, it makes sense that the concrete one is used to talk about the nonphysical one.

A great many ASL signs for abstract concepts – emotions, ideas, personal interactions, and so on – incorporate a visual image of a concrete thing or activity. For example, the signs described in the introduction to this chapter, roughly glossed as THINK–BOUNCE and THINK–PENETRATE (see Figs. 6.1 and 6.5), give a visual depiction of communication as objects moving from one person to another.[3] Anger can be shown as fire in the abdomen or as explosions; affection can be shown as closeness of articulators; authority can be shown as height, to name only a few other examples.

Not only do these signs demonstrate that metaphor exists in ASL, but they also shed light on the innumerable twists and turns and connections within the ASL user's conceptual system. A vast array of concepts are linked by metaphor to concrete concepts; a great deal of meaning can therefore be expressed by visual images of concrete objects and actions. Metaphorical signs can be taken as evidence for conceptual connections between pairs of domains of thought.

---

[3] There is no standard writing system for ASL, and the proposed writing systems use various combinations of symbols that are not part of the regular alphanumeric set. For convenience in writing, and to keep articles on signed languages accessible to the nonspecialist, many sign linguists use *glosses* to represent signs. The convention is to choose a word of the relevant spoken language to represent the sign in question; the word should have roughly the same meaning as the sign. Glosses are written in capital letters; various additional diacritics have been developed to handle grammatical features of the signed language. The conventions used in this text are outlined in Appendix 1.

Though certain choices of English words for ASL signs have become fairly conventional, there is no standard "glossing dictionary" for ASL; thus, it can be difficult to recognize a sign from its gloss. Moreover, the semantic match between the gloss and the sign can be quite poor. For this reason, for all my crucial examples (and wherever else space permits) I have presented a photographic illustration and a semantic description of the sign along with the gloss.

CONCEPTUAL MAPPINGS EXPLAIN ICONICITY AND METAPHOR

Recent years have brought a groundswell of interest in and research on iconicity and metaphor. This book unifies these developments with an approach based on *conceptual mappings*: sets of correspondences between domains of thought and linguistic forms. Each domain or form has some structure (e.g., scenario, participants, shapes, movements), and we can link parts of the structure of one domain to the structure of another. For example, one of ASL's iconic mappings is shown in Figure 3.3: A pair of fingers iconically represents a pair of human legs. The fingers have a structure consisting of two long, thin objects connected at the top; the same is true for the legs. The mapping between the two images links the left finger with the left leg, the right finger with the right leg, and the connection at the hand with the connection at the hips.

For a metaphorical example (given in detail in Chapter Six), consider again the communication examples mentioned above. These examples show us precisely how the domains of *communicating ideas* and *throwing objects* are linked for English speakers: The *idea* corresponds to the *object*; *telling* or *explaining* the idea corresponds to *throwing* the object to someone; and *understanding* the idea corresponds to *catching* the object. Once again, relevant pieces of one domain are "mapped" (to borrow a term from mathematics) onto relevant pieces of the other domain.

These mappings are not random; we do not, for example, map the right fingertip onto the left knee joint or map the process of explaining onto the tossed object. Instead, the mappings used in iconicity and metaphor preserve the part/whole structure of each domain or form. Thus, in iconicity, the parts of the referent are represented by analogous parts of the linguistic form; and in metaphor, on the whole, participants are mapped to participants, relationships are mapped to relationships, and processes are mapped to processes.

As we shall see, mappings give a precise and pithy explanation of how iconic linguistic items can exist and why linguistic metaphors come in groups with consistent patterns. The most popular current linguistic theories, however, have no room to accommodate conceptual mapping in language.

MAPPINGS AND LINGUISTIC THEORY

The most widely accepted linguistic theories are *formalist*, as opposed to *cognitivist* (see also Chapter Two): They treat language as a set of arbitrary symbols that are manipulated according to rules or constraints, arranged in allowable patterns, and assigned meaning by some interpretation mechanism. These theories usually divide language up into a number of components such as the *lexicon* or word list, the *phonology* or acceptable physical forms, the *syntax* or rules for arranging words in acceptable orders, and the *semantics* or rules for assigning meaning to sentences. Components are seen as *autonomous*; that is, rules for one component do not affect any of the others.

Such a model has no mechanism whereby the semantic component can influence the physical forms of language. It is thus not capable of handling the intimate form–meaning connection in iconic words, signs, and grammatical inflections, nor can it handle other forms of motivation such as metaphor. Cognitivist models of language, on the other hand, are particularly apt for describing networks of conceptual connections and their influence on linguistic forms.

Because iconicity and metaphor pervade signed languages and are not rare in spoken languages, I argue (Chapter Eleven) that an accurate theory of language requires a cognitivist approach or, at the very least, some type of approach that can handle conceptual structure and its impact on language.

A PREVIEW OF THE BOOK

The rest of this book illustrates and expands on the themes that I have brought up here. Chapter Two gives an introduction to the issue of motivation in language and provides some background material on cognitive linguistics. Chapter Three goes in detail through a few examples of linguistic iconicity and outlines the progress of thought on how iconicity functions in ASL. In Chapter Four, I present a theoretical treatment of iconicity, the Analogue-Building Model. Finally, Chapter Five provides a comprehensive survey of types of iconicity in signed and spoken languages.

In Chapter Six, we begin to discuss metaphor. There I give examples of ASL metaphors (and English ones, for comparison) and show how to describe them using mappings; we will see how metaphor and iconicity are linked in signed languages. Chapter Seven demonstrates how different aspects of a single sign can be motivated by different metaphorical and iconic mappings. Chapter Eight looks at four ASL metaphors that all draw on a single concrete domain: the vertical scale. In Chapter Nine, I show how metaphor and iconicity are intertwined with the grammar of ASL, and in particular, ASL's spatial system of verb agreement.

Chapter Ten applies the insights of the previous chapters to an ASL text: "The Treasure," a poem by Ella Mae Lentz. We will see how the poet blends several conventional metaphors involving the vertical scale to produce a novel and powerful framing of the struggle to get ASL recognized as a true language.

Finally, the last chapter outlines the implications of this line of inquiry for linguistic theory. Chapter Eleven suggests that metaphor and iconicity account for the remarkable degree of shared grammatical structures in the world's signed languages. Given the omnipresence of metaphor and iconicity in signed languages, and their substantial presence in spoken languages, there is no doubt that linguistic theories must be able to handle them. Theories that cannot accommodate these processes will not be successful in explaining and describing the human language capacity.

CHAPTER TWO

Motivation and Linguistic Theory

ARBITRARY, PREDICTABLE ... OR *MOTIVATED?*

Let us look at the impact that metaphor and iconicity have on linguistic theory.

As we have seen, iconic linguistic items are related to their meanings through physical resemblance. We should note, however, that there are many different possible iconic representations of a single visual or auditory image; for example, one could represent different parts of the image, use different scales or perspectives, or preserve different levels of detail. As Klima and Bellugi (1979) observed, the signs meaning *tree* in ASL, Danish Sign Language, and Chinese Sign Language are all equally iconic but different in form: in ASL TREE (see Fig. 3.1), the hands and forearms are positioned to resemble a tree growing out of the ground; the Danish equivalent uses the hands to trace the outline of a tree's branches and trunk, top to bottom; and the Chinese sign meaning *tree* uses two curved hands to trace the outline of a tree trunk, from the ground up.

Clearly, the meaning *tree* and the associated visual image do not *determine* the signs' forms, as they are all different – but neither are the forms unrelated to the meaning. Instead, the forms all bear different types of physical resemblance to the image of a tree. The nature of these forms, given their meaning, is neither arbitrary nor predictable but rather *motivated.*[1]

---

[1] ASL does have a system for iconic "representative elements," which are discussed later in detail: the classifier system (see Chapters Three and Five). Within that system, the choice of element for a particular referent and perspective (e.g., a V handshape for a "two-legged" human) is completely determined (that is, signers have a fixed set of choices within that system). My point here is that the system itself is motivated but not determined by the actual shapes of the referents.

8

In using the term *motivation,* I intend that two conditions be met: that one can observe a *tendency* rather than a strict rule, and that one can attribute the tendency to some *reason* external to the linguistic system. If there is no general tendency, only a single example, then any number of stories could be told about that example – it could easily be due to chance or to some unusual and idiosyncratic circumstances that would not shed light on other linguistic phenomena; scientific linguists would not wish to base their theories on these cases. But once a pattern exists, one can certainly look for common factors that might cause the pattern: In my data, these might consist of conceptual metaphors, iconicity or physical resemblance, conceptual associations, and so on.

It is actually quite common for linguistic phenomena to be motivated rather than strictly predictable. Spoken language has less iconicity than signed language, but it exhibits many other kinds of motivation in its patterns of form and meaning. For example, individual word roots are usually not iconic (e.g., there is nothing about the form *dog* to motivate its connection to the meaning "dog"), but their extensions to new meanings, on the whole, are motivated by natural human processes of conceptual association. To continue the example, once the form *dog* has taken on the meaning "dog," there are perfectly good reasons why it is extended to uses like *dogged persistence*: We believe that dogs are patient and persistent, and it is natural and common to use a creature's name to describe an associated characteristic. Nevertheless, we could not have said with certainty that any term meaning "dog" would take on that new meaning. The original form–meaning connection is arbitrary, but the extension to a new meaning is motivated.

As a second example, consider the English word *back*. The original meaning (ca. 1000 A.D.) was "the outer surface of a vertebrate that is nearest to the spine." After a few hundred years, the word began developing meanings such as "the area behind a person or object," prepositional uses such as *in back of the house*, adverbial uses meaning such things as "returning along the same path previously traveled," and verbal uses such as *to back up*. It even came to refer to earlier times, as in *We can't go back to 1900 and change what was done*. All of these extended meanings are motivated. There are good reasons for each extension: The spinal area of a human being is *behind* that person and thus associated with the area behind that person and with the path that the person has traveled to reach a current location; there is a common metaphor where the past is referred to as being behind us. Moreover, English (and other languages) uses these same kinds of extension over and over (cf. *side, front, head*).

It should be noted that de Saussure (1983 [1915]) used the word *motivation* in a slightly different sense. In all the cases mentioned above, the motivating factor is external to the linguistic system; de Saussure, on the other hand, noted that at times the linguistic system itself can provide powerful motivation for the formation of new items. For example, if a new count noun *brin* were coined, the plural of this noun, *brins*, would be built on the model of myriad other English plurals such as *tins*, *fins*, and *pens*. The existence of a regular pattern for combining morphemes motivates the creation of new meaningful items based on that pattern. This type of motivation is also called *analogy*. Language-internal analogical motivation is a cognitive process that most likely can be shown to emerge from interconnections in neural network structures (cf. Elman et al. 1997); nevertheless, it is not the focus of our discussion. This book will continue to use *motivation* to refer to language-external forces that can influence the nature of linguistic items.

As can be seen, spoken languages are highly motivated. Signed languages use the same kinds of conceptual motivations that spoken languages do – for example, association and metaphor. The main difference is that in addition, many or most basic word roots and inflections are iconically motivated.

THE GOALS OF LINGUISTIC THEORY

If these processes are not completely predictable, should a linguist even be bothering with them? Shouldn't linguists restrict themselves to describing the predictable, rule-governed parts of language? As will be shown, there is a difference of opinion on this matter.

Language and human communication is such a complex area that it is hard to know how to begin studying it. Language is deeply interwoven with our experiences of the world: Our social interactions, our cultural institutions, even our thoughts, are often framed and mediated by language. The structure of language is not easy to discern; there are patterns at many levels, and the boundaries between levels are not clear. In a sea of complex interacting phenomena, where can a scientific inquiry start?

Chomsky (e.g., 1957, 1965, 1981) pioneered an approach to this problem that has dominated the field ever since. The proper area of a linguist's inquiry, he said, is the language user's knowledge of the structures of his or her language. This knowledge consists of a grammar of the language, and the grammar can be modeled as if it were a system of exceptionless rules. Language is to be treated as completely separate from other human cognitive abilities; no factors from outside the linguistic system can affect the rules of that system.[2] Moreover, language is divided into several components: the *lexicon* (or word list), the *phonology* (or smallest meaningless elements), the *syntax* (or ordering of words), and the *semantics* (or meanings), and each component itself is considered to be autonomous from the others.

The effect of this set of assumptions was monumental. Linguists were freed to look at each aspect of a language separately, without having first to understand how all the aspects fitted together. Moreover, they were handed a powerful modeling tool with which to describe each aspect. At last, the problem of language seemed tractable; decades of intense modeling efforts, based on Chomsky's assumptions (which I will call the *formalist* approach to language), ensued.

Chomsky's approach is a typical one in the physical sciences: If a system is too complex to understand, break it down into parts and try to understand each part. The hope is that once each part is understood, the pieces can be put back together to yield an understanding of the whole. It is a powerful strategy, and physicists have successfully modeled many complex systems using it; yet it has limits. It works only when the parts of the system are truly independent enough that they can be understood on their own.

The danger of this "piecewise" approach is that if the autonomy assumptions are not well founded, they can lead to models in which the true explanation of a phenomenon is not allowed to figure in the rules describing that phenomenon. These models are descriptively accurate, to be sure, but they simply reproduce by fiat what a truly explanatory theory would attribute to external causes. This, many argue, has been happening in linguistics.

As a case in point, Ohala (1983) found that many types of sound change in spoken languages could be explained by perceptual similarities of the sounds involved. For example, in many languages, /kw/ becomes /p/, but not vice versa (e.g., Proto-Indo-European **ekwos* became Greek *hippos* "horse"). Ohala noted that the two sounds are extremely similar in their acoustics, with /kw/ possessing an extra set of frequencies that /p/ lacks. If noise happens to interfere with those frequencies, then /kw/ can easily be mistaken for /p/. But the reverse error, where /p/ would be misheard as having /kw/'s extra frequencies, is quite unlikely (as Winitz et al. 1972 [cited in Ohala 1983] demonstrated in

---

[2] The end product of the system can be constrained by factors such as memory load; for example, humans cannot use sentences with three or more levels of embedded clauses, because such sentences are too complex to process. But the grammatical rule systems themselves cannot be structured by such considerations.

the laboratory). Children making these errors would incorporate the "incorrect" /p/'s into their vocabularies, eventually causing a /kw/ to /p/ sound change. In a theory where the phonology is strictly autonomous, this change could only be stipulated by rule; yet human perceptual errors plus the sounds' properties easily explain this sound change and its direction.

This and other examples of semantic and perceptual motivations suggest that language is not in fact autonomous from the rest of human cognition. Unfortunately, the autonomy claims that justify the formalist school's approach have been elevated to the status of doctrine. Rather than being seen as a set of simplifying assumptions that are intended to help tame a complex system, they are now taken as truths about the nature of language. Linguists routinely argue (e.g., Bickerton 1981, 1984) that language is a completely self-contained system, with genetically preprogrammed modules that interact with each other and other cognitive processes only through well-defined interfaces.

The years of work based on assuming the autonomy of language and its components have not been wasted; our understanding of many complicated linguistic structures has advanced a great deal. But it is time to take the evidence seriously and to build theories that treat the complex interconnections of language, perception, and cognition.

Another difficulty of rule-based linguistic theories is the assumption that these rules should have no exceptions. But this leaves no room for the vast range of linguistic phenomena that are motivated: not fully predictable, yet far from random. As we noted above, a linguist could not have *guaranteed* that a word like *back* would take on the meaning "the area behind something" – yet given the frequency with which body-part terms become prepositions in the languages of the world, and the conceptual association between the body part and the area near it, the linguist certainly would not have been surprised. There must be a place in linguistic theory for consistent, less-than-predictable tendencies that happen because of clearly describable reasons.

A number of linguistic schools of thought have moved away from treating language as a self-contained, rule-based formal system and are looking for external explanations for linguistic phenomena. One group is the *experimental phonologists* (e.g., Kingston & Beckman 1990; Ohala 1983, 1990; Ohala & Jaeger 1986), who work on the sound component of spoken languages. They look for explanations of sound patterns in the characteristics of the human vocal and auditory systems, plus the acoustics of the sounds themselves. Another group is the *functional linguists* (e.g., DeLancey 1981; Givon 1979, 1984; Hopper & Thompson 1980, 1985). They seek to understand language by looking at the functions that it serves in communication; thus, they are concerned with motivations for both the form and the meanings or uses of linguistic items.

A third group is the *cognitive linguists,* who try to describe linguistic phenomena in ways that are consistent with (and motivated by) what is known about the human cognitive apparatus. This book is written in the cognitivist framework, and so I will spend some time discussing its assumptions and procedures.

COGNITIVE LINGUISTICS

The aim of cognitive linguistics is to build a theory of language that is consistent with current knowledge about the mind and the brain. Cognitive linguists draw on results from cognitive psychology and neuroscience on memory, attention, categorization, sensory perception, and the neural underpinnings of thought. Rather than inventing a new kind of rule-system for every aspect of language, we try to build our theories using the kinds of processes that are known to occur in other areas of cognitive functioning. This leads to a number of differences between cognitivist theories and formalist theories.

First of all, language is not assumed to be autonomous from other cognitive functions. Of course, there will be language-specific structures (dealing with, e.g., the language's word ordering), but they will be the same *kind* of structures that one sees in other parts of the mind. For example, Langacker (1987, 1991a, 1991b) uses general cognitive functions such as *figure/ground* structure, *scanning, viewpoint,* and *schematization* in his theory of language.

This assumption, it should be noted, leads to a different notion of theoretical economy. All scientists want their theories to be as simple as possible while still explaining the data. The formalist notion of simplicity is (roughly speaking) to have as few formal rules and exceptions to the rules as possible. Simplicity is calculated for each component, however, and different components can have completely different kinds of rules. Cognitivists, on the other hand, think that an economical theory is one that uses processes that are known to be part of mental functioning; we prefer not to create new types of rules for language and its substructures.

Just as language is not assumed to be autonomous from general cognition, the pieces of language are not seen as autonomous from each other. First of all, *meaning* is not separated off from *form.* Of course it is possible to consider the form patterns of a language (e.g., what sounds a spoken language allows) and the meaning patterns of a language (e.g., how many color distinctions it makes) separately from each other; these constitute the phonology and semantics of cognitivist theories. But there is no autonomous syntax, where forms are arranged into patterns without regard to their meaning. All linguistic items, even syntactic structures, are considered to be meaningful (even if only in a schematic way). Meaning is a primary determiner of how linguistic items are fitted together to create larger structures.

Second, most cognitivist theories make no ironclad distinction between *lexical* items, *morphological* items, and *syntactic* items.[3] That is, words, inflections, word orderings, and so on are all seen as form–meaning pairs. For formalist theories, the lexicon is the repository of all "exceptions," things that must be stipulated; it should be possible to generate everything else by rule. For cognitivist theories, *every* conventional item in the language, be it a word, an inflection, an idiom, or a clause structure, is remembered separately, along with the generalizations that link items.[4] This makes it easy to accommodate tendencies and partial generalizations such as the ones discussed in the first section of this chapter. Cognitive linguists are not much concerned with "redundancy" in our theories. It is known that the brain has immense memory capability; there is room for exceptions and generalizations at all levels of structure.

Indeed, recent examinations of child language acquisition (Tomasello 1999) suggest that children proceed by treating each linguistic item they learn as a unique individual. They memorize how that particular item can combine with other items, and only much later do they create generalizations over items that could be formalized as rules. This process, taken together with what is known about self-organization in neural architectures, suggests that children are not deducing rules or setting parameters; rather, the generalizations "emerge" from masses of individual examples.

In the same vein, there are no rules or derivations in cognitive linguistics. Complex structures (e.g., clauses, sentences, inflected words) are of course formed from combinations of simpler structures, but there is no assumption that this is done as a sequence of steps. Instead, cognitivist theories allow these combinations to occur "all at once." Linguistic items have slots or "elaboration sites" (Langacker 1987) where they can incorporate or combine with other items (e.g., verbs have slots for their main participants); this combination process can be based on form, on

---

3 De Saussure, it should be noted, also took this position.
4 It is not that the word as such has no status in cognitive linguistics. Rather, there is no radical difference between syntax and morphology; patterns at both levels, though different in their specifics, are expected to be similar in kind.

meaning, or on both. This theoretical stance is motivated by the fact that the time-depth of language processing is extremely short, on the order of 500 milliseconds or 100 neural "steps": There is no time for lengthy derivations (Rumelhart, McClelland, & the PDP Research Group, 1986).

The lack of derivations also means that cognitivist theories don't name one structure as "primary" and others as "derived" from it (e.g., passive sentences as derived from active sentences). Both structures are formed in the same way, by combination of simpler linguistic items.

Another important precept of cognitive linguistics has to do with the nature of linguistic categories (i.e., forms, such as English phonemes; meanings, such as the concept "green"; and form–meaning pairs, such as the word *dog*, the "subject – predicate" sentence structure, or the syntactic class "verb"). Linguistic categories are categories of human cognition and display all the same characteristics.

We know a lot about the nature of human categories; they are not like the categories of logic, strictly bounded with necessary and sufficient conditions for membership. Instead, their boundaries can be fuzzy and they show prototype structure (see, e.g., Rosch 1977, 1981; Rosch & Mervis 1975): There are better and worse members of the category. This structuring shows up in a number of psycholinguistic tests devised by Rosch and her associates.

To illustrate the notion of prototypes, consider the category "chair." There are many types of chairs, some more familiar than others. Yet if English speakers are asked to visualize a chair, they will probably form a mental image that has four legs, a seat, and a back. This is the *prototype* of the category: loosely speaking, the best example, the one that comes first to mind. (See Lakoff 1987 for a discussion of different kinds of prototypes.) Armchairs and lawn chairs are different in various ways from the prototypes but are still felt to be good members of the category. Beanbag chairs, on the other hand, while they still serve the same function as other chairs, lack most of the typical qualities; they are highly nonprototypical category members.

Cognitive linguists assume that all linguistic categories may show prototype structuring. This has been largely exploited in theories of semantics (e.g., Lakoff 1987), but theories of other linguistic phenomena have begun to use this fact. For example, it is possible to come up with a semantically based definition of the classes "noun" and "verb," if one treats them as categories with prototype structure; the prototype of "noun" is simply a *thing*, and the prototype of "verb" is an *action* (cf. Hopper & Thompson 1985, Langacker 1991b).

Finally, cognitive linguists place a great deal of emphasis on semantics. Some theories (e.g., Langacker's Cognitive Grammar) might even be called "semantics-driven," unlike the "syntax-driven" formalist theories: Rather than having meaningless sentences generated by the rule systems of autonomous syntax, the meanings of linguistic items guide how the pieces of utterances are put together. There is much common sense to this approach, given that the purpose of language is to communicate meaning.

Formalist theories of semantics often focus on the "truth conditions" for sentences: The approach is to pin down the circumstances under which a sentence would be true, and to consider those circumstances to be the "meaning" of the sentence. Thus, a sentence like *The cat is on the mat* would be true if a particular cat actually were on a particular mat, and it would be considered to "mean" that configuration of feline and textile. This approach has a number of drawbacks; the most significant one is that it has no place for viewpoint or perspective. Active and passive sentences with the same truth conditions, for example, would be considered to have the same meaning, though they clearly focus attention on different aspects of the same event.

Semantics as treated by cognitive linguists does not focus on what is "true" in the world; instead, it focuses on the conceptual system of the language user. A word or utterance picks out or *profiles* a piece of conceptual structure. Thus, English *cat* picks out the knowledge we have about domestic felines; in particular, it draws attention to our category of "cats," and especially to a prototypical member of that category. *The cat is on the mat* provides the conceptual cues we need to construct a mental model of a situation where a cat and a mat, already salient in the discourse, exist in a particular prototypical spatial arrangement. This is not an "objectivist" theory of semantics; it is not rooted in a theory of objective truth.

The usual opposite of *objective* is *subjective*: If linguistic meaning is not grounded in the truth of reality, people have claimed that it must be completely random or arbitrary. This is a subjectivist view of meaning: that linguistic concepts could just be "anything at all," that there are no constraints on possible nouns, verbs, and grammatical inflections. The subjectivist approach to meaning is popular in many academic circles (e.g., postmodernism and deconstructionism), but it is not the view held by cognitive linguists.

To cognitivists, meaning is neither based on objective "reality" nor completely arbitrary and subjective. Instead, conceptual structure and linguistic semantics are grounded in our *experiences* as embodied beings. All humans share the same kind of sensory organs, neural structures, and bodily experiences; these experiences shape the kinds of concepts that we develop and that we attach to our linguistic items.

A good example of this comes from the color terms of the world's languages (Lakoff, 1987). At one point, it was believed that color words were completely subjective; that is, they could carve up the spectrum in any way at all. Berlin and Kay (1969) found that though languages differ greatly in their basic terms for colors, there are remarkable regularities. They asked speakers of many languages to pick out from a chart of 320 color chips the *best example* of each basic color word. It turned out that virtually the same best examples were chosen for all languages.

In other words, all languages with a basic term for a color in the blue range would choose the same best example, regardless of the boundaries of the term; if the language's basic term covered the ranges of English *blue* and *green,* the best example would not be something like turquoise, in the middle of the two ranges; instead, it would be the same as either the best example of English *blue* or of English *green.*

Why should all languages have the same best examples of their color terms? Kay and McDaniel (1978) found an answer for this question, based on the neurophysiology of color vision. There are three types of cells in the retina: red/green detectors, blue/yellow detectors, and light/dark detectors. The red/green and blue/yellow detectors respond most strongly to particular wavelengths of light. Loosely speaking, those wavelengths constitute the best examples of the world's most basic color terms. Thus, the nature of the human perceptual system has a significant impact on the sorts of concepts we develop; color concepts are neither objective (i.e., existing independent of humans) nor subjective (i.e., completely arbitrary) but are based on experience.

Semantics, meaning connected with language, is not separable from all our other kinds of knowledge; it incorporates many of the myriad structures in our conceptual systems.[5] The most successful models of human knowledge group what we know into substructures: for example, Fillmore's (1982) *frames,* Schank and Abelson's (1977) *scripts,* and Lakoff's (1987) *idealized cognitive models.* All these terms refer to the fact that concepts tend to cluster together in related groups. As Fillmore (1982) wrote, "By the term 'frame' I have in mind any system of concepts related in such a way that to understand any one of them you have to understand the whole structure in which it fits..." (p. 111). For

---

[5] As Slobin (1996) suggests, we may have to modify or cast our thoughts in a certain way to fit them into the specific semantic categories that our language manifests; nevertheless, semantic categories can clearly contain large amounts of conceptual information and structure.

example, to understand the concept of a "menu," one had better know about restaurants, waiters, ordering food, and so on; all these concepts group together in the frame of "eating at a restaurant." Cognitivist theories of semantics draw heavily on frames and their relationships; other semantic tools include *metaphor* and *conceptual mappings,* terms defined (and used) in later chapters.

To sum up, cognitive linguists treat the language capacity as a part of the general human cognitive capacity. We seek to use general cognitive operations such as conceptual mapping, profiling, and selective attention; knowledge structures or schemas; and mental imagery in describing linguistic phenomena. We believe that linguistic categories are categories of human cognition, with the same types of prototype-based, fuzzy structures. In addition, we believe that linguistic structures at all levels of complexity (roots, inflections, word orderings, discourse patterns) carry meaning and that the interactions and behavior of these structures are usually motivated by the interactions of their meanings.

The cognitive linguistics framework is especially apt for the treatment of iconicity and conceptual metaphor (the main focus of this book). As shall be shown, iconicity involves an intimate interrelationship between form and meaning; this is easy to describe in cognitivist theories, which do not separate off linguistic form from meaning. Moreover, iconicity and metaphor do not *determine* the nature of the linguistic items discussed in this book, but they surely *motivate* the nature of those items. Cognitive linguistics has a place for the two aspects of iconic and metaphorical motivation: the less-than-fully predictable patterns (the *tendency*), and the conceptual structures that cause the patterns (the *reason*). Describing these patterns is definitely part of the linguist's job.

CHAPTER THREE

Iconicity Defined and Demonstrated

ICONICITY AND RESEMBLANCE DEFINED

In this chapter, we begin to look closely at iconicity in language: After establishing a definition of iconicity, we examine examples of iconicity in signed and spoken languages in some detail. Once we have gotten a sense of how iconicity manifests itself in language, we briefly review how linguists have treated iconicity. This discussion focuses on iconicity in signed languages and traces a development of sophistication in sign linguists' theories. The next chapter presents a cognitive model of iconicity in signed and spoken languages, and the following chapter (Chapter Five) gives a survey of types of iconic items in both modalities.

Let us start by considering the results of Pizzuto, Boyes-Braem, and Volterra (1996). This study tested the ability of naïve subjects to guess the meanings of signs from Italian Sign Language (LIS). Because one simple definition of iconicity is "form–meaning resemblance," we might expect that we could use "guessability" (also called *transparency*) as a measure of a sign's iconicity. Yet Pizzuto et al. found strong culture-based variation: Some signs' meanings were easily guessed by non-Italian nonsigners; some were more transparent to non-Italian Deaf signers; and yet others were more easy for Italian nonsigners to guess. That is, some transparency seemed to be universal, some seemed linked to the experience of Deafness and signing, and some seemed to have a basis in Italian culture.

In interpreting these results, we can see the need for a definition of iconicity that takes culture and conceptualization into account. Iconicity is not an objective relationship between image and referent; rather, it is a relationship between our mental models of image and referent. These models are partially motivated by our embodied experiences common to

Figure 3.1. TREE.

all humans and partially by our experiences in particular cultures and societies. This point is crucial to the theory developed in this and following chapters.

Iconicity is common in both signed and spoken languages, and it is present at all levels of linguistic structure, including morphology and syntax as well as individual words. It is not a "simple" matter of resemblance between form and meaning but a sophisticated process in which the allowable phonetic resources of a language are built up into an "analogue" of an image associated with the referent. This process involves a substantial amount of conceptual work, including *image selection, conceptual mapping,* and *schematization* of items to fit the constraints of the language. Iconicity exists only through the mental efforts of human beings; it is dependent on our natural and cultural conceptual associations.

Let me give a strict definition of those items which I consider purely iconic. In iconic items, some aspect of the item's physical form (shape, sound, temporal structure, etc.) resembles a concrete sensory image. That is, a linguistic item that involves only iconicity can represent only a concrete, physical referent (with one class of exceptions; see the discussion of DEGREE below).[1] Thus, ASL TREE (Fig. 3.1), whose form resembles

---

[1] As the preceding sentence suggests, by *concrete* and *physical* I mean the sort of thing that we can perceive more or less directly with our sensory systems. This includes sounds, sizes, shapes, body postures and gestures, movements and locations in space, durations, and so on. I do not mean only those things that are solid and tangible.

Figure 3.2. THINK–PENETRATE.

the shape of a prototypical tree, is purely iconic: Its form directly resembles its meaning.

There is more than just iconicity, however, in signs such as THINK–PENETRATE (Fig. 3.2), whose form resembles an object emerging from the head and piercing through a barrier. THINK–PENETRATE, which can be translated as "she finally got the point," has a nonconcrete meaning. The image of an object penetrating a barrier is used to evoke the meaning of effortful but ultimately successful communication (cf. the discussion in Chapter Six). This use of a concrete image to describe an abstract concept is an instance of *metaphor*, and THINK–PENETRATE is thus metaphorical as well as iconic.

To begin with, we will look only at iconic items that describe concrete objects or processes: sounds, shapes, durations, locations, and so on; discussion of metaphorical iconic items will be delayed until Chapter Six. This strict separation of metaphor and iconicity allows for a cleaner treatment of both processes; it lets us apply the theory of conceptual metaphor (e.g., Lakoff 1992) to metaphorical items in a straightforward way. (See Holtemann 1990, Wilbur 1987, and Wilcox 1993 as well.)

Our next task is to take apart our intuitive notion of "resemblance." There is no such thing as "resemblance" or "similarity" in the absence of an observer who makes a comparison: Resemblance is not an objective fact about two entities but is a product of our cognitive processing.[2]

---

[2] Peirce (Buchler, 1940), in his discussion of iconic items, noted that just as for arbitrary items, one must have an "interpretant" who knows the relationship between form and meaning; iconic items do not have meaning without such a person.

Specifically, when we compare two entities (for similarity), we attempt to set up *structure-preserving correspondences* between our *mental models* of the two entities (cf. S. Wilcox 1998). This means that for each entity, we figure out its relevant parts and the relations between the parts: This is the perceived structure of the entity. Then, given the structure of one entity, we look for corresponding structure in the other entity. The more correspondences we can find, the more we believe the two entities resemble each other.

For example, take the process of comparing a pair of human legs (Fig. 3.3A) and the index and middle fingers extended from a fist (Fig. 3.3B). The human legs consist of two thin parts, approximately three feet long (for an adult), each with a joint in the middle; these two parts are joined at the top and have perpendicular pads (i.e., feet) at the bottom. The extended index and middle fingers consist of two thin parts, approximately three inches long, each with two joints along their length; these two parts are joined at one end and have hard surfaces (i.e., nails) near the other.

We could in theory set up correspondences between these two entities in an unlimited number of bizarre ways – for example, the right foot could correspond to the middle finger's second knuckle, the left knee could correspond to the entire index finger, and so on – but the most natural thing to do when comparing is to set up correspondences that *preserve structure*. This enables us to note similarities *and* differences in the most efficient way: Once we have a good sense of how (if at all) the two structures correspond, we can see at once how they differ in corre-

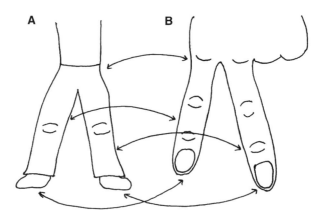

Figure 3.3. Structure-preserving correspondences between (A) human legs and (B) extended index and middle fingers.

sponding subareas. (Gentner and Markman [1996] called these *alignable differences*).

For example, the right foot is the bottommost part of the right leg, which in turn is half of the leg-pair structure. There are parts of the finger-pair structure that bear an analogous relation to the structure as a whole: For example, the middle finger's pad and nail area is the endmost part of the finger, which in turn is half of the finger-pair structure.

The lines in Figure 3.3 show a set of structure-preserving correspondences: each leg with each finger, the hips with the knuckles of the hand, the feet with the fingertips. On the basis of these extensive correspondences, we can say that there is a strong resemblance between the legs and the fingers. We can also identify clearly some ways in which the two entities differ: in size, in number of joints, in having or lacking perpendicular (footlike) ends, and of course in function.

It is the notion of alignable differences that provides concrete support for this structural view of similarity. Gentner and Markman (1996) found, for example, that subjects could list alignable differences more easily than other differences and that they used alignable differences more in judging degree of similarity. They argue that these results are not consistent with other models of similarity (e.g., models based on "mental distance" or shared features), which, because they are not based on structural alignment, cannot distinguish alignable and nonalignable differences.[3]

A set of correspondences between two entities is often called a "mapping." Thus, linguistic iconicity can be redefined as "the existence of a structure-preserving mapping between mental models of linguistic form and meaning."

EXAMPLES OF SPOKEN-LANGUAGE ICONICITY

The following examples illustrate some of the vast range of ways in which linguistic items are iconic. (See Chapter Five for a more complete survey of iconicity in signed and spoken language.) Examples are taken from English and ASL, not because these languages are special or specially related but because they are the spoken and signed languages most likely to be familiar to the reader.

---

[3] Gentner and Markman (1996: 21–23) did note that we may judge similarity differently when performing different mental operations. For example, although the comparison process seems to rely on alignment of entities' structures, the process of similarity-based retrieval from long-term memory may be based on shared surface similarities rather than shared structural relations. They referred to this as the "plurality of similarity." I will assume that the structural alignment model of similarity is the appropriate one for iconicity.

We start with a spoken-language lexical item: the onomatopoeic English word *ding*, which refers to the sound of a bell. Figure 3.4A shows an amplitude waveform plot of the sound of a bell being struck; note the sharp onset, the initial loud tone, and the long, gradual fade of the sound. Figure 3.4B gives the waveform of *ding* /dɪŋ/ spoken by an American woman; as we can see, the phonetic resources of English have been assembled into a remarkably faithful analogue of the sound. The stop /d/ provides a sharp onset; the vowel /ɪ/ is a loud, clear tone; and the nasal /ŋ/ furnishes a muffled die-off. The connecting arrows between Figure 3.4A and Figure 3.4B show the mapping between the two sound images. Note how not only the allowable *sounds* of English but also the *time ordering* of the sounds has been exploited in creating this linguistic item: The sound representing the onset, /d/, occurs first, whereas the sound representing the die-off, /ŋ/, occurs last.

At this point, we should notice a few things that are true of all iconic linguistic items. First of all, this form *ding* uses the phonetic resources of English and conforms to English phonotactic constraints. The average English speaker can certainly use his or her vocal tract to create a more faithful or realistic rendering of the bell's tone – most likely, that would involve eliminating the vowel and elongating the nasal while holding the

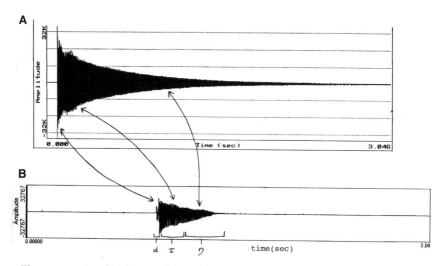

Figure 3.4. Amplitude waveforms of (A) a Japanese bowl-shaped bell's sound and (B) an American woman speaking the English word *ding*; arrows indicate correspondences.

voice at a single pitch: /dŋŋŋ/.[4] Such an imitation, however, could never be accepted as an English word, as it violates several phonotactic constraints: the need for a vowel in a monosyllabic word and the standard length and pitch contours of English utterances. (See Liddell 1992 and Rhodes 1994 for discussions of these issues.) Thus, onomatopoeic words are not "mere" vocal mime.

Second, *ding* is an established part of the English lexicon. Though there are a number of other ways to represent the bell sound that conform to English's rules (e.g., *ting, doon, pim*), none of them has become conventionally established as an English word. This point is important because it further demonstrates the difference between free mime and iconic language. Clearly, an English speaker does not reinvent a word like *ding* each time she or he wants to talk about a bell; instead, she or he uses the conventionalized items of the language. The speaker may not even notice in the moment that *ding* is iconic. However, there is also a productive system[5] (analogous to but weaker than classifier systems in signed language) that allows English speakers to invent and use such "nonce-words" as *ting* and *pim* to describe the details of particular sounds in ways that conform to English phonotactics (cf. Oswalt 1994).

In *ding,* our first example, sounds represent sounds and time-ordering represents time-ordering in an English lexical item. The second example is a syntactic construction that is present in nearly all languages: When one clause precedes another, the default interpretation is that the event described by that clause occurs *before* the second clause's event. That is, if I say I *jumped into the pool and took off my shoes,* people listening to me will assume that my shoes got wet (see Fig. 3.5). Haiman (1985b) showed that if languages want to override this default interpretation, they must do something special: for example, add an explicit time-ordering word such as *before* or *simultaneously* to one of the clauses.

Figure 3.5A is a sketch of two specific events in sequence: a person jumping into a pool, then taking off shoes. Figure 3.5B gives the two-clause sentence quoted above that describes this sequence. The connecting arrows between the sketched events and the clauses show how their parts correspond.

Note that this iconicity is purely temporal: The only parameter of the sentence that maps onto its meaning is the temporal ordering of its

---

4 Some people are more gifted at sound imitations than others; would be imitators are often strongly influenced by the phonotactics of their native language. See Chapter Five for more discussion of imitations.

5 A *productive* system is one in which elements can combine to generate new elements; for example, verb morphology in English is productive in that suffixes such as *-s* and *-ed* can attach to any newly coined verbs.

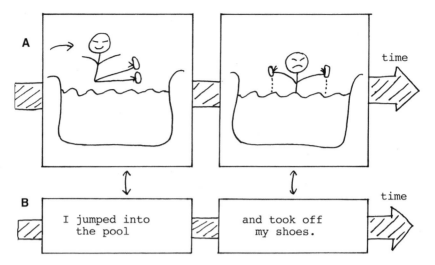

Figure 3.5. The parallel temporal structure of (A) a specific sequence of events and (B) an English two-clause sentence that describes them; arrows show correspondences.

clauses. The individual words in the sentence need not be iconic at all. Moreover, this example shows that iconicity does not manifest itself only in lexical items: the *S1 and S2* sentence structure is itself an iconic form–meaning pair.

Figure 3.5 shows the iconic mapping for a specific sentence and its referent; Figure 3.6 gives the general case, treating the syntactic structure itself as a meaning-bearing element of the language. Figure 3.6A gives a model of two generic events in sequence, and Figure 3.6B gives the two-clause construction. Again, the connecting arrows show how the parts correspond.

EXAMPLES OF SIGNED-LANGUAGE ICONICITY

We have seen how sound and time can be used iconically in spoken languages, at both the lexical and syntactic levels. Now let us consider some examples from signed languages.

Before getting into form–meaning correspondences, I will give a quick introduction to the form component of signed languages. (For more detail, see, for example, Wilbur 1987.) Signed languages are articulated with the hands, arms, upper body, and face. The area from roughly the signer's waist height to just above the head, and from the body forward to arm's length, is known as the *signing space*; this is where signs are

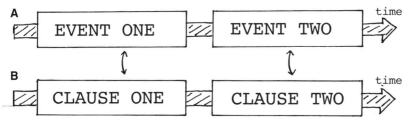

Figure 3.6. The parallel temporal structure of (A) a generic sequence of events and (B) an English two-clause syntactic structure for describing such sequences; arrows show correspondences.

made. Most people know that configurations of hands and arms are used to create signs; it is less generally known that facial expressions (including brow raises, eye blinks, and various mouth configurations), head nods and tilts, and shifts of the body and shoulders have grammatical functions in signed utterances.

One popular way to describe the structure of signs was pioneered by Stokoe (1960). In Stokoe's model, signs are simultaneous combinations of *handshape,* the configuration of the hand and fingers; *location,* the place on the body or in space where the sign is made; and *movement,* or motion of the articulators in space. Later theorists added the parameters of *orientation,* the direction that the palm "points"; and *nonmanual signals,* lexically and grammatically significant facial expressions or body postures. The illustrations show pairs of signs that differ only in one of these parameters. Figure 3.7A, THINK, and Figure 3.7B, KNOW, differ in their handshape; Figure 3.8A, SUMMER, and Figure 3.8B, DRY, differ only in their location; Figure 3.9A, AIRPLANE, and Figure 3.9B, PLANE-FLY, differ in their movement; Figure 3.10A, BRIEF, and Figure 3.10B, TRAIN, differ in their orientation; and Figure 3.11A, LATE, and Figure 3.11B, NOT-YET, differ in their nonmanual signals.

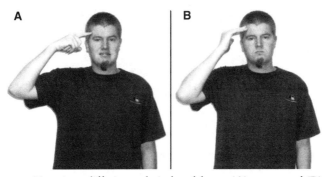

Figure 3.7. Two signs differing only in handshape: (A) THINK and (B) KNOW.

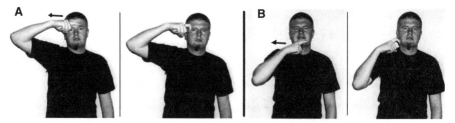

Figure 3.8. Two signs differing only in location: (A) SUMMER and (B) DRY.

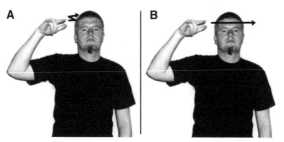

Figure 3.9. Two signs differing only in movement: (A) AIRPLANE and (B) PLANE-FLY.

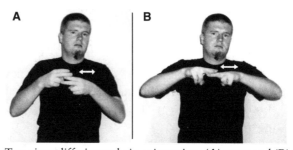

Figure 3.10. Two signs differing only in orientation: (A) BRIEF and (B) TRAIN.

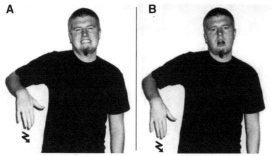

Figure 3.11. Two signs differing only in nonmanual signals: (A) LATE and (B) NOT-YET.

ASL phonologists have of course added many details to this brief description of sign structure; notably, Liddell and Johnson (1989) developed a model for treating signs as a sequence of *holds* and *movements* at, to, and from locations in the signing space. But this brief introduction will suffice for our purposes here.

The first example of signed-language iconicity is on the lexical level: the ASL sign TREE. Figure 3.12A gives an image of a "typical" tree. We can note that it grows out of the ground; has a straight, bare lower trunk; and then spreads out into a network of branches. ASL TREE, in Figure 3.12B, provides an analogue of those three elements, using the shapes of the hand and forearm articulators: The horizontal nondominant forearm represents the ground, the vertical dominant forearm represents the trunk, and the spread fingers of the dominant hand represent the branches.

This is probably the most-often cited type of iconicity in signed languages: where articulators make a "picture" of some referent. But the process is more complex than it appears. First note that not all trees look like Figure 3.12A – some do not grow straight, some have different kinds of branches, some grow out of cliff walls instead of level ground – yet the same sign TREE represents them all. Figure 3.12A is an image of a *prototypical* tree, one that serves as the category's exemplar. This choice of image is conventional and language-specific.

Second, note that the image in Figure 3.12A could have been represented with articulators in a number of ways, incorporating different details. For example, the branching structure could have been shown in more detail, perhaps with two hands, and the ground could have been ignored, or vice versa; or the tree's verticality and the ground's flatness

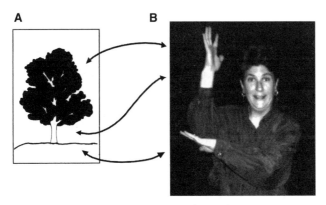

Figure 3.12. Structure-preserving correspondences between (**A**) a prototypical image of a tree and (**B**) American Sign Language TREE.

could have been shown by an upright index finger beside a flat palm-down hand.

In fact, different signed languages do exactly this: As mentioned in Chapter Two, Klima and Bellugi (1979: 21) give the signs meaning "tree" in a number of languages, and all are iconic representations of an image like Figure 3.12A, but each realizes different details of the image in different ways. The choice of iconic representation, especially for frozen signs like TREE, is an established though somewhat arbitrary fact about the language.

Finally, we must note (as we did for *ding*) that TREE uses only phonet-ically acceptable forms of ASL: the spread-fingered handshape, the straight forearms, the allowable contact between the dominant elbow and the back of the nondominant hand. All iconic form–meaning pairs that have become part of a language conform to the phonotactics of their language, even if it is humanly possible to create a more "realistic" ana-logue (i.e., one that has more correspondences with its referent).

In TREE, the shapes of the articulators represent the shapes of the ref-erent (what Mandel [1977] called "substitutive depiction," and what I prefer to call "shape-for-shape iconicity"). With this kind of iconicity, the movement of the articulators is free to represent the movement of the referent; thus, the upright forearm can sway from side to side to show the tree's movement in the wind.[6] But there is a second type of iconicity in ASL ("virtual depiction" in Mandel [1977]; "path-for-shape iconicity" here) where the articulators trace the shape of the referent: Here, the *path* that the articulators "create" in space is what resembles the refer-ent, not the articulators themselves. One example of this is the ASL sign DEGREE, which consists of an iconic representation of a diploma (a salient image associated with academic degrees).

Figure 3.13A gives a prototypical image of a diploma: paper rolled into a cylinder and tied with a ribbon. Figure 3.13C shows DEGREE: Both hands assume the F-shape (index finger and thumb create a circle; other fingers are spread); starting near each other, they separate, so that the thumb–index circles trace out a horizontal cylinder. Figure 3.13B shows the shape of the reified trace. The arrows show the points of correspon-dence between the two images, Figures 3.13A and 3.13B.

We can note first of all that this type of iconicity draws on our ability to track an object's path through space and see it as an independent entity. Note also that the representation is a featureless cylinder; no other distinguishing characteristics – for example, the festive ribbon –

---

[6] In practice, this option is available for only a conventionally limited subset of shape-for-shape iconic forms.

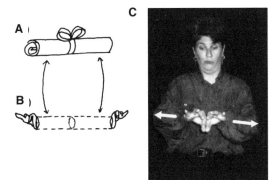

Figure 3.13. Structure-preserving correspondences between (A) a prototypical image of a diploma and (B) the reified cylinder traced out in (C) American Sign Language DEGREE.

have been retained. The sign's form is clearly more schematic than a mental image of a typical diploma. Moreover, if someone did not know the meaning of this sign, that person would have no reason to assume that the image represented was that of a diploma; it is an equally good representation of, say, a stick.

Finally, notice that the cylinder is traced with a very specific hand-shape (Boyes-Braem 1981). Although there are many ways to create circles using the hands and fingers, and all of these would leave a cylindrical trace, ASL has singled out particular hand-circles as its conventional tracers. In particular, the F-hand is used for relatively long and thin cylinders. A different shape (for example, the 7, where thumb and ring finger touch) would not create a legitimate ASL sign.

Iconicity can also appear in the morphology and syntax of signed languages. ASL's temporal aspect system, for example, consistently uses time iconically: The temporal structure of most aspectual inflections reflects the temporal structure of the event types they describe.

The example we will look at in detail is what Brentari (1996) calls the *protracted-inceptive* (or PI) inflection. According to her, this inflection can occur on any telic verb; it denotes a delay between the onset of the verb's action and the accomplishment of that action – in effect, a "protracted beginning" of the action. PI's phonetic form involves an extended hold at the verb's initial position while either the fingers wiggle (if the handshape is an open 5) or the tongue waggles (if the handshape is more closed); after this hold, the verb's motion continues as normal.

Figure 3.14 demonstrates this inflection with a specific verb. Figure 3.14A shows a situation in which PI inflection is appropriate: A person who intends to leave the house is temporarily delayed (perhaps by

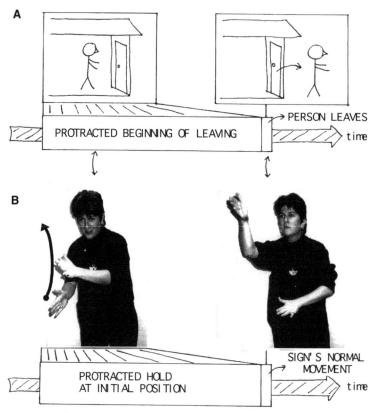

Figure 3.14. Structure-preserving correspondences between the temporal structure of (**A**) a situation in which a person is delayed but eventually leaves and (**B**) the sign LEAVE inflected for protracted inception.

another person needing to talk); eventually the person does leave. Figure 3.14B shows two phases of the sign LEAVE inflected for PI: first the long initial hold and then the verb's normal movement.[7] The associated time lines explicitly show the temporal structures of both form and referent.

It is easy to see the correspondences between the two temporal structures. A delay in leaving (referent) is represented by a delay in the verb's normal motion (form); similarly, the eventual accomplishment of leaving (referent) is represented by the eventual performance of the verb's normal motion (form).

[7] This sign is often given the more colloquial English gloss SPLIT, because a different sign with similar meaning is often glossed as LEAVE. I have not followed this tradition, as the gloss SPLIT might be confusing to people unfamiliar with ASL or colloquial English.

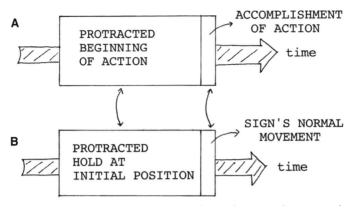

Figure 3.15. Structure-preserving correspondences between the temporal structure of (A) a situation in which an action is delayed and then carried out and (B) the hold–movement structure of the protracted–inceptive inflection.

Because PI is an inflection that can apply to many verbs, Figure 3.15 diagrams its iconicity in a more abstract, verb-independent way. Figure 3.15A presents the concept of a delayed event, Figure 3.15B describes the hold–movement structure of the inflection, and the connecting arrows show how form and referent have similar temporal structures.

We must touch on one last issue in our introduction to the iconicity of signed languages. Signed languages have two main types of iconic signs: the highly productive *classifiers,* and the less-productive *frozen signs* (Supalla 1978). Our two examples of iconic signs, TREE and DEGREE, are both frozen signs;[8] it is useful now to contrast them with ASL's classifier system.

Classifiers (cf. Dixon 1986) are linguistic elements that refer to "classes" of referents rather than specific kinds of referents. One common type is *noun* classifiers, which function as nouns; English has a few examples of these, including the *flock* in "a flock of sheep," referring to a group of animals, and the *drop* in "a drop of blood," referring to a small amount of a liquid. Some languages have noun classifiers accompanying every noun.

A typologically rarer phenomenon is *verb* or *predicate* classifier systems (cf. McDonald 1982). Predicate classifiers function as verbs and contain an element that categorizes the subject of the verb. For example (Talmy 1985a), Atsugewi has a complex system of verb roots for motion and location that each identify the type of object to which they refer: small round objects, small flat objects, and runny gooey objects, to name

---

[8] TREE can function as a classifier under some circumstances, however.

only a few. Thus, in sentence 1, the classifier root -*st'aq'* refers to runny matter, and the surrounding affixes tell us where and why the matter moved.

(1) /ˆ-w-	ca-	st'aq'-
3rd pers. subj.	from wind blowing on it	for runny matter to move/locate
ic't-	a	/
into liquid	3rd pers. subject	

→[c'wast'aq'ic'ta]

"Icky stuff blew into liquid."

Signed-language classifier systems are similar but highly iconic, forming what one might call a set of iconic building blocks for the description of physical objects, movements, and locations. (See, for example, Engberg-Pedersen 1993, McDonald 1982, Supalla 1986, and Wilbur 1987 for several different analyses of this type of sign.) Each classifier form contains a handshape that identifies some class of entities, plus movements, locations, and orientations that may further describe the entity's appearance or else its path or location in space. Signers can freely create new signs from this set to describe a huge variety of different situations.

For example, to describe a person walking up a hill on a winding road (see Fig. 5.3 and the discussion there), an ASL signer could choose a handshape (index finger vertically extended from a fist) that represents a human, a back-and-forth movement pattern that represents movement of a referent from side to side, and an upward direction that represents upward movement. Putting these components together, the signer would have a classifier form involving an extended-index-finger handshape moving on a winding path that slants upward. To show a second person accompanying the first, the signer could extend the middle finger as well; to show an up-and-down path, the hand would move upward and downward.

There are different appropriate classifier forms for each type of referent; in general, the choice of classifier is based on perceptual properties such as size and shape and interactional properties such as how the referent could be handled by a human. Often there are several classifiers that could describe a given referent; they draw attention to different aspects of the referent (e.g., a person's hand or feet rather than the entire body), and the signer will choose the one that best fits his or her purpose. (Wilbur, Bernstein, & Kantor 1985 have shown that this is typical of classifier systems in the world's languages.) Moreover, classifier forms are not universal; different signed languages have different forms and different criteria for applying them to referents.

Iconic frozen signs often use the same set of building blocks as classifiers, but they cannot be freely varied to show differences in their referents. (It is for this reason that they are called "frozen.") For example, the sign TREE would not be made differently to show a tree growing out of a hillside, and the frozen sign HOUSE represents the image of a pointed roof and walls, even if the house in question has a flat roof.

Frozen signs tend to represent a whole category, rather than a specific referent; the image that is chosen to represent the category can be a prototype or salient category member, or it can be an action or item metonymically associated with the category. Classifiers are *less* specific than frozen signs in that they identify larger classes of referents (e.g., *long, thin objects* rather than *pens* or *logs*), but *more* specific in that they show what an individual of that type is doing in a particular situation.

APPROACHES TO ICONICITY IN LINGUISTIC THEORY

The preceding examples have served to demonstrate a few major types of iconicity in signed and spoken languages. Before proceeding to give my account of linguistic iconicity (Chapter Four), I will spend some time on how other linguists have treated this topic. My main thrust will be on the development of thought about signed-language iconicity, with a few words on spoken-language iconicity.

There is a long tradition (mentioned in Chapters One and Two) of minimizing and dismissing iconicity in language. I have already cited de Saussure's doctrine of the "arbitrariness of the sign"; this doctrine was embraced by most linguists who followed him. De Saussure's statement was aimed at countering a naïve view of iconicity, one that would attempt to derive the bulk of all languages' vocabularies from iconic origins (i.e., even words like *cat, dog,* and *girl*). Yet for years it was used to shut down discussions of any iconic aspects of language. Even Peirce, founder of the field of semiotics, accepted this perspective.

Peirce (Buchler 1940)[9] devoted a great deal of attention to iconicity. For him, icons (i.e., iconic items) represent their objects mainly by their similarity to the object. He distinguished iconic *images,* those which simply resemble their referents, from iconic *diagrams,* which are systematic arrangements of signs, none of which necessarily resembles its referent

---

[9] Buchler (1940) is an edited volume of Peirce's papers. The quotation comes from an unpublished manuscript of Peirce, circa 1900.

but whose relationships to one another mirror the relationships of their referents.

Peirce (like de Saussure) discounted the importance of iconic images to language while acknowledging the importance of iconic diagrams in motivating syntactic forms:

In the earliest form of speech, there probably was a large element of mimicry. But in all languages known, such representations have been replaced by conventional auditory signs... But in the syntax of every language there are logical icons [i.e., diagrams] of the kind that are aided by conventional rules. (p. 106)

As our examples have suggested, however, both images and diagrams are in fact prevalent in signed languages.

Another philosopher and semotician, Goodman (1968), had a different view. He challenged the doctrine of the arbitrariness of the sign, saying,

Descriptions [i.e., languagelike representations] are distinguished from depictions [i.e., pictorial representations] not through being more arbitrary but through belonging to articulate [i.e., discrete] rather than to dense [i.e., continuous] schemes... The often stressed distinction between iconic and other signs becomes transient and trivial; thus does heresy breed iconoclasm. (pp. 230–1)

In other words, linguistic symbols may be either iconic or arbitrary; the crucial fact is that they take part in a system of conventional linguistic contrasts among a limited number of possible symbols. This view is much more compatible with the data presented in this book.

Through the years when formalist theories (e.g., Chomsky 1957, 1965, 1981) dominated the field of linguistics, iconicity continued to receive little attention. Given the assumptions of formalist linguistics, the dismissal of iconicity made sense. Formalists believe that language and its components are strictly autonomous from each other (cf. Chapter Two); there is no convenient way to describe form–meaning resemblances in that framework. Linguists of this type were hard at work modeling language with formal systems; there was always more to do with the data they had. Iconicity in spoken languages is limited enough that it seemed reasonable to ignore it.

The functionalist and cognitivist schools of linguistics, not sharing the autonomy assumptions and being interested in motivation of all sorts, were not content to leave linguistic iconicity unexamined. Starting in approximately the 1980s, articles, books, and conferences began to appear on this topic. Notable examples are Haiman (1985a), *Iconicity in Syntax,* and Hinton et al. (1994), *Sound Symbolism.* Though both books include phenomena that would not fit the definition of pure iconicity given here (i.e., they involve metaphor or some other kind of motivation), they present a concerted effort to seriously address iconic motivation.

Iconicity in Syntax consists of chapters on how iconicity manifests itself in the syntax of spoken languages. Among the many points addressed is the fact that word order or order of morphemes in a polysynthetic word is often iconic for order of events or for degree of perceived "conceptual closeness" (a metaphorical use of iconicity). *Sound Symbolism* takes a serious look at sound-for-sound iconicity in spoken languages. The introduction gives a useful classification system; the chapters investigate sound symbolism in many languages and show that just as in ASL, each language has a *system* within which words resemble their meanings yet conform to the language's phonotactics. Thus, even without the impetus of signed languages, some linguists were beginning to investigate and incorporate iconicity in their theories of language.

Sign linguists, unlike "speech linguists," never had the option of ignoring iconicity; iconicity is simply too pervasive in signed languages. Even the lay observer (perhaps *especially* the lay observer) can immediately notice the resemblance between some signs and their meanings. This led to trouble for signed languages and Deaf people.

The earliest attitude toward signed-language iconicity (and one that many people still hold) was that signed languages were simply a kind of pantomime, a picture language, with *only* iconicity and no true linguistic structure (see discussion in Lane 1992). Stokoe discredited this attitude in 1960, with his proof that ASL does have formal linguistic patterning: Possessing its own lexicon, phonology, morphology, and syntax, ASL is a true language. Over the years, however, sign linguists have had to work hard to fight the entrenched myth of signed languages as pantomime. Even now, talking about iconicity to Deaf people and sign linguists can be a touchy matter – as if admitting that signed languages do have a lot of iconicity is tantamount to agreeing that they are not languages.

Sign linguists, at least in the early days, took two basic approaches to iconicity: strongly arguing against its presence/importance (with the goal of proving ASL, etc., to be true languages), and reveling in its multifarious manifestations, excited by the differences between signed and spoken languages. Over the years, understanding of ASL's iconic items has grown and changed: It is quite clear now that the items are there, *and* that they form a linguistic system.

As mentioned in Chapter One, studies like those by Hoemann (1975), Frishberg (1979), and Klima and Bellugi (1979: 1) were among those that downplayed the presence of iconicity in signed languages. These studies showed that historical change could disrupt the iconicity of signs (Frishberg 1979; but cf. Chapter Eleven) and that nonsigners could not readily guess the meaning of signs from their forms (Hoemann 1975; Klima & Bellugi 1979:1), which meant that signed languages were conventional as well as iconic. It was of course important to demonstrate that signed languages have linguistic systems as well as iconicity, but the devaluation of iconicity exceeded what was strictly necessary.

Other studies were more enthusiastic about signed-language iconicity. Mandel (1977) and DeMatteo (1977) are among those who marveled at the differences between signed and spoken languages. Mandel (1977) wholeheartedly embraced the existence of iconicity in ASL and set out to catalogue the devices used. By comparing a number of ASL forms and their meanings, he put together a list of the ways in which signs are iconic, arranged into a hierarchy of types. He noted that in some signs the articulators sketch the outline of an image; in others, the articulators themselves resemble the referent; and in a third type, the articulators point out a referent (for example, a body part) that is present in the signing situation.

DeMatteo (1977) argued that ASL's iconic forms are truly analogue representations of visual imagery. He noted the presence of forms that seemed to vary in an unlimited number of ways in correspondence with their meanings; for example, the verb MEET, with two hands coming together in the 1-shape, can be varied to express meanings like *almost meet, turn away*, and so on.

DeMatteo sketched out a model to handle these phenomena. It involves mental images of varying schematicity, a set of rules that maps aspects of the image onto a linguistic form (including pragmatic selection of the most important aspects), and a set of analogue rules that tell us how the sign is to be modified in representing variations on the image. There is much that is useful in this proposal (and indeed it resembles to some degree the proposal in Chapter Four); its main flaw is that, like Mandel's work, it misses the existence of a system of iconic elements.

Klima and Bellugi (1979) set forth a measured compromise between the iconicity enthusiasts and detractors.[10] They affirmed the presence of iconicity in ASL on many levels but noted that it is highly constrained in a number of ways. The iconicity is conventionally established by the language, and not usually invented on the spot; and iconic signs use only

---

[10] The citation above (Klima & Bellugi 1979:1) refers specifically to their earlier work on the transparency of ASL vocabulary, reviewed in the first chapter of this book.

the allowed forms of the sign language. Moreover, iconicity appears not to influence on-line processing of signing; it is "translucent," not "transparent," in that one cannot reliably guess the meaning of an iconic sign unless one knows the signed language already. To use their phrase, iconicity in signed languages is submerged – but always available to be brought to the surface and manipulated.

Boyes-Braem's (1981) dissertation fits into this early stage of figuring out how to handle signed-language iconicity. This work was a survey of ASL's handshapes and their uses. She noted that although much of the time handshapes were meaningless formational components of the language, certain groups of signs with similar meanings also shared handshapes (cf. Frishberg & Gough [1973] on "sign families"). Many of these groups used the handshape as an iconic representation of a physical referent.

Boyes-Braem gave a model of how this iconic representation was created. For her, a concept was first given a "visual metaphor" – in my terminology, a visual image associated with the concept. Next, ASL handshapes were selected to represent this "metaphor," either by convention or in a new way. Finally, the handshapes could manifest in different ways, owing to allophonic variation (i.e., regular processes internal to the form component of the language). The major advance over DeMatteo's model is the recognition of the role of *convention* in choosing iconic representation. As we will see, the model of iconicity in Chapter Four shares a lot with Boyes-Braem's model. At the time when she was writing, however, the study of linguistic semantics was not far advanced. For example, she did not have a thorough explanation of similarity, based on structure-preserving mappings between mental images; instead, she broke images down into features (e.g., +linear, +surface, ±full) and relied on matches between these features.

At this stage, linguists began to investigate the *system* that underlies sign language iconicity. There was somewhat of a backlash against the theories of Mandel and DeMatteo, notably by Supalla (1978, 1986, 1990) and McDonald (1982); at that time, an understanding of signed languages' classifier systems began to emerge. At the same time, linguists such as Armstrong (1983, 1988) and Stokoe (1986) continued to maintain that iconicity was an important phenomenon that illuminated the impact of modality on linguistic systems.

McDonald made the point that for a linguistic analysis, it does not suffice to say that a sign resembles its referent, or even *how* it resembles it. The iconic signs of ASL fall into a *language-internal system*; for example (as we saw for ASL DEGREE), one kind of circular handshape (the F) is consistently used to trace out thin cylinders; other shapes are not gram-

matical. Without understanding the system, one cannot know the grammatically correct way of describing a scene with classifiers; one can only
recognize that correct ways are iconic (a subset of the myriad possible
iconic ways). She argued against focusing on the signs' iconicity; though
the system is clearly iconically motivated, linguists would do better to
spend their energy on figuring out the rules for grammatically acceptable
forms. McDonald also disagreed with DeMatteo; in her view, iconic
signs are not true analogue representations but instead present discrete
categories of shape, size, and movement.

Supalla (1978) was even more direct in discounting the importance of
iconicity. In refuting DeMatteo's notion that ASL uses "continuous
visual analogues," he wrote:

We have found that these verbs are composed of internal morphemes (hand
classifiers, movement roots and base points) along with external morphemes
that add further meanings to the verb form in terms of number or aspect, or
change it into a noun. We have also found that these morphemes are discrete
in form and meaning like those in spoken languages, and that the meanings
of these morphemes are much like those found in many spoken languages.
(p. 44)

These words reflect a continuation of the effort to prove that ASL is like
spoken languages, and thus a true language.

One of Supalla's ongoing projects (e.g., 1978, 1986, 1990) has been
to establish the nature of ASL's classifier system; indeed, he was one of
the first to apply the term *classifier* to that system. His 1986 article is a
catalogue of types of classifiers in ASL. At every stage of description, he
points out the places where classifiers' iconic representations are
"parametrized." For example, in Supalla (1978), he introduced a list of
seven "movement roots," each with a specific meaning, which are combined to yield more complex movements, and he described a closed set
of six ways that the nondominant hand can be used to describe land-
marks in a motion event. In all cases, he provides evidence that these are
discrete units with specific meanings, not a continuously varying free-
form mime system.

Supalla's intent seemed to be to show that iconicity is largely irrelevant to the classifier system, as the system is composed of units just like
the noniconic units of spoken languages. It must be noted that at least in
the case of movements, his arguments are less than convincing: His seven
movement roots can be combined to create any path through space, and
because they do not result in any constraints, they have no explanatory
power. Moreover, he states that there are times (such as describing a precise path or a particular, unusual shape) when signers use "continuous"

rather than "discrete" movements; he links this type of signing to specific purposes and claims that it occurs much more slowly than normal, "discrete-morpheme" uses. Thus, even within his discretized, parametric model of the classifier system, Supalla has found (as Klima & Bellugi suggested) that iconicity is still accessible.

While McDonald and Supalla were emphasizing the systematic nature of ASL's classifiers and downplaying the impact of iconicity, other linguists maintained a different view. Armstrong (1983, 1988) contested the doctrine of the arbitrariness of the sign, arguing that spoken languages could be viewed as impoverished given their relative lack of iconicity; this lack is a necessary consequence (as Stokoe [1986] also noted) of the fact that audible signs by their nature resemble far fewer concepts than do visible signs. This is a theme I shall return to in Chapter Four. Armstrong has suggested that had linguistics begun with signers, iconicity rather than arbitrariness might have been regarded as a defining principle of human language.

At this point in the history of signed-language research, cognitive linguists began to appear on the scene. Researchers such as Liddell (1990, 1992, 1995, 1998), van Hoek (1996), Wilcox (1993, 2000), S. Wilcox (1998), and Brennan (1990, 1994) began to introduce the concepts of visual imagery, conceptual structure, and metaphor to descriptions of signed language in a systematic way. Though most earlier accounts of iconicity simply appealed to the notion of "imagery," the tools of cognitive linguistics allow a more precise analysis.

Many of these linguists' works are cited in the following chapters, but explicit mention of a few is useful here. Elisabeth Engberg-Pedersen does not explicitly adopt the cognitivist model, but her work fits well within the paradigm. Her (1993) book focuses on the use of space in Danish Sign Language, showing that many of these uses are iconic and others are metaphorical as well. For example, she discussed motivations for choosing particular loci to represent particular types of referents. One metaphorical motivation relates closeness and intimacy: Loci with which the signer feels intimate or identified are placed closer to the signer, and others are farther away. She also discussed the TIME LINE structure in Danish Sign Language (cf. Chapter Seven), classifier predicates (which she prefers to call *polymorphemic verbs*), and verb agreement.

Brennan's work on iconicity and metaphor is cross-referenced throughout the following chapters. Her 1990 book provides evidence for these phenomena in British Sign Language, plus a model of metaphorical/iconic word formation that in many ways resembles the model in Chapter Four. One difference between her work and others' in the cognitive framework is her use of the term *metaphor*; she does not make a distinction between pure iconicity and metaphor-linked iconicity and instead uses *metaphor* to describe the iconic mapping itself. Many elements that she calls metaphors (e.g., the EMANATE, ABSORB, and BALANCE structures) in the framework provided here would be called *image-schemas* and treated as purely iconic.

Liddell has introduced a number of cognitivist concepts to the study of signed languages, notably *conceptual blending* (1998) in classifier signs. It is his 1992 manuscript "Paths to Lexical Imagery," however, that is essential to our discussion of iconicity. In that paper, he mounted an attack on the arbitrariness-of-the-sign doctrine, using linguistic iconicity as a major example. He notes that the iconic items in signed and spoken languages are completely analogous: They resemble their referents in structure while conforming to the phonotactics of their language. After looking at other types of motivation in language (e.g., compounds, acronyms), he concludes that rather than arbitrariness, *motivation* seems to be the central principle of language. We will return to these points noted by Liddell throughout this book.

S. Wilcox (1998) analyzed iconicity using the Cognitive Grammar framework of Langacker (e.g., 1987, 1991a,b). He has noted, as I do, that iconicity is a relationship not between words and the world but between our mental conceptions of a linguistic item's form and its meaning; because of this, he used the term *cognitive iconicity*. He has proposed that owing to the pervasive influence of metaphor and iconicity on their structure, all signed languages will share certain morphological structures. I will return to this proposal in Chapter Eleven.

The next chapters will bring together and integrate these insights within the cognitivist framework. We will see that linguistic iconicity works in the same way, regardless of modality. The early models of DeMatteo and Boyes-Braem will be revisited in light of new developments in cognitive linguistics. Mandel's catalogue of signed-language iconicity will be expanded and compared to a similar catalogue of spoken-language iconicity. Finally, the connection between iconicity and conceptual metaphor in signed languages will be clearly defined and described.

CHAPTER FOUR

The Analogue-Building Model of Linguistic Iconicity

THE ANALOGUE-BUILDING MODEL: IMAGE SELECTION, SCHEMATIZATION, AND ENCODING

The examples of Chapter Three have demonstrated that both signed and spoken languages have iconicity, and that iconicity manifests not only at the lexical level but also at morphological and syntactic levels. This is enough to show that form–meaning resemblance should be included on the list of phenomena that all reasonable linguistic theories explain. Other questions about iconicity immediately arise. How are iconic items created? How is the form–meaning resemblance modeled in users' minds? Are new iconic items created on-line? How does iconicity interact with other ways in which meaning motivates form? This chapter proposes answers to some of these questions.

The purpose of this chapter is to provide a general framework and a set of tools for precise description, modeling, and analysis of iconic linguistic items. As we shall see, this framework can be applied equally well to iconicity in either the spoken or signed modality and at any level of linguistic structure. The fact that iconicity is more common in the signed modality is a simple consequence of this framework as well.

To model iconicity fully, we need to talk both about structure-preserving mappings of meaning onto form and about creation of particular forms ("analogues") that are amenable to such mappings. In most iconic items, we create an analogue of the referent's image out of the phonetic "stuff" of our language: sounds, movements, shapes. How exactly do we determine the form of that "stuff"? What processes would be necessary to create a valid linguistic form that nonetheless preserves the structure of its referent?

I offer here some tools for thinking about how iconic items arise in languages, in the form of an "analogue-building" model of iconicity. The

model owes a great deal to the thinking of DeMatteo (1977), Boyes-
Braem (1981), Brennan (1990), and Liddell (1992); it is more general
than any one of those treatments, however, being applicable to both
signed and spoken languages and to lexical, morphological, and syntactic iconicity, and it incorporates recent cognitive linguistics work on
semantics.

The basic model is diagrammed in Figure 4.1, using ASL TREE as an
example. It can be summarized as follows: To create an iconic item, one
selects an image to represent, modifies or *schematizes* that image so that
it is representable by the language, and chooses appropriate forms to
show or *encode* each representable part of the image. Moreover, when
modifying the image or "translating" it into linguistic form, one makes
sure that the new image preserves the relevant physical structure of the
previous stage.

I would like to make it clear that this model is not intended to represent what goes on in a language user's mind each time he or she utters an
iconic item. This is a model for the *creation* of iconic items; once created,
these items can be stored and used just like any other linguistic item. As
Brennan (1990) pointed out, these items can also be modified by language-internal morphological processes such as compounding.

Moreover, though the model is presented as having stages, I am not
making a claim that the stages represent a *sequence* that the language
user goes through. For the purposes of exposition, it is easiest to separate
out the aspects of analogue building into stages, but the cognitive
processes for each aspect could easily occur simultaneously: For example, the aspects may be viewed as providing sets of constraints that could
be integrated together and satisfied all at the same time. (Langacker

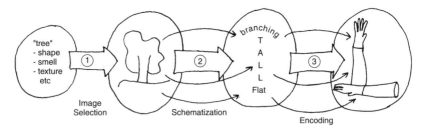

Figure 4.1. Analogue-building process for American Sign Language (ASL) TREE,
showing **(A)** the initial concept *tree,* **(B)** prototypical visual image of a tree, **(C)**
image schematized to fit ASL's categories, and **(D)** image encoded as TREE, and
the three processes of (1) image selection, (2) schematization, and (3) encoding;
arrows show structure-preserving correspondences between **B, C,** and **D.**

[1987] took a similar position on the status of "derivational stages" in his models.)

Image Selection

Let us go through each part of the model. The analogue-building process begins with a concept that needs a linguistic representation. Such concepts are potentially multimodal and densely packed with information. For example, the concept "tree" probably contains images from many different sensory modalities: visual images of various tree species and individuals, tactile images of how bark and leaves feel, auditory images (for hearing people) of leaves rustling and branches groaning in the wind, kinesthetic images of climbing trees or cutting wood, even images of smells and tastes associated with trees.[1] Along with this plethora of sensory images, there is no doubt encyclopedic information about how trees grow from seeds or cuttings, their life cycles, their uses, and so on.

Out of this potentially vast amount of information, we *select* a sensory image to stand for the entire concept. This image must be in a modality that the language can directly represent – for example, auditory for spoken languages, visual for signed languages, temporal for either one. For ASL TREE, the image is as described in Chapter Three, a tree growing out of flat ground, with branches atop a bare trunk.

Note that there are often a number of appropriate images to choose from, and the choice can vary from language to language and culture to culture. The particular image used for a given language represents a choice made by the user(s) of the language who created that iconic item; that choice of image may be somewhat arbitrary (within the appropriate alternatives), but it becomes conventionally established in the language.

The image selected by ASL for *tree* is fairly typical for our culture, though (as pointed out earlier) there are many kinds of trees that look significantly different. Nevertheless, that single image has achieved the special status of representing the concept "tree" in general for ASL.

Selecting a single image to stand for a complex associated concept is an example of the cognitive process *metonymy,* which has been treated by a number of cognitive linguists (Fauconnier 1985, Kövacecs & Radden 1998, Lakoff & Johnson 1980, etc.). The association between image and concept can be more or less direct and compelling: In the case of *ding,* for example, where the concept in question is simply "the sound

---

[1] In this chapter, I am not taking any stance about the "boundaries" of concepts in the mind: It matters little to my theory whether the concept "tree" *contains* these sensory images or instead is merely *closely linked* to them.

of a certain type of bell," it would be absurd to choose any auditory image other than our image of that sound itself. In the case of TREE, the image chosen is a prototypical exemplar. For DEGREE, the image chosen is a visual representation of an important object associated with the degree: a diploma. The degree itself is a nonphysical title, rather than a physical object, and so a salient object is chosen for the purposes of creating an iconic sign. The different types of metonymic associations between concept and selected image deserve study and comparison with the types of metonymic links between English words (catalogued by Leite 1994 and Kövacecs & Radden 1998); this issue receives further attention in Chapter Five.

Schematization

Now that an appropriate image has been selected, we set about representing it using the resources of our language. The first step in that process is to make sure that the image is in a form that our language can handle. If there is too much vivid detail in the image, we must chunk it or otherwise modify it so that every significant part fits a semantic category of the language. Moreover, we must be guided by a sense of the level of complexity that the phonetic resources of our languages can handle. This process of pulling out important details is called *schematization.*

In our example, the relatively vivid image of a tree growing out of the ground is distilled into three main components: a flat level surface, a tall vertical shaft emerging from it, and a complex branching structure atop that shaft. More vivid details, such as the contour of the ground, the shapes of the branches, and the existence of leaves on the branches, are all lost; nevertheless, the resulting schematic image preserves most of the structural relationships of the original (presumably the most important ones in some language-specific sense – the ones the language cares most about).[2] We can still set up a structure-preserving mapping between the two images.

We should note that the original sensory image is *already* schematized to some degree, owing to the constraints of our perceptual and cognitive systems. The process of integrating sensory signals into a coherent image involves a great deal of schematization (see, e.g., Marr's 1982 model of vision). Moreover, even though we may perceive many vivid details of

---

[2] There is, I do not doubt, a set of important features and relationships that is language-neutral and depends only on the human cognitive equipment. But languages focus in on specific members of this set, either "arbitrarily" or in a way that is harmonious with the rest of their structure.

specific images, over the long term we tend to retain only a generic image.[3]

Even such a schematic image, however, often cannot be directly encoded into linguistic forms. For one thing, we cannot *fit* everything we know into the linguistic signal. Thus, there must be some kind of weeding-out process in which we retain only those details important to our language.

For example (Choi & Bowerman 1991), when analyzing spatial relations between objects, English speakers learn at an early age to pay attention to whether one object is contained within another; this schematic notion of *containment* governs the use of the preposition *in*. Korean speakers, on the other hand, do not class together all instances of containment; instead, they look (among other things) for cases where two objects fit tightly together and represent those situations using the verb *nehta*. *Nehta* would describe a ring fitting tightly on a finger or a videocassette inside its case but not an apple sitting in a large bowl; as we can see, tightness of fit is not a parameter that English speakers tend to use. ASL signers, of course, would divide up these cases in yet a different way, choosing appropriate classifier handshapes and locations to give an iconic representation of each situation.

Slobin (e.g., 1996) has called this categorization process *thinking for speaking*, where we cast our thoughts into the specific mold that our language finds easy to represent. Our sensory images, like any concept that we wish to communicate, must be reformulated in terms of a *language-specific system* of schematic semantic categories.

Encoding

The next step is to encode our schematic image into linguistic form. We have already analyzed the image into pieces that fit the semantic categories of our language; now, we choose a physical form to represent each piece, and we make sure that this substitution process preserves the overall structure of the original image. The result of this process is an iconic linguistic form–meaning pairing.

In our example, the schematic image of a tree consists of a branching structure above a tall, thin support, which rests on a flat surface. Reviewing the allowed forms of ASL, we note that a spread hand can

---

[3] This is attributable to the nature of neural network systems, which are good at generalizing from specific examples. (See, e.g., Rumelhart, McClelland, & the PDP Research Group, 1986.)

represent the branching structure, an upright forearm can represent the tall support, and a horizontal forearm and palm can represent a flat surface. Moreover, we see that these different articulators can be arranged in a way that preserves the spatial structure of the original image: Fortuitously, the hand grows out of the forearm in just the way that the branching structure grows out of its support, and the other hand and forearm can easily be placed beneath the first one just as the flat surface supports the tall shaft. Putting these things together, we arrive at the iconic linguistic form of ASL TREE.

It is crucial to note that there are two levels at which languages make somewhat arbitrary choices about how the encoding process will work.4 These are the levels of choosing particular iconic building blocks for linguistic forms, and of choosing particular composites of these building blocks to retain as lexical or syntactic items in the language. These language-specific choices are an important part of what makes the encoding process different (more *constrained*) than free mime or imitation.

First of all, each language has its own set of conventionally chosen iconic "tools" for representing the pieces of schematized images. Boyes-Braem referred to ASL's tools as "morphophonemic primes"; Brennan called some of them "visual metaphors." In the terminology of cognitive linguistics, a good alternative name might be *iconic image-schematic items*.

Each tool consists of a link between a semantic category (e.g., "flat," "branching," "tall") and a phonetic form (e.g., "horizontal forearm," "spread hand," "upright forearm"). Table 4.1 shows a number of these tools for ASL and for English. Note first of all that each tool is based on a structure-preserving correspondence between form and meaning: In every case, the phonetic form resembles (or even is an *example* of) the semantic category.5 Putting these tools together in an appropriate way will of course result in a linguistic form that resembles its referent.

But also notice that these tools are highly language-specific.6 As discussed in the previous section, the semantic categories are language-spe-

---

4 As Bolinger (1985) said in his discussion of onomatopoeic words such as *bash,* the word is not totally arbitrary but *is* chosen, and "choice is the conduit for arbitrariness."

5 It would be interesting to look closely at the exact types of relationships between semantic category and phonetic form in these iconic "tools": For example, is there always at least some superordinate category that both belong to? I note that, though the V hand-shape is not an example of the category "legs," both are members of the category "branching structures."

6 Of course, not all tools are peculiar to a particular language. The temporal dimension may well be used iconically in all languages in analogous ways, and there may be other iconic universals within the spoken or the signed modalities, if not across modalities. (My thanks to Eve Sweetser for this point.)

TABLE 4.1. Selected Iconic "Tools" for American Sign Language and English: Conventional Building Blocks for Iconic Forms

FORM		MEANING
English[a]		
Initial *p-, b-, pl-, kl-, kr-*	↔	Abrupt onsets
Fricatives *th-, s-, sh-*	↔	Noise of air turbulence
Medial *-i-, -I-*	↔	Low-pitched sounds
Temporal order	↔	Temporal order
American Sign Language[b]		
Forearm	↔	Flat surface
V-shape	↔	Legs
Path of F	↔	Narrow cylinder
Spatial arrangement	↔	Spatial arrangement
Temporal order	↔	Temporal order

[a] See Oswalt 1994 and Rhodes 1994.
[b] See, for example, McDonald 1982 and Supalla 1986.

cific (though in a broad sense, they may be similar cross-linguistically because of universals in the human perceptual system); the phonetic forms are taken only from the allowable forms of that language; and the language uses only a conventionally established subset of the form–meaning pairs that resemble each other.

As a demonstration of the second point, note that ASL uses an extended index finger as one way of representing long, thin objects. This use is clearly motivated by the resemblance between an extended finger and a long, thin object. Yet ASL would never use an extended ring finger for the same meaning, even though the resemblance is equally good: A fist with ring finger extended is not an allowable handshape of ASL. Similarly, English would never use a velar fricative to represent noise, because velar fricatives are not part of English's phonetic inventory.

To demonstrate the third point, consider ASL's conventional "tracers." As we saw in the sign DEGREE, ASL uses the F-handshape – thumb and index finger touching in a ring, other fingers spread – to trace out long, thin cylinders. Clearly, it is the path of the thumb–index ring through space that is crucial in creating a cylindrical trace. Now, notice that ASL has three other allowable handshapes where a single finger (middle, ring, pinky) forms a ring with the thumb – yet none of these handshapes can be used as cylinder-tracers. We must conclude that the allowable iconic tools (basic form–meaning pairs) of a language are conventionally established; they are chosen in a somewhat arbitrary way from the set of possible iconic form–meaning pairs. As Boyes-Braem (1981) wrote, "The actual use of even very 'daily' hands is therefore highly restricted by relationships established within the language" (p. 67).

We should also note that there is a continuum of conventionalization: Certain iconic tools may be very common in a language, whereas others might occur only a few times (possibly not even meriting the status of "tool"). For example, ASL TREE uses both very common tools – the flat-surface–horizontal-forearm and tall-thin-object–vertical-forearm pairings – and a relatively rare one – the branching-structure–spread-hand pairing. The use of that rare pairing may have been motivated by the nice way in which it preserves the structure of the original image, as the hand is conveniently located at the end of the forearm.

We have seen how languages have specific sets of iconic tools. As mentioned above, there is a second level at which conventional, language-specific choices become important: the preservation of particular combinations of tools as a permanent representation of a meaning. For example, ASL users are aware of the language's iconic tools and can use them on-line to construct new representations of objects in space (i.e., the classifier system); similarly, English speakers can invent new words like *ting* and *kaboom* to describe sounds (cf. Oswalt 1994 on comic-book sound words). These forms come and go and can be invented as needed. A single image could have several equally valid iconic descriptions of this type. But these transient iconic representations can also become "frozen," conventional parts of the language. When a permanent association develops between a referent image and a particular representation of that image, the iconic representation is then part of the language's lexicon.

For example, there are many ways in which ASL users can put their iconic tools together to encode the flat-tall-branching schematic image. They can use an index finger to show the tall trunk and a curved claw-shaped hand to show the edges of the branching structure, for example, or use tracers to sketch out the outlines of the image. Either of these ways is a valid ASL encoding of the image, and indeed we may find ASL users creating forms like these to describe specific trees in specific situations. But only one iconic representation has developed a long-term, conventional association with the concept "tree": the double-forearm, spread-hand form. As always, the choice of conventional representation for a concept is somewhat arbitrary, within the alternatives allowed by the system; factors such as ease of articulation can influence this choice as well.

The same kind of conventionalization occurs in spoken languages. Though in the moment, an English speaker may say *sploosh* or *ka-toosh* to represent various different sounds created by a rock falling into water, the iconic item that has been elevated by convention to the status of an English word is *splash,* and it covers all cases of noisy falls into liquid.

Once a form–meaning pair has been conventionally adopted as part of a language's lexicon or grammar, users may stop accessing its iconic origins on-line, and it may even undergo changes that make it less transparently iconic (cf. Brennan 1990, Klima & Bellugi 1979). One example is the "opaque" sign HOME, where an O-shaped hand touches the cheek first near the mouth and second near the ear; this sign developed as a compound of the iconic signs EAT (O-shape at the mouth) and SLEEP (spread hand's palm at the cheek, suggesting a pillow).

These changes are not at all surprising, as we see the same effects for any sort of derivational morphology. Derived items of all sorts can take on semantic nuances not predictable from their parts. At that point, users of the item are clearly not re-deriving it on-line each time they use it but instead have given it some kind of independent representation. Over time, any such items can become so remote from their derivational origins that typical users would not know how the item arose. This does not prove that those derivational patterns are no longer productive in the language or perhaps never even existed; it simply means that items can become dissociated from the processes that created them.

It is useful to note, in addition, that iconic items often *resist* regular changes that affect all other items of the language (e.g., Hock 1986). Thus, for example, the English "great vowel shift" altered Middle English vowels so that all stressed syllables containing /i/ shifted to the diphthong /ai/: *eye* was previously pronounced /i/, *high* was /hi/, and so on. When this change took place, the original forms with the vowel /i/ were lost. Yet notice that to describe a soft, high-pitched noise, English has two words: the older *peep* or /pip/, and the newer *pipe* or /paip/. In this case, the original form (with the high front vowel /i/ that English uses iconically to represent high-pitched sounds) was retained in the language. It seems that the iconicity of some items is important enough to language users that it is preserved even when all similar items are undergoing regular rule-governed change.

ADDITIONAL DEMONSTRATIONS OF THE MODEL

As we have concluded the step-by-step discussion of the Analogue-Building Model, I will now give more examples of how to use it in describing iconic items, including grammatical structures and items from spoken languages.

Let us think again about English *ding,* a word representing the sound of a particular sort of bell. The analogue-building process for this word

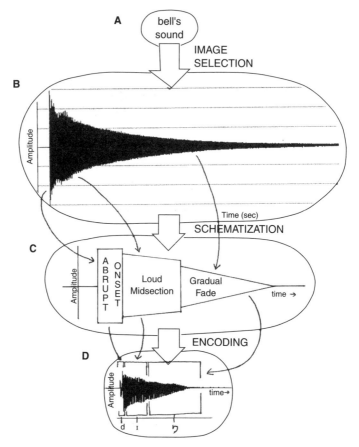

Figure 4.2. Analogue-building process for English *ding,* showing (A) initial concept, (B) auditory image of bell's sound, (C) image schematized to fit English's categories, and (D) image encoded as *ding* /dɪŋ/; arrows indicate structure-preserving correspondences between **B, C,** and **D.**

is diagrammed in Figure 4.2. Our starting point is the concept "the sound of a bell" (Figure 4.2A); as noted above, this concept is relatively simple and concrete (as compared to "tree" or "degree"), and the obvious image to select in the auditory modality is that sound itself, shown in Figure 4.2B. This sound image has a relatively high pitch and resonates for a long time.

Fig. 4.2C shows the bell's sound after it has been schematized to fit the categories that English uses for iconic descriptions of sounds: The schematic image consists of an *abrupt onset;* a *loud, high-pitched midsection;* and a *gradual fade.* Note how the temporal structure of the schematized image matches that of the original auditory image; there is clearly a structure-preserving mapping between the two.

Finally, Figure 4.2D shows the result of the encoding process. English conventionally uses initial stops to represent abrupt onsets, vowels with significant high-frequency components (high second formants; e.g., /i/, /u/) to represent high-pitched sounds, and final nasals to represent long, resonant sounds.[7] (As usual, the phonetic forms chosen to represent these categories are in some sense themselves exemplars of those categories.) In this case, the stop chosen is /d/, the vowel is /i/, and the nasal is /ŋ/; arranged in the proper order, they give us the iconic form *ding*. Other equally well formed English representations of the sound can be created (e.g., *ting, pim*), but *ding* is the form that English speakers have adopted for this kind of bell sound.

The Analogue-Building Model works in a straightforward way to describe the sketching type of iconicity in signed languages as well as the shape-for-shape type we have seen demonstrated for TREE. Figure 4.3 diagrams the model for ASL DEGREE.

The initial concept, an academic degree (Figure 4.3A), is fairly abstract – it is a social marker of respect bestowed on those who have completed a course of study. The concept is no doubt connected with much knowledge about classes and study and achievement, but these are too abstract to be of use in constructing an iconic form. There is, however, a physical symbol of achieving a degree, and that is the *diploma*. Traditionally, the diploma is presented as a rolled-up scroll to a new graduate. It is the visual image of this scroll, shown in Figure 4.3B, that ASL has chosen for creating its iconic sign DEGREE.

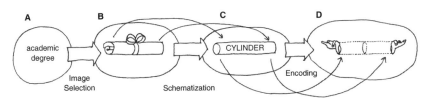

Figure 4.3. Analogue-building process for American Sign Language (ASL) DEGREE, showing (**A**) initial concept, (**B**) prototypical visual image of a diploma, (**C**) image schematized to fit ASL's categories, and (**D**) image encoded as DEGREE; arrows indicate structure-preserving correspondences between **B**, **C**, and **D**.

---

[7] It is instructive to note that English and French have made different language-specific choices on how to represent the long, resonant die-off of bell sounds: English uses the velar nasal /ŋ/, as in *ring* and *ding-dong*, whereas French uses the bilibial nasal /m/, as in *bim bim bom*.

Figure 4.3C gives the schematized image used in this sign: a simple cylinder. It should be noted that it is not impossible to use the resources of ASL to give a more detailed representation of a diploma, ribbon and all. But such a representation would be long and unwieldy as a lexical item. The actual sign DEGREE represents a distillation of the most salient aspects of a diploma into a form that is quick and easy to articulate. Thus, ease of articulation as well as the need to fit the language's semantic categories drives the schematization process.

Finally, in Figure 4.3D we see the creation of a virtual cylinder in space via the tracing action of two thumb–index-finger circles. The original image and the schematized image can clearly both be mapped onto this cylinder in a structure-preserving way. The tracing of this cylinder has become, via the process outlined here, the conventional ASL item meaning "degree."

Our final example is grammatical rather than lexical: the iconic ordering of clauses to represent the temporal ordering of the events described. Though most if not all languages display this pattern (Haiman 1985b), we will once again discuss it as it manifests in English.

The initial concept is simply *temporal sequence*: events happening in a particular order (Fig. 4.4A). This concept was perhaps derived from many experiences of specific events occurring in an order, but now the details have been abstracted away to leave a general notion of temporal ordering. The sensory image chosen to represent this concept (Figure 4.4B) is a *temporal* image: it relies on our ability to localize events in time and perceive their sequentiality. Figure 4.4B uses the device of a time line to represent our temporal sense; the particular temporal image is of an event followed by another event.

It should be noted that our temporal sense is not nearly as vivid or precise as our visual or auditory senses. To us, time has only one dimension: the sense of how long it has been since a particular event occurred. People vary on how accurately they can measure durations without the help of a timepiece or other external aid; although some people may have a highly refined sense of duration, others do not. Language tends to represent time using rough approximations of relative durations (i.e., *long* or *short* times) and notions of simultaneity and sequence (i.e., ordering of events). Though words for more exact measures of time (e.g., *minutes, seconds, years*) do exist, such notions are rarely (if ever) presented in the grammatical structure of a language (cf. Comrie 1985, Talmy 1987).

Our initial concept, temporal sequence, is in fact one of the basic notions about time. The image of one event following another that represents the concept is already highly schematic, containing no specific details about how long each event took and how much time elapsed

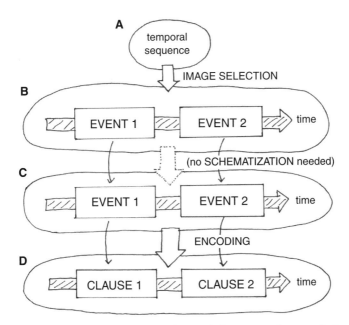

Figure 4.4. Analogue-building process for English's iconic clause-ordering construction, showing (A) the initial concept of temporal sequence, (B) and (C) the already-schematic temporal image of two events in sequence, and (D) the image encoded as the clause-ordering construction; arrows indicate structure-preserving correspondences between B, C, and D.

between them. No further schematization is needed, as this image already fits the time-describing semantic categories of English. The diagram reflects this by simply repeating Figure 4.4B ("sensory image") as Figure 4.4C ("schematized image").

The final stage, encoding, exploits the fact that English words themselves are articulated in a sequential order. English (like most other languages) has set up a convention where the order of elements in an utterance can represent the order of elements in a temporal image. In this case, the entire cluster of elements representing the first event (i.e., the clause describing that event) will come before the cluster of elements describing the second event. The iconic linguistic item created here (Figure 4.4D) is a two-clause construction expressing temporal ordering.

ICONICITY AND MIME COMPARED

At this point, it is fruitful once again to compare linguistic iconicity and nonlinguistic mime or imitations. The two processes do resemble each other in many ways: Both are in fact analogue-building processes. But the crucial difference is that linguistic items are constrained to fit the semantic and phonetic categories of the language, whereas mime is constrained only by the imitator's conceptualizing power and physical skills.

Let us contrast linguistic and nonlinguistic iconic representations of the bell's sound pictured in Figure 3.4A. This particular sound results from the striking of a bowl-shaped bell; the tone is fairly high-pitched and steady, begins loud, and fades away over a long period of time. As we have already seen, the iconic word *ding* (Figure 3.4B) is an analogue of that sound which fits the phonotactic constraints of English: It contains a vowel, and its pitch and duration are typical of English words. But an imitator would be free to create a sound that adhered much more closely to the actual sound image. The imitator could match the pitch of the bell's tone and the temporal fade in a way that violates English constraints, and there need not be a shift in vocal quality from vowel to nasal: The whole sound could have the same quality, just as does the original. Figure 4.5 presents the waveform of an imitation of the bell, transcribable as [tŋŋ].

We can compare the mime process, diagrammed in Figure 4.6, with the linguistic analogue-building process (Figs. 4.1 through 4.4).

Note that many of the stages are the same: Both imitator and language user start with a concept to communicate, select a sensory image to represent that concept, and create an analogue of that image in some modality (visual, auditory, temporal, etc.); in both cases, the end product preserves significant parts of the structure of the original image. But at every stage, in mime, the element of *conventionalization* is lacking. The imitator gets to choose any image she or he wishes to represent the concept, in any modality; there is no shared tradition influencing the choice. At the next stage, the imitator must pick out salient aspects of the image to produce, but she or he is not constrained by linguistic categories and may be as detailed or fanciful as desired. And at the encoding stage, the only limitation on the imitator's form is the imitator's skill in controlling his or her voice or body. The end product of the mime process may bear

Figure 4.5. Amplitude waveform of an American woman's imitation of the bell sound in Figure 3.4, transcribable as [tŋŋ].

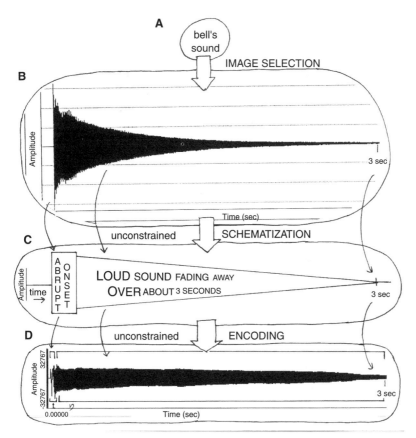

Figure 4.6. *Mime* analogue-building process for [tŋŋŋ] showing (A) initial concept, (B) sensory image of bell's sound, (C) image schematized without regard for English's constraints (e.g., retaining the image's exact duration), and (D) image encoded as [tŋŋŋ]; arrows show structure-preserving correspondences between B, C, and D.

no resemblance whatsoever to forms of the imitator's language; in fact, it may not even be in the same modality (for speakers creating visual/gestural mime).

Languages have devices for incorporating free mime into sentences, even though these imitations may not fit the structure of the language; this serves as an acknowledgment that mime is something that language users may occasionally want to do, even though they have the powerful linguistic system to draw on for expressing their thoughts. As Langacker (1987) noted, the English *go + [noise]* construction lets the speaker insert any sound imitation (or even a gesture) into the *[noise]* slot: *the bee went [bzzz], the gun went [kts], the girl went [hand on hip pose].* Similarly, the

ASL device called the *body classifier* (Supalla 1986) or *referential shift* (Engberg-Pedersen 1993; see Chapter Five) allows the signer temporarily to imitate any upper-body movement that another person performed. It should be noted as well that imitations often conform at least partially to the phonotactics of the imitator's language. For example, it is fairly common for English speakers to imitate cats' sounds using the form [mraw]. This violates English's structure in that [mr] is not an allowable initial cluster; on the other hand, [m], [r], and [aw] are in fact allowable sounds of English, though the human vocal tract could have produced a less English, more catlike imitation. Rhodes (1994) coined terms that are useful for describing this partial conformity: forms that fit a language's structure are called *tame,* whereas forms that do not completely fit are *wild.* A form like [mraw] for cats' sounds is wilder than /miaw/ but tamer than [ŋyyy], which uses only non-English sounds.

The Analogue-Building Model of linguistic iconicity, as presented thus far, seems to suggest that a tame iconic form–meaning pair would arise only directly from the *linguistic* schematization and encoding process diagrammed in Figures 4.1 through 4.4: That is, that the very first time a person wants to express an image iconically, he or she creates a form that fits perfectly into the semantic and phonetic constraints of his or her language. It is clear that the process *often* happens in this way; for example, the classifier system in ASL can be seen as a means for on-line production of linguistically correct iconic representations. But it may also happen differently: A piece of mime – a wild form like [mraw] or [kts] – will be *reschematized* and *reencoded* until it fits the language's constraints.

Reschematization and reencoding involve elements of both the mime and linguistic analogue-building processes. Figure 4.7 shows how it might work. The first three steps are just the normal process of developing an imitation: image selection, schematization, and encoding that are not subject to the language's constraints. Let us say that the result is a form like [tŋŋŋ] for a bell's ringing.

Now the nonlinguistic imitation itself is reschematized: Its sensory image is taken as the input to the *linguistic* schematization process. In our example, [tŋŋŋ] is reschematized as a high-pitched sound with an abrupt onset and a gradual fade (Figure 4.7E). This new schematic image is then encoded according to the phonotactic constraints of the language; the resulting tame form, /tɪŋ/ (Figure 4.7F), preserves the structure both of the original image and the wild form, but it possesses a vowel and conforms to English's standard pitch and durational patterns.

It may well be that if a particular wild form becomes popular among users of a language, there will be a tendency for that form to be

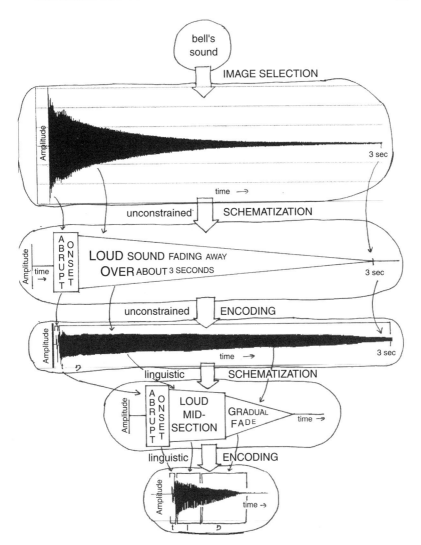

Figure 4.7. Reschematization and reencoding of the imitation [tŋŋŋ] into the English form *ting* /tɪŋ/, with the stages of (A) the initial concept, (B) the auditory image of the, bell's sound, (C) the image schematized without regard to English's categories, (D) the image encoded, as [tŋŋŋ], (E) a reschematization of the image to fit English's categories, and (F) the image reencoded as /tɪŋ/, an allowable English word; arrows show structure-preserving correspondences between **B** through **F**.

reschematized and reencoded as a tame form. One reason for this would simply be that users of a language get used to formulating and expressing their thoughts in ways that conform to the language's structure; the more a wild form is used, the more it may get "hooked in" to the language-specific representation process.[8]

This process of reschematization and reencoding may even continue for tame forms that fit the language's categories perfectly well: The forms may continue to change until they approximate some "norm" or "typical" structure for the language (instead of using "odd" or marked phonetic elements). It seems fairly clear, in fact, that this process of further taming is at work in ASL. Frishberg (1979) showed how over time, iconic signs become more "typical," by, for example, moving to a more central location in signing space, or by becoming more symmetrical.

Although wilder forms may have a tendency to become tamer, even at the cost of giving up some correspondences with their referents, this does not mean that languages have a tendency to become less iconic overall. For one thing, many or most languages have productive or semi-productive conventional means of producing tame iconic form–meaning pairs – e.g., ASL's classifiers, English's onomatopoeic words – and there is no reason why these systems should die away. We see individual lexical items undergoing further change that hides their origins, not destruction of the productive iconic formational processes themselves. For another, iconicity at the grammatical level – for example, temporal structure of clauses and inflections – doesn't seem to be further tamed in the same way that unusual sound or shape combinations can be. It may be that only certain types of iconic items are affected by the taming process.

IMPLICATIONS OF THE ANALOGUE-BUILDING MODEL

The purpose of presenting this Analogue-Building Model has not been to make a definitive statement about what goes on in the mind/brain of a person creating an iconic linguistic item; that, of course, must be discovered through experiments, not introspection. Instead (to paraphrase Langacker 1987:6), the purpose has been to bring out the phenomena

---

[8] This process can also explain/underlie the *nativization* of (noniconic) borrowings from other languages: The sound image that does not fit the constraints of the new language is reschematized and reencoded into the new language's categories. For example, the basic Japanese syllable canon requires consonants and vowels to alternate; English words borrowed into Japanese become significantly restructured, as in *beisuboru* for *baseball*. The English /beysbal/ is treated as a sound image to be represented by Japanese allowed combinations.

that must somehow be involved and give linguists a framework in which to discuss them. My major points have been (1) that iconicity is common in both signed and spoken modalities, and at both lexical and grammatical levels of structure; (2) that iconic items are language-specific, systematic, and conventional; and (3) that iconicity involves the *selection, schematization,* and *encoding* of sensory images in a way that preserves the structure of the original image. I have unpacked the notion of "similarity," shown that it is based on establishing a structure-preserving mapping between two images, and worked that notion into a model of the production of linguistic forms that resemble their referents while still meeting the semantic and phonetic constraints of their languages.

Iconic items appear to be far more common in the signed modality than in the spoken modality; it was this very tendency, coupled with official disdain for iconicity, that led to such difficulty in recognizing signed languages as true languages. Armstrong (1983), Stokoe (1986), Brennan (1990), and Liddell (1992), among others, have argued that this tendency is simply a consequence of the relative ease of creating iconic items in the signed modality. The Analogue-Building Model makes it easy for us to explain why this is so.

Recall that the first step in the analogue-building process is to select a sensory image that both is associated with a concept and is in a modality appropriate for the builder's language. It is a simple fact that we have far more visual and kinesthetic images associated with many more concepts than we have auditory images: All objects we interact with, all spatial relationships, and all human and animal motor programs generate in us either visual or kinesthetic images, or both; and Rosch's (e.g., 1977) criteria for the basic level in human categorization include the existence of characteristic visual and motor images for the entire category. On the other hand, relatively few objects, spatial relationships, or motor programs have a characteristic sound. As Liddell (1992) has said, it is difficult to sound like a carpet or a wall.

Thus, users of a visual/gestural language will be able to draw on a far wider range of sensory images than will users of aural/oral languages. A much greater percentage of the language's concepts have the potential for iconic representation.

This shows only that signed languages have a greater *potential* for iconic items. The fact that signed languages actually do have a huge number of iconic items suggests that there is some motivation for realizing that potential. It would not be out of line to propose that *languages are as iconic as possible,* given the constraints of their modality (cf. Armstrong 1983, Brennan 1990, Liddell 1992). Only the relative poverty of auditory imagery in our experience and the lack of precision in our auditory and vocal systems (e.g., in creating and detecting localized sounds) have kept spoken languages from being richly iconic; recent work has shown that such languages have found other rich ways to motivate their structures on the basis of cognitive processing (e.g., Lakoff 1987; Langacker 1987, 1991a). Iconicity is clearly not a flaw in signed languages; rather, it is the general tendency of all languages, frustrated and redirected in the spoken modality.

I wish to note in closing that the cognitive linguistics framework that has been employed here is particularly apt for describing linguistic iconicity. Iconicity is clearly a process that involves the manipulation of mental imagery: in particular, the creation of a valid linguistic form to more or less "match" a referent image. As we have seen, the cognitive linguistics framework contains all the tools needed to fully describe this phenomenon: mental imagery itself, the notion of mappings between images, ways of characterizing language-specific semantic categories, and ways of discussing language's iconic encoding patterns. These tools have come together in a reasonable working model of iconicity.

Formalist linguistic theories, as we have seen in Chapter Two, posit a sharp boundary between the language capacity and general cognitive abilities and treat language as a set of autonomous "modules," with one module handling phonology, another syntax, and yet a third handling semantics. Such theories would have a difficult time treating iconicity in such a natural way as it has been treated here.

Iconicity by its very nature involves an intimate connection between form and meaning. The construction of an iconic form must be guided at every step by an awareness of the referent image – otherwise, how could the resulting form end up resembling its referent? A theory with strictly autonomous phonological and syntactic components would have a difficult time showing how the autonomous semantic component could participate enough in the creation of forms to make iconicity *possible,* let alone *common* (as it is in many languages). If semantics really were a separate module, one would not expect to find iconic linguistic items. The existence of linguistic iconicity supports theories that integrate form and meaning.

CHAPTER FIVE

Survey of Iconicity in Signed and Spoken Languages

INTRODUCTION

Now that we have a basic understanding of the type of conceptual machinery needed to create iconic linguistic items, let us turn to a survey of the iconic patterns that we can see in signed and spoken languages.[1] This survey focuses on the iconic "tools" that are standard in different languages: the conventional ways in which forms are chosen that preserve the structure of schematic mental images.

In surveying these tools, we will be looking at both "frozen" and productive examples of their use.[2] As we saw in Chapter Three, although the tools can usually combine in a relatively free and productive way, combinations of tools can become established parts of a language's lexicon. I assume here that these no-longer-productive, frozen combinations derived from an earlier, more-productive stage of tool use and I continue to use them as exemplars of the language's tools.

In this survey, we will see both the range of imagery that can be represented iconically by the modality and the range of form parameters that are exploited in these tools. The survey does not present an exhaustive list of the iconic tools of any language; for example, there is no list here of all the ways in which English uses its consonants to represent onsets of sounds. Instead, we will note general principles – for example, the fact that spoken languages do use initial consonants to represent the beginnings of sounds. Specific examples are drawn from English, for spoken languages, and from ASL, for signed languages; these languages were

---

[1] We will not be looking at iconicity in writing systems here, though there is a fair amount of evidence pointing to the iconicity of, for example, Chinese characters.

[2] For ASL, the productive forms are classifiers, and the no-longer-productive forms are frozen signs (cf. Chapter Three).

chosen for their familiarity to the reader. This section relies heavily on Haiman (1985a); Hinton, Nichols, and Ohala (1994); Mandel (1977); and Supalla (1978, 1986) for their analyses and examples.

ICONICITY IN SPOKEN LANGUAGES

The discussion of iconicity in spoken languages will bring few surprises, because we have already seen examples of the main types in Chapter Three (i.e., *ding* and *S1* and *S2*). Basically, the aural/oral modality is suited for iconic representations of *sound images* (including sounds of animate origin, such as human or animal vocalizations, and sounds of inanimate origin, such as explosions, rustles, or bells), *temporal images*, and *human speech* itself.[3] Speech is listed as a separate category, though it is definitely an animate sound, because the phenomenon of quoted speech has some special characteristics (e.g., its potential complexity of word choice and voice quality).

Sound images are represented via what we might call "sound-for-sound" iconicity. As we have seen through our discussion of *ding*, spoken languages have conventional ways of choosing speech sounds to fit the pieces of an auditory image. The resulting words can be treated as normal nouns and verbs, as they are in English, or they can be separated off into a special adverblike class (sometimes called *ideophones*), as in many African and Asian languages (see, e.g., Alpher 1994). Words of this class can serve important functions in the language. For example, in Japanese, they are used to show subtle distinctions of meaning. According to Shibatani (1990), "In comparison to English, many Japanese verbs have very general meanings. *Naku*, for example, covers all types of crying that are expressed in specific English verbs such as *weep* and *sob*. ... This lack of specificness of the verb meaning is compensated by the presence of onomatopoeic words." Table 5.1 gives his list of combinations with *naku* along with their closest English equivalents; he comments that "...one may argue that the differences [in meaning] between *weep* and *sob* ... are more expressive in Japanese" (p. 863).

"Time-for-time" iconicity occurs when the temporal characteristics of the speech stream are used to represent temporal characteristics of referent images. This happens both within individual words and on a larger scale, in the ordering of clauses in a sentence or sentences in a story. On the word level, as we saw above, speech sounds that represent parts of a

---

[3] In principle, it is possible for spoken languages to use mouth gestures iconically: The biting, chewing, and sucking motions of the mouth articulators could be used to represent concepts with similar meanings or even similar event structure.

TABLE 5.1. Japanese Onomatopoeic Words for Weeping

cry	*waa-waa naku*
weep	*meso-meso naku*
sob	*kusun-kusun naku*
blubber	*oi-oi naku*
whimper	*siku-siku naku*
howl	*wan-wan naku*
pule	*hii-hii naku*
mew	*een-een to naku*

---

referent sound are arranged in the same temporal order as their referents: For example, initial consonants represent onsets while final consonants represent ends of sounds. In addition, an unusually long vowel can be used to emphasize the long duration of an event, as in We *had to wait a loooong time*. Repetition, another kind of lengthening of the utterance, can also be used to signal long duration, as in We *waited and waited* or We *waited a long, long time*.

On the sentence level, the order of clauses often represents the order in which the events in each clause occurred. Notice that this is an example of iconicity in the *grammar* of spoken languages.

Another type of linguistic iconicity that we have not yet discussed shows up in spoken languages. This is the ability to use language to represent other language – that is, the ability to directly quote other people's speech. For example, English speakers can say *John said,* and immediately follow the verb of speaking with the words that John used. This, too, is a grammatical rather than a lexical device.

Quoted speech fits well into the Analogue-Building Model of iconic processes. The sensory image to be encoded is the speaker's memory of an earlier speech event: what that person said, the quality of his or her voice, the emotional affect, and so on. This image is basically already in an encoded form: The speaker need only attempt to reproduce, with his or her own voice, the words that were said and (to some degree) the way in which they were said. Note that speakers are free to reproduce more or less of the original person's intonation and affect; a quoted tirade can be presented in a flat, bland way, or it can incorporate the loud pitch, angry intonation, and even the angry facial expressions and gestures of the original speaker.[4]

---

[4] Acting (e.g., in plays) is thus also iconic, according to my model: It is a representation of human behaviors that resembles the behavior itself. This is a *culturally* conventional form of iconicity rather than one that is purely based on *linguistic* devices.

Spoken languages also have ways to "quote" not just speech but also sounds or even gestures. One such example (as discussed in Chapter Four) is the English *go* + *noise* construction, noted by Langacker (1987), as in *John went, "No way!"*; *The baby birds went, "[i], [i], [i]"*; or *And then she went [speaker puts hands on hips and frowns]*. In this construction, speakers can follow the verb *go* with a reproduction of the referent person's words, sounds, or gestures.

RELATION BETWEEN CONCEPT AND IMAGE IN SPOKEN-LANGUAGE ICONICITY

We should recall that these iconic devices are means of encoding schematic sensory images. Though the types of *images* representable via iconic means in spoken languages are limited to sound images, temporal images, and quoted speech, the types of *concepts* given iconic representation are not so limited. This is because any concept that is somehow associated with these kinds of sensory images can enter into the analogue-building process.

Thus, a concept such as "the destructive impact of one thing into another" can be named by the iconic English word *crash*. This concept is not primarily an auditory one, but such impacts nearly always have a characteristic sound image associated with them. It is that sound image that receives iconic representation as *crash*. Then the iconic word is used to talk about the concept as a whole. Even abstract concepts that can in some way be associated with a sound image can thus be represented iconically in spoken languages (cf. Oswalt 1994).

The following examples show specific metonymic connections that lead to iconic words for nonauditory concepts. First, a number of actions produce characteristic sounds; this gives rise to iconic items such as to *whack* something and to *bash* pots and pans together. Sometimes these actions have visible physical aftereffects, and these effects can be named by the sound as well: a *rip* in one's dress, a *ding* on the car's bumper. Finally, sometimes the sound-producing actions are created with a characteristic object; the sound can then name the object: a *whip*, a *snap* on a shirt.

It turns out, of course, that the vast majority of concepts are not closely enough associated with a sound image, as we saw in Chapter Four. For this and other reasons, iconicity is less common in spoken than in signed languages. There are fewer concepts that are appropriate for iconic representation in the spoken modality; and, as we will see in the following section, there are far fewer parameters that the spoken modality can exploit. The smaller amount of iconicity in spoken languages, which has been attributed to the inferiority of iconic representations, could just as well have been attributed to the inferiority of the spoken modality in establishing iconic representations.

ICONIC DEVICES IN SIGNED LANGUAGES

As we know, many different kinds of concepts have associations with visual images or body actions. We will explore now the range of signed-language features that can be exploited to create iconic representations of these concepts, using ASL as an example. The signed-language examples are from ASL; cross-linguistic surveys show that many of these devices are shared by other signed languages (e.g., Newport 1996); and we can expect other new and interesting devices in other signed languages. That is, this is not an exhaustive account of the possibilities; it will serve, however, to get the newcomer acquainted with the vast iconic potential of signed languages.

In brief, ASL's iconic devices draw on our perception of hands, arms, and fingers as having overall shapes, locations, and movement; on our ability to "see" the path that a moving object traces out in space; on our knowledge that the signer's body is a human body, like other human bodies in shape and function; on our additional knowledge that animal bodies often resemble human bodies in shape and function; on our ability to recognize the body movements that go along with particular activities; on our perception that body gestures take place over time and in space; and on our knowledge of the movements of signing itself. I will illustrate each of these points using both frozen signs and classifiers, wherever possible, and including both lexical and grammatical examples.

Physical Entities Represent Themselves

Objects and people that are actually present during a signing event can be understood as representing themselves in the discourse. On some level, this is true for any communication, spoken or signed; thus, to refer to a person standing nearby, one can always point to that person. (This is called *direct deixis*.)[5] But signed languages incorporate this pointing into their grammar and vocabulary in conventionalized ways: There are many kinds of signs that consist basically of pointing in a specific way at a meaningful location or thing.[6] For example, some ASL frozen signs for

---

[5] Thanks to Kevin Moore for comments on the topic of deixis.
[6] Peirce would call these signs *indexical* rather than *iconic*; Mandel (1977) referred to this as *presentation*.

Figure 5.1. NOSE.

body parts use the fact that the signer's body is always present during signing and they name the body part by pointing to it in a conventional way (e.g., NOSE [Fig. 5.1], BODY, HEAD). Another example comes from Providence Island's signed language, which uses deictic or pointing signs as names for entities such as the ocean or the island's town; signers are always aware of where these places are, and there are few enough notable locations around that pointing is not ambiguous (Washabaugh, Woodward, & DeSantis 1978).

A third, more complex example is the type of pronoun system used by ASL and most other signed languages (Newport 1996): pronouns consist of "pointing gestures" directed at the spatial location of their referent. As we will see in detail in the section on space later in this chapter, pronouns can be directed at nonpresent but *projected* referents as well as at present ones. This can easily be seen as deriving from direct deixis: Once the image of the referent has been projected onto signing space, it is available to be pointed at (Liddell 1990).

Shape of Articulators Represents Shape of Referent

We turn now to cases in which the signed material is not simply a pointing gesture directed at a known referent but in some sense "creates" an image of that referent. One major way in which signed languages can do this is by focusing on the shapes of the articulators themselves and using them to encode images of similar shapes. (Mandel [1977] referred to this as *substitutive depiction,* in that the articulators are "substituted" for the parts of the image; I prefer the term *shape-for-shape iconicity.*) Many of ASL's classifier forms work in this way: Certain handshapes and hand–forearm configurations have been conventionally selected as the proper way to represent particular shapes of objects. These same configurations and a few others are used in iconic frozen signs as well. In each case, signers know by convention which parts of the articulators encode which parts of the referent; they also know which parts of the articulators "don't count" – that is, do not participate in the iconic mapping.

Our example of Chapters Three and Four, the ASL frozen sign TREE (see Fig. 3.1), uses this kind of iconicity. As described in detail there, the nondominant hand and forearm represent the ground, the dominant forearm represents a tree trunk, and the spread dominant hand represents the branches. The upper arms and the rest of the signer's body are not part of the iconic mapping and do not encode any part of the image of a typical tree. Similarly, in the sign BOOK, two flat B-hands touching at the pinky edge repeatedly come together at the palms and open again; here the flat handshapes encode the cover and pages of a book, whereas the wrists, forearms, and so on "don't count" in the mapping.

Some shape-for-shape iconic representations are more detailed and exact than others; that is, some signs and classifiers of this type have more iconic correspondences with their referents than others do. In terms of the Analogue-Building Model, we could say that the referents' visual images are schematized to different degrees. At the highly schematized end of the continuum, we have semantic classifiers (Supalla 1986) representing broad classes of referents. Examples are the *vehicle classifier* (illustrated in Fig. 5.2), in which the 3-handshape (thumb, index, and middle fingers extended from a fist) with thumb pointing upward represents a vehicle of some sort, and the *person classifier,* in which the 1-handshape (index finger extended from a fist) pointing upward represents

Figure 5.2. The sideways-3 *vehicle* classifier.

a person. Here, the only match between referent image and linguistic form is the broad outline (i.e., horizontal oblong vs. vertical rod).

At the weakly schematized end, we have signs like TREE and classifiers like the inverted V for human legs (see Fig. 3.3) that preserve a fair amount of the referent image's structure. Somewhere in the middle are the element classifiers (Supalla 1986) in which, to use one example, spread hands with wiggling fingers can represent moving water or flames.

Movement of Articulators Represents Movement of Referent

Another form of iconicity frequently appears together with shape-for-shape iconicity. When the articulators themselves are configured to represent a referent's shape, the signer can move that configuration around to represent movement of the referent (Mandel's *temporal motion*). Thus, signing the PERSON classifier (index finger extended upward from fist) and moving it upward in a zigzag path represents movement of an actual person upward in a zigzag path, most likely on a winding road up a hill. (Fig. 5.3 illustrates this classifier construction.) Similarly, an articulator can be placed at a particular point in signing space to represent the existence of the referent at a particular point in space. So, for example, the passage of a car or truck beside a wall can be represented by a sideways-3 VEHICLE classifier moving along and past an unmoving tall, flat object classifier (flat hand with fingers upward).

Figure 5.3. The upright-1 *person* classifier moving upward and left on a winding path.

It should be noted that just as certain parts of articulators conventionally don't count as part of the iconic image, certain movements don't count, either. These are the movements that are necessary for setting the stage, so to speak. They are distinguished from iconic movements by special path-shapes and nonmanual signals such as eye gaze and head nodding (cf. Engberg-Pedersen 1993 for Danish Sign Language). For example, the fist with thumb extended upward is used as a classifier for movable objects. If the signer wishes to state that an object is in a particular location, she or he will move the fist classifier to the corresponding location in signing space; the movement will arc downward to that spot and end abruptly there, and the signer's head will nod as the fist reaches the location that counts iconically.

How schematized are iconic uses of motion? That is, how freely can an articulator's motion imitate the motion of its referent? This is a matter of some debate. Signers do certainly create a vast number of movement paths. Some researchers (e.g., DeMatteo 1977) argue that any movement can be freely imitated. Supalla (e.g., 1978), on the other hand, has argued that only a small range of "movement morphemes" are allowed and that their combinations generate most of the paths that signers actually produce. For example, in Figure 5.3's representation of a person walking on a winding path up a hill, signers would combine an "upward" movement, a "forward" movement, and a "back-and-forth" movement to produce a relatively simple uphill path. The exact details of the path's twists and turns would usually not be shown, though Supalla does allow that if a signer wishes to be extremely exact, she or he can show every twist and turn of the path. Supalla claims as well that when the dominant and nondominant hands both represent entities located in space, they can be in only six or eight relative locations; all scenes described in this way must be schematized to fit these relative locations.

Supalla's claim is that movements and locations in classifiers are discretized and thus morphemic. This is part of the larger debate, summarized in Chapter Three, on whether ASL's iconicity makes it different from spoken languages. As I pointed out there, it is difficult to evaluate the claim that there are discrete movement elements because the set proposed by Supalla can be put together to generate all possible movement patterns. Moreover, discrete movement elements would not necessarily be morphemic rather than iconic. It is certainly consistent with the Analogue-Building Model that paths should be schematized into simpler, language-specific elements; the schematic nature of Supalla's proposed movement elements would not detract from their iconicity.

A Special Set of Patterns: Representation of Body Parts

Shape-for-shape iconicity (and its corollary, movement iconicity) can be used, as we have seen, to encode the shape of just about any kind of physical object. There are some noteworthy patterns in ASL, however, in which the signer's body parts are assigned to represent human or nonhuman body parts in systematic ways. Some of these patterns are based on shape similarity alone; others are based as well on similarity of function between articulator and referent.

The patterns fall into several types: The signer's articulators can represent human body parts of the same type (e.g., hands representing hands), animal body parts that correspond to the signer's articulators on the basis of an overall mapping between the two body types (e.g., hands representing forepaws), and human or animal body parts that do *not* correspond to the signer's articulators (e.g., hands representing human feet).

There are a number of standard ways in ASL for parts of the signer's body to represent different human body parts or unrelated animal body parts. In these cases, the articulators in question often both "look like" the referent and move like or share some other higher-level structure with the referent. For example, hands attach to arms via wrists in much the same way as feet attach to legs via ankles, so it makes sense that one conventional way to represent *feet* is with the signer's hands. (This pattern shows up in frozen signs like WALK or SHOES as well as in productive, classifier-like depictions of people moving their feet.)

Another example of this sort is illustrated in Figure 3.3, which shows structure-preserving correspondences between the inverted V-handshape (index and middle fingers extended from a fist) and human legs. ASL uses this handshape as a classifier to show the movement and position of *human legs,* and it occurs as well in frozen signs such as FALL and TOSS-AND-TURN. The V-shape with fingers bent can also represent *animal legs* (both fore and hind), as shown in Figure 5.4.

There are many more instances of this kind of iconicity. To name just a few more, the dominant forearm and hand can encode an *animal's tail*; both index fingers together can encode *human legs*; and two F-handshapes (thumb and index finger form a circle, other fingers extended) held near the eyes can encode *eyes and eyelashes*. Most of the time, these forms are used productively to show the movement and location of their referents. Figure 5.5 shows the use of the two index fingers for legs, in a construction denoting *effortful walking* (as in slogging through mud).

The next group of cases draw on the fact that many other animals have the same general body type as humans: four limbs; a torso; a head

Figure 5.4. The bent-V *four-legged* classifier.

with eyes, nose, ears, and a mouth. Because of this, it is natural for us to see correspondences between certain animal body parts and certain human body parts, the ones that have analogous structural relationships to the whole body (cf. Chapter Four, Gentner & Markman 1996). Moreover, it is natural to use human body parts to refer to the corresponding animal body parts, and signed languages like ASL have incorporated this tendency into their linguistic forms. For example, to represent a cat washing its paws and face, a signer could mime licking

Figure 5.5. The double-index-finger *legs* classifier used to show *effortful walking.*

Figure 5.6. CAT.

the backs of his or her curved and flat hands and rubbing them against his or her face.[7]

Sometimes an animal's body parts can look significantly different from the corresponding human body parts (e.g., pointy ears, long trunks for noses); they can also have parts that humans do not possess (e.g., fur, whiskers). ASL signers can combine two kinds of shape-for-shape iconicity to show these body parts. The hands (being mobile and easily positioned in the appropriate place) will represent the shape of the animal's body part (e.g., an F-shape for whiskers); that shape will then be placed at the part of the signer's body that corresponds to the referent's correct location on the animal's body (e.g., the signer's cheek, to represent whiskers). This kind of sign draws on both general shape-for-shape iconic devices and the correspondence between animal bodies and the human body; both kinds of devices are part of ASL's set of iconic tools.

As another example, to show large elephant ears waving forward and backward, a signer could place flat B-hands (for the ears' basic shape) at his or her own ears, to show that the hands represented large, flat ears, then angle them forward and back. Also, to show animals eating or biting, a handshape appropriate to the size and shape of the animal's jaws can be placed in front of the signer's mouth; for each bite, the handshape and the signer's mouth open and close.

Signs for kinds of animals are often made using this type of combined iconic mapping; they encode a salient body part of the animal, which then is associated metonymically with the concept of the animal itself.

---

7 This could be considered an extension of the *body classifier*, discussed later in this section, to nonhuman referents: Once the mapping between signer's body and animal body is established, the signer's movements freely represent the animal's movements.

Figure 5.7. EAGER.

Examples from ASL include *whiskers* in the sign CAT (Fig. 5.6), *ears* in HORSE and MULE, and a *beak* in BIRD and DUCK.

Finally, the signer's body can be used to represent a human body; the signer's movements and poses can be understood to represent the movements and poses of a human being. These forms draw on our ability to recognize the motor programs our bodies use in daily life. This natural mapping from signer's body to referent's body shows up in a number of ways in ASL, ranging from free, mimelike imitations of human actions to highly conventionalized and frozen names for particular human activities.

The most mimetic, least stylized instances are called *body classifiers* by Supalla (1986). Here, signers are free to do any action at all, with the understanding that their movements represent the actions of some referent person (i.e., someone else, or themselves at a different time). This iconic device is roughly analogous to quoted speech in spoken languages – but for signed languages, what is reported is not sound but body movement, both linguistic and nonlinguistic (i.e., both signing and other actions). Thus, body classifiers are often used to show, for example, someone waving arms, frowning, standing with hands on hips, or signing.[8] (See the section below on *role shift* for additional discussion.)

Frozen versions of body classifiers are often used to name sports or activities. Thus, KARATE is signed with flat hands on straight wrists circling as if performing a stylized karate block, and a sign glossable as EAGER (Fig. 5.7) is made by rubbing the palms together and leaning

---

[8] Of course, in describing a situation with body classifiers, the signer may not represent *exactly* what the person did in the situation; instead, the signer may choose, for example, to represent an angry yet expressionless person by giving an exaggerated frown. This is again analogous to reported speech in spoken languages.

slightly forward. Most signs of this type are *metonymic*, in that they use a *part* of the sport or activity (e.g., the karate block or a stereotypical gesture associated with eagerness) to name the *whole* concept.

More conventionalized are forms known as *instrument classifiers* (Supalla 1986). In these, the signer describes or names objects by showing interactions with them. In many or most cases, the object itself is not directly represented by the articulators; instead, the articulators form stylized versions of the handshapes and body movements needed to manipulate the object. For example, to show manipulation of a smallish flat object, ASL signers would bring their fingertips and thumb together in a flattened O-shape; this is a language-specific schematic version of a hand configuration that people actually use in picking up, say, an index card. Notice that no part of the hand corresponds to the object itself; instead, the hand as a whole represents the hand of a person grasping the object. Movement of the hand will then show how the object is manipulated. In other examples, to show the manipulation of small rounded objects, ASL uses an F-handshape (thumb and forefinger together, other fingers extended); and to show grasping of a handle, ASL uses a fist handshape.

Frozen versions of instrument classifiers can name actions, sports, and objects; they often combine with body classifiers and shape-for-shape iconicity. So, for example, BASEBALL (shown in Fig. 5.8) uses two fists touching as if gripping a baseball bat ready to swing; TEA uses the F-handshape moving around above a curved C-shaped hand, as if swishing a teabag around inside a cup; and the verbs FIND, GIVE (see Fig. 9.5), and MOVE all use handshapes derived from instrument classifiers.

Figure 5.8. BASEBALL.

The use of body and instrument classifiers is strongly motivated by the distinctiveness of body actions: Sometimes it is easier to produce and recognize body movements associated with an object than an analogue of the object itself. For example, showing the action of turning a crank makes it clear that the long, thin object in question is in fact a crank. Similarly, showing the way that an object must be lifted can give us the shape and size of that object more clearly than a "sketch" of the object itself. The existence of these forms shows that we categorize things in our environment not just by shapes, sizes, or other "objective" criteria but also by the way we interact with them.

Shape of Articulators' Path Represents Shape of Referent

So far, we have looked only at cases where the articulators' shape and configuration represents the referent's shape; now we turn to ASL's second major iconic strategy. Here, the signer's articulators trace out a *path* in space whose shape resembles the referent's shape. This strategy is possible because of our general cognitive ability to look at a moving object and perceive the shape of its path as a whole. Note that while using this strategy, the signer has no way to represent the referent's movement through space; the articulators' movement shows static extent in space rather than movement of the referent over time. (Mandel [1977] called this *atemporal motion*.)

ASL uses a number of conventional handshapes as "tracers," as we saw in Chapter Three in our discussion of ASL DEGREE. For example, index fingertips trace out lines, flat hands with fingers together (the B-shape) trace out planes, curved hands (the C-shape) trace out curved surfaces, and thumb-and-forefinger circles (the F-shape) trace out small cylinders. Just as with shape-for-shape iconicity, only certain parts of the articulators are understood as counting – that is, as leaving behind a trace; for example, the extended three fingers of the F-handshape leave no trace when the thumb-and-forefinger circle traces out a cylinder. And just as with path-for-path iconicity, only certain parts of the motion count as part of the path; movements required for setup are not included.

As Mandel points out, this method (which he calls *virtual depiction*) enables signers to make their clearest, most detailed specification of shapes: They are not limited to the general outlines of fingers, hands, and arms but can "sketch" in the air many details and subtleties.[9] For

---

[9] The degree of detail depends partly on the signer's choice and partly on conventional schematization of the referent image. It is not clear whether there are form-based constraints on the complexity of path-for-shape paths.

Figure 5.9. A classifier-based description of a floor lamp; the signer first articulates LAMP, then traces a long, thin vertical cylinder, and finally traces a ruffled conical section at the top of the cylinder.

example, a description of a floor lamp might begin with the lexical sign LAMP, followed by both F-hands sketching out a vertical cylinder, and then both spread hands tracing the shape of the lampshade; this sequence is illustrated in Figure 5.9. Once the lamp has been described, subsequent references to it might use the less-detailed shape-for-shape classifiers; in particular, the fist with thumb extended upward (for movable objects) or the fist with index finger extended upward (for tall, thin objects).

Path-for-shape iconicity is very common in the description of physical objects, as might be expected; the example of the floor lamp above is typical. Quite a few path-for-shape descriptions have become frozen signs naming particular referents; our familiar example DEGREE is of this sort, as is HOUSE, in which both B-hands trace the silhouette of a pointed roof and vertical walls. (This is the schematic image of a prototypical house; it is used whether or not the roof is actually pointed.)

Shape-for-shape and path-for-shape iconicity can combine in interesting ways. Recall that ASL has a number of conventions through which the signer's hands and fingers represent human and animal body parts (the "special patterns" dicussed above). All of these conventions can combine with path-for-shape iconicity. As we know, the signer's body parts can represent *noncorresponding human or animal body parts* (e.g., hands for feet, fingers for legs, etc.); when the signer wants to specify that the body parts have a particular shape, the hands can sketch out a path that gives the details of the shape. One example is the usual way of describing high-heeled shoes: the dominant hand sketches the outline of the heel and toe on the nondominant hand, which represents a foot.

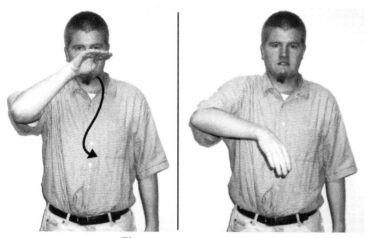

Figure 5.10. ELEPHANT.

Similarly, signer's body parts can represent *corresponding animal body parts*: path-for-shape iconicity can again give additional information about the shape of these parts. The frozen sign ELEPHANT (Fig. 5.10), for example, traces the elephant's trunk starting at the signer's nose; a classifier-based description of a lion's claws would sketch them out at the signer's nondominant hand. Finally, path-for-shape iconicity can show the exact shape of a *corresponding human body part or accessory*. One example of this is the frozen sign EYEGLASSES, where the thumbs and index fingers of both hands trace the approximate shape of lenses in front of the signer's eyes; another, more productive use is the usual way of showing hairstyles and lengths, by tracing the outline of the hairstyle on the signer's own head and body.

Locations in Signing Space Represent Locations in Mental Spaces

There are a number of different mapping systems by which locations in signing space can represent locations in some mental space, either real or imagined; these systems are more or less comprehensive, in that they can set up correspondences either with a very limited chunk of signing space, with the entire space around the signer, or with some intermediately sized section of signing space.[10]

---

[10] There is an extensive literature (e.g., Engberg-Pedersen 1993; Kimura 1990; Klima & Bellugi 1979; Liddell 1990; Padden 1988; Poizner, Klima, & Bellugi, 1987) and ongoing debate on the nature of the use of space in signed languages. Some supporting evidence for the current position is presented in this chapter, and some is in Chapter Nine's discussion of spatial and agreement verbs.

Let us start with a use that can be fairly limited. The space-for-space iconic principle is deeply involved in both shape-for-shape and path-for-shape iconicity: In both cases, there is a structure-preserving mapping between signing space and some imagined space, such that relative distance and direction between locations is preserved. This mapping may be limited to the area of space occupied by the iconic sign or classifier. For example, in TREE, the spread fingers of the dominant hand are above and adjacent to the dominant forearm rather than directly adjacent to the nondominant forearm; this corresponds to a mental image in which the tree's branches are above and adjacent to the tree's trunk. Similarly, in HOUSE, the sketched diagonal planes are above the sketched vertical planes, corresponding to the way in which a roof sits on top of a house's walls. In both of these examples, the area occupied by the sign maps onto the area occupied by the referent in some mental space, but no further iconic mapping attaches to locations that are outside that area.

We also see this principle at work in path-for-path iconicity, where the movements of articulators through various locations in signing space represent the movement of an entity through locations in some real or imagined space. In this case, more of signing space can be assigned meaning; the area through which the articulators move is usually mapped as part of an iconic "landscape."

There are uses of classifiers, however, that involve a comprehensive and thorough mapping between most of signing space and a mental space. In these cases, the signer is explicitly describing a complicated scene or landscape. A typical example is the description of a room; the signer can establish in space the limits of the room and proceed to name objects and place them in the signing-space locations that correspond to their real-world locations. Generally, a large percentage of signing space gets used for these descriptions.

Another use of space-for-space iconicity is woven into ASL's verbal and pronominal agreement system. Locations in space, or *loci,* are set up to represent people or places in a discourse; Liddell (1990) has shown that in many cases, a full-scale iconic image of the referent is mapped onto the locus.

Liddell's chapter deals with ASL anaphora and verb agreement, which involve (loosely speaking) associating a place in signing space with a particular referent and displacing signs' locations toward that place to indicate pronouns' referents or verbs' arguments. Liddell showed that these places often "contain" full-size mental images of the referent.

The evidence is as follows. ASL verbs and pronouns can also be directed at a person who is present in the signing context; in those cases,

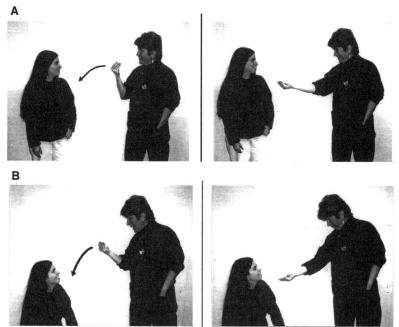

Figure 5.11. The sign I-GIVE-(TO)-YOU, inflected for agreement with **(A)** an addressee of the same height as the signer and **(B)** a shorter addressee.

verbs have a characteristic "height" – they are directed toward a specific area on the person's body. For example, GIVE is directed at the person's chest and ASK at the person's chin. Thus, the taller the person in question, the higher the articulation of the sign's endpoint (Fig. 5.11).

Liddell noted that even when the referent person is not present, the height of the verb still reflects the referent's actual height (Fig. 5.12): Verbs agreeing with a taller person are still directed at a higher level in space. The only way for this to happen would be if signers are actually accessing a mental image of the person, height and all, and mapping it onto signing space. Different parts of the mental image are being mapped in a structure-preserving way onto adjacent pieces of signing space[11] (Fig. 5.13). We must note that in this type of iconicity, the space

---

[11] Note that this is much like the process involved in iconicity, where an image of the referent can be mapped onto an image of the form; it's enough like it that I prefer to treat projection of images onto signing space as a form of iconicity. The difference between the image projection in anaphora and in "normal" iconicity is that in the latter case, the articulators provide a physical configuration on which to ground the image, whereas in the former case, all the conceptual work is done by the mapping process.

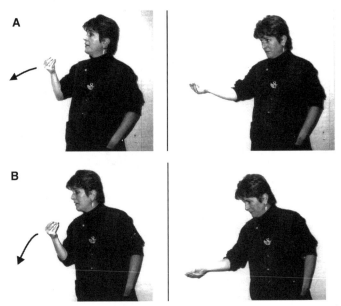

Figure 5.12. The sign I-GIVE-(TO)-HIM/HER/IT, inflected for agreement with (**A**) an absent person of the same height as the signer and (**B**) a shorter absent person.

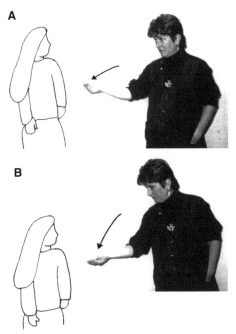

Figure 5.13. Projection of (**A**) same-height person and (**B**) shorter person onto signing space, with appropriate adjustment of I-GIVE-(TO)-HIM/HER/IT.

between loci need not be iconically mapped in any way; if the signer establishes one referent to the left, and another to the right, she or he is not necessarily claiming that the two referents are in fact located in that spatial configuration.

It has been claimed (e.g., Klima & Bellugi 1979; Poizner et al. 1987) that ASL uses space in two ways: the grammatical agreement system, in which referents are iconically established at points in space but the rest of signing space has no iconic meaning; and the locative system, in which space, direction, and relative location are all iconically significant.[12] These ways have been considered to be completely separate systems. But as we can see from the above discussion, this does not seem to be the case. Rather, there is a continuum of iconic uses of space, from the least-iconic grammatical uses (where the spatial loci themselves are all that is mapped) to the most-iconic descriptive uses (where the majority of signing space is given iconic meaning), and many uses are intermediate on the continuum. This position resembles that of Engberg-Pedersen (1993); see Chapter Nine for a detailed study of this issue in the context of ASL's spatial modulation system for verbs.

Size of Articulation Represents Size of Referent

In both shape-for-shape and path-for-shape iconicity, the size of the shape created can iconically represent the size of the referent. We need to consider two different aspects of this process: representing *relative* sizes of the referent's parts and representing the *absolute* size of the referent as a whole.

In general, the shapes created by path-for-shape iconicity are proportionally accurate – that is, the relative sizes of each part of the shape correspond well to the relative sizes of parts of the referent image. This is less true for shape-for-shape iconicity, because the shapes created are more schematic and are limited to the shapes of the articulators themselves; yet for complex shape-for-shape signs like TREE, the sign's parts still correspond remarkably well to the referent image's parts.

The *absolute* size of the image can be represented in several ways. The first two strategies depend on contextual information. If the iconic sign uses the signer's body to represent body parts, then the body provides the context in which we can figure out the referent's size. For example, if classifiers are used to sketch a bracelet around the signer's nondominant wrist, we understand that the bracelet is about the same size as the wrist. Second, if a signer has set up an entire scene in signing

---

[12] These are usually referred to as *syntactic* or *pronominal* and *topographic* or *locative* uses of space, respectively.

space, we can rely on the scene's context to establish the relative sizes of objects within it. Thus, if we know that the signer is giving a classifier-based description of a bedroom, with windows, bed, dresser, and desk all located in signing space, we can easily figure out the probable absolute sizes of each piece of furniture.

The third possibility is for the signer to explicitly indicate the absolute size of the object. Generally, when employing this strategy, the signer either will use a lexical sign such as BIG or SMALL or will indicate the object's general dimensions using flat B-handshapes or extended index fingers.

Size-for-size iconicity shows up in the nonmanual component of ASL as well.[13] For example, let us look at the ways in which lips and mouth encode relative sizes in ASL. We will be considering two separate paradigms, and both involve a contrast between compressed, smaller mouthshapes and relaxed, wider mouthshapes. The first paradigm is used for descriptions of distances and times: When discussing a short distance or brief time, the signer must squint and tighten the lips in a tense "smile"; this is illustrated in Figure 5.14A with the sign NEAR. In contrast, to indicate long distances and times, the signer's mouth relaxes and opens wide, as shown in Figure

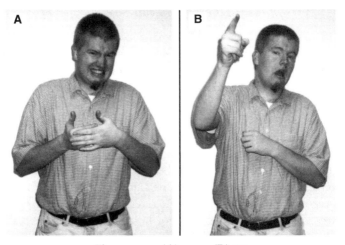

Figure 5.14. (A) NEAR; (B) FAR.

[13] Although we have not addressed this issue in this book, there is a large literature on the nonmanual components of signed languages: Shifts of the body, head nods and tilts, direction of eye gaze, raising and lowering of eyebrows, eye blinks, mouth configuration, and other facial expressions carry a great deal of grammatical information. For example, in ASL, questions that can be answered by yes or no are marked with brow raise and forward head tilt. See, for example, Baker and Cokely (1980) for more information.

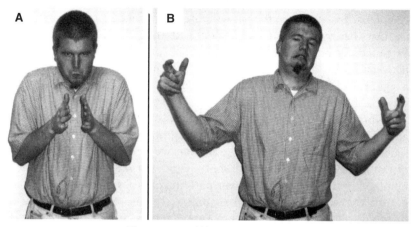

Figure 5.15. (A) SMALL; (B) BIG.

5.14B for the sign FAR. The second paradigm is used when describing the size of objects. For a small item, the signer squints and purses the lips (as if saying, "Oo"), as in Figure 5.15A for the sign SMALL. To indicate that an item is large, the signer opens the mouth wide (as if saying, "Cha"), as in Figure 5.15B for the sign BIG. Within both paradigms, the smaller, tenser mouthshapes indicate smaller referents, whereas the larger mouthshapes indicate larger referents.

Number of Articulators Represents Number of Referents

There are cases in which the number of articulators present in a sign represents, more or less directly, the number of referents. As we will see, the upper limit on number-for-number iconicity depends on the number of articulators available; for the most part, ASL restricts itself to the fingers of one hand, so numbers higher than *four* or *five* cannot be represented in this way.

To give a simple example, the ASL signs for numbers *one* through *five* each consist of a handshape with the appropriate number of fingers extended.[14] Another example is what Supalla (1986) called *pluralized*

---

[14] It should be noted that these signs are conventionalized as well as iconic: To correctly articulate the ASL number signs, one must extend not simply the correct *number* of fingers but specifically the exact fingers required by the language. A noteworthy example is ASL THREE. Most American English speakers, when indicating the number *three* by gesture, will touch thumb to pinky and raise index, middle, and ring fingers; this is in fact the ASL sign SIX. THREE is made by extending the thumb, index, and middle fingers and folding down the ring finger and pinky. As this description suggests, the ASL signs for numbers greater than *five* are not iconic in any simple way.

classifiers. For example, the fist with the index finger vertically extended is a classifier representing one person; with the index and middle fingers extended, it represents two people. The one-to-one correspondence between fingers and people works for up to four referents; beyond that, a signer uses both hands, with four fingers extended on each one, as a classifier representing *many* people.

"Number-for-number" iconicity has also worked its way into the grammar of ASL, though (as usual for grammar) the numbers represented are more limited: In the grammar, we find iconic representation of the numbers *one, two,* and *many* (Padden 1988). We can see these numbers in the spatial agreement patterns of verbs like GIVE. If the situation to be described involves one recipient, GIVE's movement is directed toward a single locus in space, representing the recipient. If the situation involves two recipients (as in *I gave it to two people*), GIVE will take on a *dual* inflection: The verb will move first from donor to one locus and second from donor to a second locus.[15] Finally, if the situation involves many recipients, the verb will have a *multiple* inflection: From donor, it will sweep across a wide arc of signing space; this arc can be understood as containing a large but unspecified number of recipient loci.

Finally, number-for-number iconicity is at work in the ASL phenomenon known as *number incorporation*. Basically, in number incorporation the handshape of a sign varies according to how many referents are being described; the handshape becomes the shape of the appropriate ASL number sign. For example, the sign HOUR, illustrated in Figure 5.16, is usually articulated with an extended index finger (ASL ONE). It can be modified, however, to mean TWO-HOURS, THREE-HOURS, and so on, by adding the additional appropriate fingers to the handshape; Figure 5.17 illustrates TWO-HOURS, with its two extended fingers. Up to *four* or *five* (and in some cases, up to *nine*) referents can be agreed with in this way. There are several subtypes of number incorporation; Liddell (1996) has made an extensive analysis of the phenomenon. Number incorporation

---

[15] The dual inflection in ASL takes on a number of forms. According to Padden (1988), "i) The verb stem is executed twice, with the inflected end point displaced the second time. or: (ii) The verb stem is doubled to a two-handed form and executed either: (a) simultaneously or (b) twice in sequence." All of these forms incorporate an iconic representation of *two*.

The dual movement pattern (directing the verb first toward one and then toward another locus) is in fact an inflected utterance of a single verb rather than uttering the same verb twice. The dual movement pattern repeats the verb stem with a second final locus; two utterances of a verb with a singular object would involve repeating the initial locus as well as the verb stem.

Figure 5.16. HOUR.

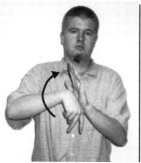

Figure 5.17. TWO-HOURS.

can combine with other types of iconicity; this is treated further at the end of Chapter Seven.

Temporal Ordering of Signing Represents Temporal Ordering of Events

The preceding sections have summarized the set of resources for iconicity, based on size, shape, and movement, that are specific to the signed modality. Now we return to a few types of iconic resources that signed and spoken languages share. The first of these is *temporal ordering*: Elements that are signed first can be understood as occurring earlier in time.

Just as with spoken languages, temporal ordering can be iconic either within an iconic description of a particular event or at the level, of the grammar within morphological and syntactic structures. The first case happens with shape-for-shape and path-for-path iconicity: When the movement of an articulator represents the movement of a referent, the time course of the articulator's motion is understood as representing the referent's position over time. For example, if a PERSON classifier (index finger extended upward from fist) moves progressively closer to a "B" classifier representing a wall, we understand that in the event being described, a person starts far from a wall and over time, moves progressively closer to it.

Our discussion of the PI inflection in Chapter Three gives an example of how time-for-time iconicity seeps into ASL's grammatical inflections for aspect: A time delay in a sign's movement iconically represents a time delay of the referent event. To give a syntactic example, a clause that is signed first can be understood as describing the first of two events. Thus, the sentence glossed as YESTERDAY, MY FRIEND COME-TO MY HOUSE; US-TWO PLAY BASKETBALL will usually be understood to mean that the friend came over *before* the two people played basketball.

Signing Represents Signing

Finally, we come to what might be called "quoted signing," because it is analogous to quoted speech in spoken languages. Here, the signs and phrasing used by the signer are intended to be a direct report of the signs and phrasing used by some referent person.

Though in spoken languages it is possible to directly portray a referent's speech, tone of voice, sounds, and sometimes even gestures, the quoted-speech mechanism is fairly limited. Not so in signed languages: The quoted-signing mechanism is part of a larger system (cf. the discussion above of *body classifiers*) in which the signer's body actions can iconically represent the body actions of a referent person. Quoted signing is the special case in which the actions are linguistic in nature.

Quoted signing often combines with the phenomenon known as *role shift* or *referential shift* (Emmorey & Reilly 1995, Engberg-Pedersen 1993). This is a device used for reporting actions and statements made at a different time or by other people. A shift begins when the signer's eye gaze moves away from the addressee and the signer's body shifts slightly to one side; at this point, the signer takes on some other persona or character. Signers can represent several characters and their interactions in a single discourse: Each character will have a characteristic gaze direction and perhaps a facial expression or posture. At times, taking on a characteristic expression is enough to signal the start of a role shift.

Thus, for example, in reporting a conversation between a mother and a small child, the signer might use three different postures and eye-gaze directions. Let us say that the child's locus has been established to signer's left and the mother's locus to signer's right. When reporting the child's speech and actions, the signer would shift slightly to the left and look upward and to the right; when reporting the mother's speech and actions, the signer would shift slightly to the right and look downward and to the left. Finally, when acting as narrator, the signer would return to center and make eye contact with the addressee. Figures 5.18 and 5.19 demonstrate the body shifts for this example: In Figure 5.18, the signer shifts into the child's role and signs MOTHER as if addressed to the mother, and in Figure 5.19, the signer takes on the mother's role and shows the mother signing SON to her child.

In role shift, the space near the signer represents the space near the referent person. If the signer is describing an interaction between two or more people in some imagined space and is taking on each of their personae in turn, each persona will create a different mapping of the imagined space onto signing space: Objects will be treated from the current persona's point of view. (Liddell [1994, 1995] used Fauconnier's [1985] theory of *mental spaces* to describe how these different mappings correspond to each other in regular ways – how they are, in fact, representations of two perspectives on the same imagined scene.)

For example, consider the case discussed above of a signer describing a conversation between mother and child. Let us assume that in the original conversation, the mother and child were facing each other and they

Figure 5.18. The sign MOTHER, articulated as if quoting a child signing to an adult.

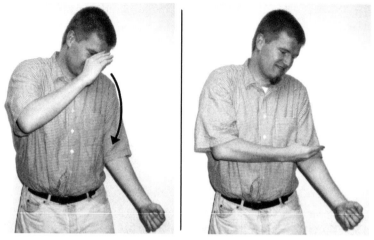

Figure 5.19. The sign SON, articulated as if quoting an adult signing to a child.

were standing next to a kitchen table. If the table is to the left of the child, it would be to the right of the mother. Let us say that during the course of the conversation, the child put a toy on the table and then the mother picked it up. How would the signer report this? Recall that the child's locus is to the signer's left; the signer would shift his or her body to the left, taking on the child's persona. The table's surface would be to signer's forward left and fairly high in signing space. The signer would use an instrument classifier to show the release of an object onto that surface. Next, the signer would shift slightly to the right, to take on the mother's role. At this point, the table's surface would be located to signer's forward right and lower in signing space; once again, the signer would use an instrument classifier located at that surface to show the grasping of an object there.

RELATION BETWEEN CONCEPT AND IMAGE IN SIGNED-LANGUAGE ICONICITY

We have just gone through the many ways in which signed languages can represent visual, spatial, and kinesthetic imagery; this corresponds to the *encoding* stage of the Analogue-Building Model, where forms of the language are chosen to create a linguistic analogue of a schematic mental image. It is useful to spend a few moments on the *image selection* stage of the model, just as we did for spoken languages, and ask: How are these mental images related to the concepts that the iconic signs eventually represent?

In discussing this topic, we will find that classifiers and frozen iconic signs behave in different ways. Classifiers are essentially descriptions of visual–gestural images – objects, things people do, and so on – and the relation between concept and image is quite direct: They are basically identical. Frozen signs, on the other hand, often have meanings that are less purely visuospatial. For example, a use of the instrumental classifier involving a flat-O handshape (thumb and fingers together, fingers bent only at the first joint) will simply mean that a human held and moved a flat object. But use of the verb GIVE, which involves the same handshape, does not necessarily entail physically handling an object; instead, it invokes a complex conceptual model of *giving* that can involve change of possession and abstract entities as well as movement and manipulation of physical objects (Wilcox 1998).

Thus, for frozen signs, the relation between concept and image is more complex: The image itself can no longer incorporate the entire meaning of the sign. We can thus focus on describing and looking for patterns in how concepts and images tend to be related. This topic deserves an extended treatment of its own; for a good start, see Wilcox's (1993) discussion of the concept–image relationship in a number of frozen signs. Nevertheless, there is space to make a few general observations here. Iconic frozen signs in ASL display at least the following added links in the chain between what is iconically portrayed and what is actually referred to.

One common pattern is for *parts* to stand for *wholes*. If the concept is a category of things that all have roughly the same shape, sometimes the selected image is a memorable part of that shape. This is a common way to name types of animals. For example, the sign CAT (see Fig. 5.6) consists of the F-shaped hand (index finger and thumb touching, other fingers extended) brushing against the signer's cheek; the thumb and index finger touch the cheek, and the palm is directed forward. The image presented here is of the cat's whiskers, a well-known feature of a cat's face.[16]

If the concept is a category of physical objects that come in many sizes and shapes, sometimes the selected image is a *prototypical* member of the category. This is the case for HOUSE and TREE (see Fig. 3.1): Houses

---

[16] Note that here it is the extended middle, ring, and small fingers that count in encoding the iconic image. In the other signs we have discussed that use the F-shape (DEGREE and tracers for cylinders), it is the circle formed by thumb and index finger that counts, and the other fingers are irrelevant.

and trees come in many sizes and shapes, but the image in both signs is of a prototypical member of the category. For HOUSE, the prototype has a pointed roof and straight walls; for TREE, the prototype grows straight out of the ground, with a large system of branches above a relatively extended trunk.

Categories consisting of both physical and nonphysical events can also be represented by an image of a prototypical case, if the prototype is physical. For example, the verb GIVE (see Fig. 9.5) uses the image of handing an object to a person. Not all types of giving involve physical movement with the hands, but the prototype does.

In many cases, the image chosen for a concept will be of a typical body movement or action associated with the concept. The ASL names for sports are often of this type. Thus, BASEBALL (see Fig. 5.8) uses the image of a person holding and swinging a bat (encoded via fist-shaped instrument classifiers), and KARATE uses a person performing a stylized karate block (using body classifiers). These actions are a subset of the actions that people perform when playing baseball or practicing karate.

Body movements can also name an object that is associated with the movement; for example, CAR uses an image of a person turning a steering wheel (again encoded with fist-shaped instrument classifiers).

In some signs, an entire scenario involving the referent as well as other entities is given representation. Examples include GAS, showing gas pouring into a car's tank, and KEY, showing a key turning in a lock.

Finally, if some physical object is strongly associated with the concept, then the image of that object may be used to represent the concept. This is what we saw for DEGREE (see Fig. 3.13): The image of the diploma, an object ceremonially presented when a degree is granted, is used to represent the degree itself.

This brief set of observations barely scratches the surface of the different kinds of associations between image and concept that ASL displays; a deeper analysis must be left for future research.

Moreover, there is an entire category of iconic signs that has not yet been addressed, as they are the topic of the next chapter: *metaphorical iconic signs*, or those which name an abstract concept using a structured set of correspondences between the abstract concept and some physical concept. We will turn to this category shortly.

CONCLUSION: ONE PHENOMENON, MANY MANIFESTATIONS

The purpose of this chapter has been to demonstrate the many forms that iconicity takes in the lexicon and grammar of signed and spoken languages and to show how signed languages are far more rich in iconic devices than are spoken languages. At this point, we can reiterate the basic insight of the Analogue-Building Model: Despite its many forms, iconicity is a single process, characterized by *image selection, schematization,* and *encoding*. The richness of signed-language iconicity can be explained by the extra possibilities in the image selection process and the many additional encoding resources that are available.

CHAPTER SIX

Metaphor in American Sign Language: The Double Mapping

CONCEPTUAL METAPHOR THEORY

The crucial insight of conceptual metaphor theory (e.g., Lakoff 1992, Lakoff & Johnson 1980, Lakoff & Turner 1989) is that metaphor is not a rare, poetic device; it is not limited to formal or colorful speech or to artistic language. Rather, people use metaphors all the time in everyday speech; in fact, there are some topics that are almost impossible to discuss without metaphor.

For example, consider how English speakers talk about communication; sentences 1 through 6 are typical:

(1) We were *tossing* some ideas *back and forth.*
(2) I couldn't *catch* what you said.
(3) That *went right by me.*
(4) I couldn't *get* my point *across.*
(5) I can't *get* that idea *into my head.*
(6) I finally *got through to him.*

These completely natural and commonplace sentences all share one thing: They use the vocabulary of *throwing and catching objects* to talk about *communicating ideas.*

In fact, one can set up a single coherent system of correspondences between the conceptual domains of *sending objects* and *communicating ideas* that would explain every one of these sentences; such a system, or *mapping,* is presented in Table 6.1. The domain to which the language literally refers is usually called the *source domain,* and the metaphorically represented domain is called the *target.* All of the metaphorical sentences above (and many more; see, e.g., Reddy 1979, Sweetser 1987) are predictable from the mapping in Table 6.1. For example, the scenario of *toss-*

TABLE 6.1. Communicating Is Sending

SOURCE	TARGET
Objects	Ideas
Sending object	Articulating idea in language
Catching object (and putting it in head)	Understanding idea
Sender	Communicator
Receiver	Addressee
Difficulties in sending or catching	Difficulties in communication
Throwing object too high or far, making it difficult to catch	Articulating idea in a way difficult for addressee to understand
Failure to catch object	Failure to understand the idea
Object bouncing off wall	Unsuccessful communication

ing [things] *back and forth* involves at least two people who take turns at successfully sending objects to each other; the verb *toss* also implies that the sending is leisurely and informal. Metaphorically, repeated successful sending represents repeated successful communication; thus, for people to *toss ideas back and forth* is for them to take turns successfully communicating ideas to each other, in an informal manner.

Because examples 1 through 6 all draw on the same mapping, conceptual metaphor theorists prefer not to refer to them as different metaphors. Instead, the term *metaphor* is reserved for the underlying mapping between conceptual domains, and individual sentences that use the mapping are called *metaphorical expressions*. Typically, metaphors are given a name of the form TARGET IS SOURCE; the metaphor above has been called COMMUNICATING IS SENDING.[1] The exact name, however, is of little consequence; the metaphor is defined by its mapping.

The mapping, or statement of correspondences, represents one of the advances of conceptual metaphor theory over other ways of analyzing metaphors. A well-constructed, well-justified mapping amounts to a proof of the existence of a conceptual metaphor in the conventional resources of a particular language. The essential elements of a mapping include a list of entities (people, things, concepts), relationships, and actions or scenarios from the source domain; a similar list from the target domain; a statement of how the elements in each list correspond to each other; and (most important of all) metaphorical expressions that exemplify (and thus justify) each correspondence.

[1] It is also known as the CONDUIT metaphor because one major treatment, Reddy (1979), used that name.

These explicit statements of correspondences show clearly that metaphors in language are consistent and systematic and that they link two domains in a way that preserves the structure of both domains. They are also useful tools for showing that a given mapping does *not* exist or that a given expression does *not* fit in with others that are superficially similar: If a list of metaphorical expressions seems to share a source and target domain but no consistent mapping can be established between the two domains, then the expressions on the list cannot derive from the same conceptual metaphor. Theories of metaphor that do not emphasize a precise statement of correspondences have great difficulty teasing apart these differences.

A number of contemporary works have focused on the relationships among various metaphors in a particular language. Lakoff (1992) showed, among other things, that there is a hierarchical inheritance structure among metaphors. Thus, expressions such as *His career is on the rocks* would exemplify a specific-level metaphor where careers are conceptualized as boat trips. But both the source and the target domain are subsets of more general categories; and given examples such as *I reached a crossroads in my life,* it makes sense to state the mapping at the general level as well, where long-term purposeful activities are conceptualized as journeys.

Grady's (1997) dissertation is a comprehensive effort to determine which metaphors truly have a direct grounding in our experiences. Grady referred to these as *primary* metaphors and to the experiences from which they derive as *primary scenes.* Other metaphors consist of combinations or *compounds* of primary metaphors. Thus, for example, Grady analyzes the mapping behind sentences such as *His theory has no foundation* and *We're building the scaffolding for Construction Grammar,* usually called THEORIES ARE BUILDINGS, as a compound of the two primary metaphors STRUCTURE IS PHYSICAL STRUCTURE and PERSISTENCE IS REMAINING ERECT. A different compound, consisting of STRUCTURE IS PHYSICAL STRUCTURE and PERSISTENCE IS PHYSICAL INTEGRITY, gives rise to expressions such as *without that proof, his theory unraveled.* More detail on Grady's theories is given later in this chapter, in discussing the application of the Analogue-Building Model to metaphorical iconicity.

THE DOUBLE MAPPING OF AMERICAN SIGN LANGUAGE METAPHORICAL SIGNS

In looking at sentences 1 through 6 above, we can see a familiar characteristic of English metaphor: Words from the source domain, including nouns, verbs, and prepositions, are used to refer to the target domain. In

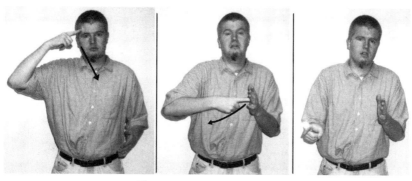

Figure 6.1. THINK–BOUNCE.

sentence 1, *tossing* refers not to throwing objects but to expressing ideas; in sentence 3, *went right by me* refers not to a missed throw but to a lack of understanding. (Notice that the data are richer than the typical philosophical/literary treatments of metaphor acknowledge; these tend to deal only with noun-based expressions such as *Man is a wolf.*) The situation for ASL's metaphor usage is different, in that it is rare for frozen lexical items from one domain to be used to describe another. What does ASL do instead?

We are now intimately familiar with ASL's resources for iconic descriptions of physical objects. In an ingenious chain of conceptual mappings, ASL hooks those resources up with conceptual metaphor.[2] A large number of ASL's metaphors have concrete, physical source domains; it should come as no surprise that ASL represents those source domains iconically using all the resources discussed in earlier chapters. Thus, the powerful communicative tool of iconicity is harnessed to the equally powerful tool of metaphor, allowing ASL signers to express a vast range of abstract and concrete concepts using vivid visual imagery.

In essence, ASL metaphorical signs are shaped by *two* mappings: a metaphorical mapping from concrete to abstract conceptual domains and an iconic mapping between the concrete source domain and the linguistic forms that represent it (Holtemann 1990). The result is that the target domain is actually presented using an iconic depiction of the source domain. For example, the metaphorical sign THINK–BOUNCE (Fig. 6.1) consists of an iconic depiction of a projectile bouncing off a wall. It denotes a failure of communication and is roughly equivalent to the English metaphorical sentence *I can't get through to him.* As we can see,

[2] Wilbur (1987) was probably the first to apply Lakoff and Johnson's (1980) theory of metaphor to signed languages.

however, the English sentence uses noniconic source domain nouns and verbs, whereas the ASL sign uses a metaphorical extension of its iconic classifier system. (The next section describes the two mappings in much more detail.)

Rather than promoting the metaphorical use of existing signs (as in English), ASL's metaphorical/iconic system tends to either (1) create new signs, (2) allow creative modifications of existing signs, or (3) allow the establishment of a metaphorical scene or object that can be manipulated meaningfully throughout a discourse. The next section presents some established metaphorical/iconic signs from the domain of communication, demonstrating tendency 1; the following section shows how a different set of communication signs can be modified creatively, demonstrating tendency 2. The discourse-level establishment of metaphorical objects will be treated in Chapter Ten, when we examine an ASL poem; for an example from normal discourse, see Wilcox (1995).

COMMUNICATING IS SENDING *in American Sign Language*

ASL has many signs that are motivated by a metaphorical mapping similar to the one presented in Table 6.1 (Wilcox 1993).[3] Some of these signs are COMMUNICATE (Fig. 6.2), COMMUNICATION–BREAKDOWN (Fig. 6.3),

Figure 6.2. COMMUNICATE.

[3] The COMMUNICATING IS SENDING signs have been discussed by Wilcox (1993); Wilcox described their iconicity and the metaphorical pattern that they share but did not explicitly set out the iconic and metaphorical correspondences between articulators, source, and target domains.

    This chapter presents my analysis of a number of ASL metaphors. Where these metaphors have been noticed before, I provide citations; in most cases (except for Holtemann 1990, Wilcox 1993) the metaphors have simply been named without detailed analysis. Explicit mappings for these metaphors are set forth here for the first time.

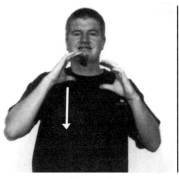

Figure 6.3. COMMUNICATION–BREAKDOWN.

INFORM (Fig. 6.4), THINK–BOUNCE (Fig. 6.1), and THINK–PENETRATE (Fig. 6.5). In the following discussion, I will show how these signs use an iconic representation of a concrete domain (i.e., *sending objects*) to refer to an abstract domain (*communicating ideas*). It will become clear how these signs share a pattern that gives evidence for the iconic and metaphorical double mapping.

Let us look closely at the sign INFORM, shown in Figure 6.4 in the inflected form I-INFORM-YOU. In this sign's articulation, both hands begin in a closed, flat-O shape; the dominant hand's fingers touch the signer's forehead, whereas the nondominant hand is in the "neutral space" in front of the signer. Both hands move toward the addressee while the fingers spread open.

The form that the articulators take in this sign is far from random. The flat-O shape, as we have seen in Chapter Five, has meaning in ASL's classifier system; it represents the handling of a small flattish object. If I-

Figure 6.4. I-INFORM-YOU.

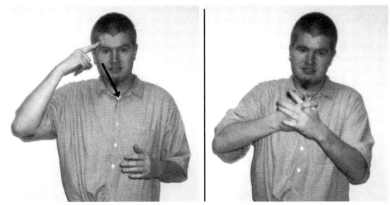

Figure 6.5. THINK–PENETRATE.

INFORM-YOU were purely a classifier description of some concrete scene, it would denote the signer's taking a flat object out of the forehead and tossing it at the addressee.[4] Table 6.2 gives an explicit list of the iconic correspondences between linguistic form and referent that this involves.

Of course, I-INFORM-YOU does *not* mean that objects are being taken out of the signer's forehead and thrown to the addressee. It means that the signer is communicating information to the addressee. Should we then assume that the form of the sign is completely arbitrary and unmotivated and that its resemblance to classifier forms is a coincidence?

Let us look at a second example. Consider the verb THINK–PENETRATE (Fig. 6.5). Here the dominant hand's index finger, extended from a fist, begins at the temple and travels toward the location established for the

TABLE 6.2. Iconic Mapping for I-INFORM-YOU

ARTICULATORS	SOURCE
[Null]	Objects
Forehead	Head
Flat-O handshape	Holding an object
Flat-O touches forehead	Object located in head
Flat-O moves toward locus of addressee and fingers open	Sending an object to someone
Signer's locus	Sender
Addressee's locus	Receiver

[4] The nondominant hand is slightly idiosyncratic – it "echoes" the dominant hand at a lower height. It is actually fairly common in ASL for the nondominant hand to "fall away" from its presumed proper height. Some signers produce INFORM with the nondominant hand symmetrical to the dominant hand; others do not add the second hand at all.

TABLE 6.3. Iconic Mapping for THINK–PENETRATE

ARTICULATORS	SOURCE
I→	An object
Forehead	Head
I→ touches forehead	Object located in head
I→ moves toward locus of addressee	Sending an object to someone
Nondominant **B**	Barrier to object
I→ inserted between fingers of **B**	Penetration of barrier
Signer's locus	Sender
Addressee's locus	Receiver

verb's object. On the way, it encounters the nondominant hand in a flat B-shape, palm inward, but the index finger penetrates between the fingers of the *B*. If this sequence were to be interpreted as a classifier description, it would denote a long, thin object (the horizontal index finger, or "I→") emerging from the head, moving toward a person, encountering a barrier, and penetrating it. Table 6.3 shows the iconic mapping for this scenario.

It is useful to note the similarities between THINK–PENETRATE and the sign DRILL, shown in Figure 6.6. In DRILL, the dominant hand assumes an L-shape, with index finger and thumb extended; the nondominant hand again forms a flat B-shape. The index finger of the L penetrates between the fingers of the B. The image chosen to stand for the piece of equipment known in English as a drill is that of a long, thin object with a handle penetrating a surface; the L of course, iconically represents the long, thin object (or drill), and the B represents the surface pierced by the drill.

Figure 6.6. DRILL.

TABLE 6.4. Iconic Mapping for DRILL

ARTICULATORS	SOURCE
Dominant L	Long, thin object with handle (in particular, a *drill*)
Nondominant B	Flat surface
L inserted between fingers of B	Penetration of surface

This is a case of pure iconicity (plus metonymic association). The iconic mapping is given in Table 6.4.

Unlike DRILL, and like I-INFORM-YOU, THINK–PENETRATE does not in fact describe a physical scene. Its actual meaning can be translated as "to get one's point across" or "for someone to understand one's point." Thus, we now have two signs whose forms are nearly identical to classifier descriptions of objects moving from the signer's head toward an addressee. Moreover, if we look closely at the meanings of the signs, we see that both contain the element of *communicating information to another person*. This parallel should make the linguist suspicious that there might be a consistent pattern motivating the forms of these signs. When we consider as well the signs THINK–BOUNCE, OVER-MY-HEAD, and IT-WENT-BY-ME, all of which both (1) resemble classifier descriptions of objects moving to or from heads and (2) pertain to communication of ideas, we begin to have strong evidence for a metaphorical mapping between the domains of *sending objects* and *communicating ideas*. As we can see, the metaphorical mapping used by these signs is very similar to the English mapping in Table 6.1.

We can now show precisely how I-INFORM-YOU and THINK–PENETRATE use classifier-type descriptions of space to refer to communication of ideas. Tables 6.5 and 6.6 list again the iconic mappings of these two signs (linking the linguistic form to the concrete conceptual domain); then, for each line of the mapping, they give the corresponding element of the abstract conceptual domain.

In Table 6.5 we can see clearly how each articulatory element of I-INFORM-YOU corresponds to an element of the domain of *communication*, through the medium of the double mapping. The signer's location corresponds to the communicator's location; the imaginary object held in the flat-O hand corresponds to the information to be communicated; and the movement of the hand from signer toward addressee corresponds to the communication of that information to an intended recipient.

Table 6.6 shows us the double mapping for THINK–PENETRATE. Notice again that the iconic representation of the source domain in THINK–PENE-

TABLE 6.5. Double Mapping for I-INFORM-YOU

ICONIC MAPPING		METAPHORICAL MAPPING
ARTICULATORS	SOURCE	TARGET
[Null]	Objects	Ideas
Forehead	Head	Mind; locus of thought
Flat-O handshape	Holding an object	Considering an idea
Flat-O touches forehead	Object located in head	Idea understood by originator
Flat-O moves toward locus of addressee and opens	Tossing an object to someone	Communicating idea to someone
Signer's locus	Sender	Originator of idea
Addressee's locus	Receiver	Person intended to learn idea

TRATE differs from that in I-INFORM-YOU: THINK–PENETRATE represents the object directly using the I→, whereas in I-INFORM-YOU, the object is implied by the instrument classifier. But we can see that in both signs, the moved or transferred object, however it is represented, corresponds to the notion of an *idea*. Once again, the explicit statement of the mappings involved proves that the two signs use the same source–target metaphorical mappings, though their source–articulators iconic mappings differ.

TABLE 6.6. Double Mapping for THINK–PENETRATE

ICONIC MAPPING		METAPHORICAL MAPPING
ARTICULATORS	SOURCE	TARGET
I→	An object	An idea
Forehead	Head	Mind; locus of thought
I→ touches forehead	Object located in head	Idea understood by originator
I→ moves toward locus of addressee	Sending an object to someone	Communicating idea to someone
Nondominant B	Barrier to object	Difficult in communication
I→ inserted between fingers of B	Penetration of barrier	Success in communication despite difficulty
Signer's locus	Sender	Originator of idea
Addressee's locus	Receiver	Person intended to learn idea

There is one exception: The mapping for THINK–PENETRATE has an *additional* metaphorical correspondence; it treats a difficulty in communication as a barrier to be penetrated. This new correspondence is completely consistent with the mapping for I-INFORM-YOU. It is not unreasonable to claim that the same metaphorical mapping motivates both signs, and that I-INFORM-YOU contains no iconic barriers because its semantics makes no reference to difficulties in communication: Only the relevant portions of the conceptual domain are given metaphorical–iconic representations.

It is important to note that not just I-INFORM-YOU and THINK–PENETRATE but *all* the signs mentioned in this section have the same, consistent way of using the domain of *sending* to refer to the domain of *communicating*: In all of them, the object corresponds to the idea, the source of the object corresponds to the communicator, and the intended recipient of the object corresponds to the person intended to understand the idea. Thus, all the signs can provide evidence for the same metaphorical mapping; taken together, they provide a good argument that ASL has the metaphor COMMUNICATING IS SENDING as part of its conventional resources. If each sign had a different way of using *sending* to refer to *communicating* (e.g., having the object correspond to the formulator of the idea, or having the source correspond to the person intended to understand the idea), the signs would not give evidence for a consistent metaphorical mapping between the domains. One would conclude either that the signs were nonmetaphorical and their forms were a coincidence, or that the particular metaphors that they drew on were not conventional parts of ASL's system. It is crucial to have at least two and preferably more data points to justify claiming that a language has conventionalized a particular metaphorical mapping.

We should note as well that signs that share a metaphorical source–target mapping need not share an iconic source–articulators mapping. Just as signers can represent the concrete, physical world in several different iconic ways, so, too, can they use these different iconic means to represent the concrete source domain of a metaphor.[5] This fact

---

[5] In particular, different signs represent the idea/objects as if they had different shapes: by a 1→ as if pointlike or long and thin, or by instrument classifiers such as flat-O (for flat objects), F (for small, rounded objects), and A$_s$ (for objects to be grasped by a fist). Wilcox (1993) has argued that these different shapes represent different special cases of the COMMUNICATING IS SENDING metaphor and that different thought processes metaphorically treat ideas as objects to be manipulated in different ways: Ideas to be selected or discriminated are seen as small, rounded objects; ideas to be discussed and ordered are seen as flat objects; and ideas to be controlled are seen as graspable in a fist. But it may be that the process (or even just the *verb*) of *selection* is what requires the selected objects to be small and round, that the process or verb of *control* is what requires fist-graspable objects, and so forth. I would guess that these verb-frames have their own metaphors, specifying shapes of objects, which then are combined with IDEAS ARE OBJECTS; IDEAS ARE OBJECTS by itself need not supply the shapes. (Cf. Grady, Taub, & Morgan, 1996 on "primitive" and "compound" metaphors.)

shows that the double-mapping model is a useful way to describe metaphorical–iconic phenomena in ASL: A single-mapping model, which described signs in terms of a direct mapping between articulators and an abstract conceptual domain, would miss what THINK–PENETRATE and I-INFORM-YOU have in common (i.e., the source–target mapping); it would also miss the fact that the source–articulators mappings are often identical to the mappings used by ASL's productive classifier forms.[6]

Earlier discussions of signed-language metaphor are commendable for noting the existence of systematic cross-domain correspondences. These works (e.g., Brennan 1990, Wilbur 1987, Wilcox 1993; Holtemann 1990 is an exception), however, either did not recognize the need for explicit mappings or did not spell out the details of both the source–target and the source–articulators mappings. The precision inherent in explicit tables of correspondences gives both a more substantial justification of these ASL metaphors' existence and a more complete characterization of their nature and scope.

TOPICS ARE LOCATIONS

Let us look at another metaphor for communication. The sign POINT (Fig. 6.7) has both hands with index finger extended (1-shape). The non-dominant hand's 1 is upright, palm out, in the center of signing space, whereas the dominant 1 points forward directly at the top of the non-dominant 1. This sign can be translated as the *point* of the conversation, the *topic,* the *moral* of the story.

In a second sign, MAKE-DIGRESSIONS (Fig. 6.8), the nondominant hand's shape and location are the same, whereas the dominant 1 repeatedly moves away from the nondominant 1 and back to it, first to one side and then to the other. A good translation would be "to make repeated digressions from the point."

These two signs share both an iconic mapping and a metaphorical mapping. First, let us look at the metaphor (one that is shared by English to some degree). Possible topics of conversation are seen as areas in a landscape. The point or proper topic of conversation is thought of as an entity located at a central place. The conversation or talk itself is seen as an object that travels to different locations. When the conversation is on

---

[6] Some double mappings may be so common and simple that they *function* as direct links between the articulators and an abstract target domain; in particular, the simple "one-parameter" metaphors such as THE FUTURE IS AHEAD, discussed in Chapter Seven, may function in this way. Psycholinguistic studies could be developed to determine how entrenched and seemingly direct the connections between articulators and abstract domain have become. I still claim, however, that the articulators–target mapping is mediated, at some level, by the articulators–source and source–target mappings.

Figure 6.7. POINT.

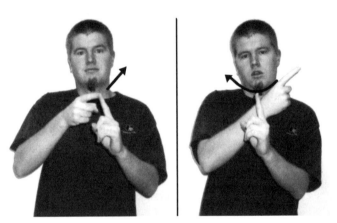

Figure 6.8. MAKE-DIGRESSIONS.

topic, the conversation/object is metaphorically seen as directed/located at the proper topic. When the conversation digresses (we might say *wanders* in English), this is metaphorically represented as the conversation's/object's moving away from the topic entity. Resumption of the proper topic (*returning or coming back* to the topic) is represented as the conversation's/object's moving back toward the topic entity.

The iconic mapping may already be obvious to the reader, but for completeness I will spell it out. The nondominant upright 1 (or 1↑) represents the topic entity,[7] whereas the dominant horizontal 1 (or 1→) rep-

---

[7] It is actually common in ASL for this upright 1 to represent an abstract entity of some sort; this is an example of a very general metaphor, ABSTRACT ENTITIES ARE CONCRETE ENTITIES.

resents the conversation/object and its movements toward and away from the topic entity. The location of the topic entity in the center of signing space represents the concept of centrality.

The iconic and metaphorical mappings together are shown in Table 6.7; the unit might be called TOPICS ARE LOCATIONS.[8]

There are several other signs that use this same pair of metaphorical and iconic mappings: MAKE-SINGLE-DIGRESSION (Fig. 6.9), MAKE-COMPLEX-

TABLE 6.7 Double Mapping for TOPICS ARE LOCATIONS

ICONIC MAPPING	METAPHORICAL MAPPING	
ARTICULATORS	SOURCE	TARGET
Locations in signing space	Locations	Possible topics of discussion
Center of signing space	Central location	Important topic
Nondominant 1↑	Located entity	Intended topic or focus of talk
Dominant 1→	Moving entity	The talk itself
Location of 1→	Location of entity	Actual topic of talk/ discussion
Movement of 1→ from place to place	Movement of entity from place to place	Change from one topic to another in the talk
1→ directed at 1↑	Moving entity at same place as located entity	Talk focusing on intended topic
1→ directed away from 1↑	Moving entity at different place from located entity	Talk focusing on unintended topic
Distance between 1→ and 1↑	Distance between moving entity and located entity	Difference between intended and actual topics
1→ returning to 1↑	Moving entity returning to located entity	Talk changing back to intended topic

[8] Wilcox (1993) included these signs in a broader metaphor she called THOUGHT IS A JOURNEY; I am not convinced that the mappings of these signs fit with the mappings of the other THOUGHT IS A JOURNEY signs, because of inconsistencies as to which entity is mapped as the traveler: the topic of conversation/thought or the thinker.

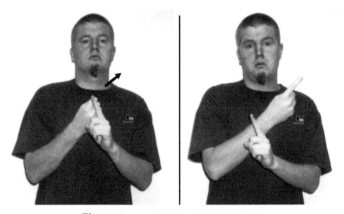

Figure 6.9. MAKE-SINGLE-DIGRESSION.

DIGRESSION (Fig. 6.10), and RETURN-TO-POINT. In all three signs, the non-dominant hand presents the 1↑ classifier, metaphorically representing the topic of conversation. For the first two, the dominant hand starts in a fist handshape, palm toward the signer and back of the hand against the nondominant 1↑; in MAKE-SINGLE-DIGRESSION, the index finger "bursts" outward from the fist to point toward the nondominant side, whereas in MAKE-COMPLEX-DIGRESSION, all four fingers burst out in that direction. As might be expected, the first sign denotes a situation where someone goes off the expected topic; the second sign is used when the person goes through several unrelated topics before (presumably) returning to the main topic (e.g., a physics teacher unexpectedly lecturing her class about football, horseback riding, cooking, etc.). Finally, in RETURN-TO-POINT, the dominant 1→ classifier starts at one edge of signing space and moves

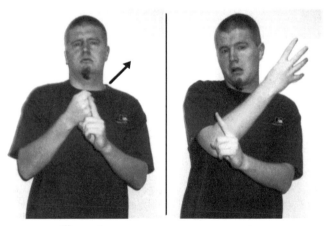

Figure 6.10. MAKE-COMPLEX-DIGRESSION.

so that the index fingertip points forward and nearly touches the non-dominant 1↑.

This iconic–metaphorical pair of mappings is in fact something that signers can play with and use for expressiveness. For example, a long, involved digression can be shown by the dominant 1→ moving a long distance from the nondominant 1↑. Adverbs that emphasize this distance can be added: An open mouth indicates that the distance is long, and a shaking and twisting of the 1→ as it moves indicates high speed. (Once again, these are part of the normal ASL system for describing movements in space.) Clearly, the same mappings from source to target and between source and articulators are used here, but the form of the sign is not frozen; it can be adapted creatively to express the nature and length of the digression.

ANALOGUE-BUILDING MODEL OF METAPHORICAL ICONICITY

Now that we have seen clearly the double mappings of some ASL metaphorical–iconic signs, we can begin to discuss how a language user might invent such signs. Once again, we can use the Analogue-Building Model to structure the discussion. As before, I am presenting this model not as a claim that the process works in exactly this way but in the spirit of setting out the issues connected with metaphorical iconicity that must be addressed.

First, we must look at the question of how metaphorical mappings arise and become entrenched parts of a language's conceptual structure. Most conceptual metaphors in language link a deeply familiar, simple, or concrete source domain with a more abstract or more complex target domain (Lakoff 1992, Lakoff & Johnson 1980, Lakoff & Turner 1989). Metaphorical source domains tend to be *directly experienced* – that is, experienced through the body, early in childhood development; they include domains such as *movement and location, up–down orientation, handling objects, vision,* and *hunger.* Metaphorical target domains tend to be less concrete and less accessible to direct observations through the senses; common target domains are *progress, emotions, communications,* and *social interactions.*[9]

---

[9] There are exceptions to this generalization: Compare Morgan's (1996) work on metaphorical "families," or groups of domains that can function as source or target for each other (e.g., in English, BUSINESS, WAR, and SPORTS are all in the same family). This is a special case, in which each domain contributes a different perspective on the other domains when used as source domain; none of the domains is more abstract than the others. It is unlikely that ASL will have such families, because nearly all ASL metaphors use a concrete domain to describe an abstract domain.

How do these particular pairs of domains become linked? One major way is for the two domains to be correlated in our experience (Grady 1997; Grady & Johnson in press, Lakoff & Johnson 1980); for example, the domains of *understanding* and *manipulating objects* are strongly linked in primary scenes experienced by all children. It is nearly universal for children to pick up and manipulate new and interesting objects and in so doing to gain understanding of their parts and functions. Situations like this one form the *experiential basis* or *grounding* for the primary metaphor UNDERSTANDING IS GRASPING, which underlies sentences such as *I couldn't get a handle on that idea* or *She grasped the implications instantly.* They provide a common, well-defined experience in which the structure of *manipulating objects* is perfectly matched to the structure of *understanding ideas.*

Other metaphors are not directly grounded in our experiences but instead piggyback on other metaphors. In Chapter Seven, we will see how MORE IS UP, a metaphor grounded in our experiences with piles of objects, is the indirect basis for metaphors such as POWERFUL IS UP and GOOD IS UP (cf. Lakoff & Johnson 1980); and in Chapter Ten, we will see how many simpler metaphors can combine into what Grady et al. (1996) called *compound* metaphors. To sum up, metaphorical links between conceptual domains are not random; instead, they are highly motivated by our experiences interacting with the world as physical creatures.

Now that we have some understanding of how metaphorical links between domains arise, we can start to incorporate these links into the Analogue-Building Model. The metaphor COMMUNICATING IS SENDING and the sign THINK–PENETRATE will be our ongoing example.

The analogue-building process models how an iconic linguistic item is developed to represent a particular concept. Up to now, the concepts we have discussed have been *concrete* ones, such as body actions, sounds, and shapes. Let us say, instead, that the concept that the innovative language user wishes to represent is *abstract*; for example, let us say that an ASL signer wishes to talk about *communication*. If a metaphorical mapping exists that connects the abstract domain to a concrete domain, and if that concrete domain can be represented iconically by the language in question, the language user is in luck: He or she can construct a metaphorical–iconic linguistic item to represent the concept. Because COMMUNICATING IS SENDING is part of the resources of ASL, our hypothetical ASL signer will be able to express concepts related to *communicating ideas* by creating an iconic form depicting *sending objects.*

Let us go through that creation process in detail; Figure 6.11 diagrams the stages. The process begins with a specific abstract concept to be expressed; in our case, the concept is *successfully communicating an*

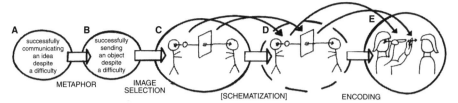

Figure 6.11. Analogue-building process for American Sign Language THINK–PENETRATE, showing **(A)** initial abstract concept, **(B)** corresponding part of concrete source domain, **(C)** and **(D)** the already-schematic associated image, and **(E)** the image encoded as THINK–PENETRATE; arrows show structure-preserving correspondences between **C/D** and **E**.

idea despite a difficulty (Fig. 6.11A). The ASL user will know what part of the concrete source domain corresponds to this target-domain concept. In the COMMUNICATING IS SENDING mapping, *successfully communicating an idea* corresponds to *successfully sending an object from one's head to another person*; *difficulties in communication* corresponds to *difficulties in sending*. Thus, the ASL user will be creating an iconic representation of *successfully sending an object from one's head despite a difficulty* (Fig. 6.11B).

At this point, the language user has a choice to make: The concrete source-domain concept is still quite general, and the analogue-building process requires a specific sensory image. First, there are many possible ways to send an object to another person: by mail, by handing it to them, by sending it through the air. The choice is made here to use the image of sending an object through the air; the image focuses in particular on the projectile movement of the object. Next, there are many different possible difficulties in sending objects through the air: The object could be aimed too high, it could go off in the wrong direction, or it could hit a barrier. Each difficulty can be overcome, sometimes in several ways: The receiver could jump or run to catch a badly aimed object, or the object could be thrown hard enough to penetrate the barrier. In the case of THINK–PENETRATE, the specific difficulty chosen is the *barrier,* and the specific way of overcoming it is to *send the object with sufficient force.* (Note that this gives the *sender* the credit for overcoming the difficulty; this carries over into the target domain as well, because THINK–PENE-TRATE also credits the communicator, not the addressee, with the success in communicating.) Thus, the complete image that is selected is of *projectile motion of an object from one's head through the air toward another person; the object hits a barrier with sufficient force to penetrate it* (Fig. 6.11C).

The image-selection stage of the analogue-building process is now complete. The next stage of the process is schematization of the image. This stage, however, is not needed for metaphorical–iconic signs, because the metaphorical mapping "preschematizes" the sensory image. That is, the mapping between source and target domains has picked out certain aspects of the source domain as particularly relevant. For our example, our sensory images of objects hitting barriers can be as specific as our memory or imagination allows (e.g., *a blue Nerf ball breaking through a fence of toothpicks*); but we already know which aspects of the image are essential for the creation of this metaphorical–iconic sign: We do not really care what kind of object or barrier is involved, as long as the crucial events and relationships are represented. Figure 6.11D, the "schematization stage," is thus drawn with dashed lines, to show that it is not necessary here.

Finally, the last stage is the encoding of the schematic image into linguistic form. This stage is the same for metaphorical–iconic signs as for purely iconic signs: Appropriate articulators are chosen that preserve the structure of the schematic image. In some sense, once a schematic sensory image is established, there is no difference in ASL between metaphorical and nonmetaphorical iconic signs: They both use the same sets of iconic "tools" for encoding, and they cannot be distinguished by their forms – only by their meanings.

In our example, the different parts of the schematic image are encoded using the classifier system. The sender's head is represented by the signer's head, through body-for-body iconicity. The moving object is represented by the tip of the extended index finger, a common ASL form for small moving objects. Finally, the barrier is encoded by the nondominant flat B-handshape, and penetration of the barrier is encoded by the dominant index finger's passing between the nondominant index and middle fingers. The result is the metaphorical–iconic sign THINK–PENETRATE (Fig. 6.11E).

With this example, I have demonstrated the extension of the analogue-building process to metaphorical–iconic signs. As we have seen, the main difference between these signs and purely iconic signs is in the image selection process: The conceptual mapping between source and target domain guides the selection of a concrete sensory image to represent an abstract concept. Moreover, little additional schematization of this image will be needed, because the source–target mapping will highlight the important parts of the image.

We should at least note in passing that metaphorical–iconic words and constructions also exist in spoken languages and can be handled with a double mapping and the analogue-building process in the same way as metaphorical–iconic signs. Some examples of metaphorical iconicity in English include *lengthening* to represent *emphasis* (e.g., *a baaaad idea*), and *temporal ordering* to represent *order of importance* (e.g., topic–comment structures such as *Pizza, I like.*) Ohala (1994) and others have noted a synesthetic "frequency code," where high-pitched sounds denote small entities and low-pitched sounds denote large entities. Finally, Bolinger (1985) provided some evidence that intonational patterns of high and low pitches, through iconicity and metaphor, convey broadly conceived notions of stress, restraint, and release.

Again, metaphor and iconicity are conceptual-mapping-based processes that function in the same way for signed and spoken languages; it is the richness of the signed modality's iconic resources that accounts for the greater frequency of iconic forms in signed languages.

SUMMARY

It is now clear that we can give a unified treatment of iconicity in signed and spoken languages; that we can fruitfully separate off pure iconicity from metaphorical iconicity; and that once that separation is made, the methods of conceptual metaphor theory can be applied to the analysis of metaphorical–iconic signs. The double-mapping approach to metaphorical iconicity lets us treat the facts in an appropriate way: Signs can share both iconic and metaphorical mappings (as in POINT and MAKE-DIGRESSIONS), they can share a metaphorical mapping but not an iconic mapping (as in I-INFORM-YOU and THINK–PENETRATE), or they can share an iconic mapping but not a metaphorical mapping (as in DRILL and THINK–PENETRATE). The iconic representation of the concrete source domain can draw on all the varied iconic resources of the language in question.

CHAPTER SEVEN

Many Metaphors in a Single Sign

So far we have looked at metaphorical iconic signs that present complete pictures of little scenes; for example, I-INFORM-YOU (see Fig. 6.4) is in effect a portrayal of ideas being taken out of one's head and tossed to someone else. In these signs, every formational parameter (movement, handshape, location, etc.) takes part in the same consistent mappings from linguistic form to a source domain and from source to target domain.

But recall how for purely iconic signs, the form doesn't have to give a complete picture: Although a single aspect or parameter of the form might resemble one aspect of the referent, the rest of the form is noniconic. Our example of this was iconic time ordering of clauses in both signed and spoken languages: Each clause may or may not resemble the event it refers to, but the temporal sequence of clauses does present an analogue for the temporal sequence of events.

The same is true for metaphorical iconic signs. As Brennan (1990) noted for British Sign Language, there are a number of signs in which only one or two formational parameters are metaphorical, and other signs in which some parameters are motivated by one metaphor and others by a different one.[1] In these cases, the conceptual mappings involved tend to be fairly sparse, consisting of only one or two correspondences, and thus they can easily be represented by a single parameter such as direction of motion. Moreover, in some signs, some of the parameters are motivated by metaphors and others are motivated by iconic imagery.

---

[1] Brennan used different terminology to describe this phenomenon (for example, she used the term *metaphor* to refer to what I would call an *image schema*).

In this chapter, we look at case studies of single-parameter iconic metaphors, signs that combine several metaphors, and signs that combine both metaphorical iconicity and pure iconicity. It should be noted that in this chapter, the term *parameters of a sign* is not restricted to the five major parameters described in Chapter Three (i.e., handshape, location, movement, orientation, and nonmanual signals). Instead, it refers to all the aspects of a sign that can be used iconically: all the directions in signing space that could be meaningful (e.g., front/back, up/down, left/right), all the parts of the body that we distinguish (e.g., head, hand, heart, gut), all the potentially meaningful qualities of handshape (grasps, tracing shapes, shape, plurality) – in short, all the iconic devices listed in Chapter Five and more besides.

THE FUTURE IS AHEAD

It is extremely common in the languages of the world for *time* to be metaphorically understood in terms of *space,* and in particular, in terms of the space *in front of* and *behind* the language user (see, e.g., Clark 1973; Emanatian 1992; Fleischman 1982a, 1982b; Traugott 1975, 1978). In this mapping, the language user (or thinker) functions as a reference point or "reference person" in space. The future is conceptualized as being *ahead* of the reference person; the past is *behind* the reference person; and the present is *co-located* with the person. Relative distance in space corresponds to relative "remoteness" in time; thus, a time one week in the future is seen as closer to the reference person than a time ten years in the future.[2] This metaphor can be called THE FUTURE IS AHEAD, and its mapping is laid out in Table 7.1.

As we can see, this metaphor uses a single spatial dimension and is thus a perfect candidate to be a single-parameter metaphor in signed languages.

Researchers have indeed noticed this kind of metaphorical–iconic representation of time in many different signed languages (cf. Engberg-Pedersen 1993 for Danish Sign Language; Cameracanna et al. 1994 for Italian Sign Language [LIS]; Frishberg 1979, Wilbur 1987, Wilcox 1993 for ASL); the phenomenon is usually referred to as the *time line.*[3] The

---

[2] This mapping is consistent with two larger (yet mutually inconsistent) mappings: In one, TIME IS A MOVING OBJECT, time is seen as a continuum of objects that flow past the language user from front to back; in the other, TIME IS A LANDSCAPE, the language user travels forward across a "temporal landscape" from past to future times. See Lakoff (1992) for details.

[3] Engberg-Pedersen (1993) also noted the existence of other time lines in Danish Sign Language – in certain circumstances, for example, the left-to-right dimension can represent the past-to-future dimension.

TABLE 7.1. Metaphorical Mapping for THE FUTURE IS AHEAD

SOURCE	TARGET
"Here"; location of reference person	Present time
Space in front of reference person	Future time
Space behind reference person	Past time
Points located with respect to reference person	Specific times
Location of events with respect to reference person	Occurrence of events at specific times
Degree of distance from reference person	Degree of "remoteness" in time

line in signing space passing from the signer's front to his or her back, perpendicular to the line of the shoulders, has become metaphorically defined as representing past and future time (Fig. 7.1). The signer's location on this line (or more specifically, the space between the signer's dominant shoulder and chin) represents present time, locations ahead of the signer represent progressively later times, and locations behind the signer represent progressively earlier times. The double mapping for the *time line* metaphor is given in Table 7.2.

Many signs incorporate location or movement along this line into their forms and, by so doing, incorporate a corresponding time or progression in time into their meanings. For example, the sign meaning WEEK (see Fig. 7.22; the dominant 1-hand with index finger extended forward, palm

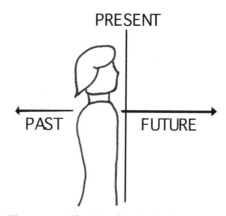

Figure 7.1. The time line in signing space.

TABLE 7.2. Double Mapping for THE FUTURE IS AHEAD

	ICONIC MAPPING	METAPHORICAL MAPPING
ARTICULATORS	SOURCE	TARGET
Area in front of signer's dominant shoulder ("origin area")	"Here"; location of reference person	Present time
Line extending forward from origin area	Space in front of reference person	Future time
Line extending backward from origin area	Space behind reference person	Past time
Points along this line	Points located with respect to reference person	Specific times
Location of signed material along this line	Location of events with respect to reference person	Occurrence of events at specific times
Degree of distance from origin area	Degree of distance from reference person	Degree of "remoteness" in time

down, moves across the nondominant palm toward the fingers) can incorporate a forward movement and future reference to mean ONE-WEEK-IN-FUTURE (cf. Fig. 7.24); it can also add a backward movement and take on the meaning ONE-WEEK-IN-PAST. Some other signs participating in this metaphor include those glossed as ONE-YEAR-IN-FUTURE (Fig. 7.2), ONE-YEAR-IN-PAST (Fig. 7.3), TODAY, YESTERDAY, TOMORROW, POSTPONE, "PREPONE," WILL, PAST, UP-TO-NOW, FORESEE, and REMINISCE (Fig. 7.4).

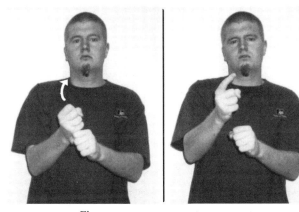

Figure 7.2. ONE-YEAR-IN-FUTURE.

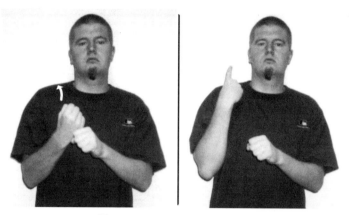

Figure 7.3. ONE-YEAR-IN-PAST.

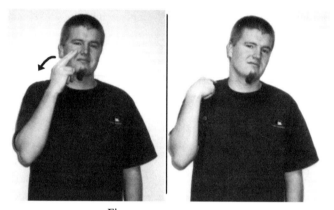

Figure 7.4. REMINISCE.

It should be noted, however, that not all signs that are located along or move along this line participate in this metaphor – that is, the line is not "dedicated" to the metaphor. This is typical for ASL's iconic system as a whole, both metaphorical and nonmetaphorical: Though hand-shapes, movements, locations, and so on may participate, even productively, in iconic mappings, they also occur in other signs where they are not used iconically. Also, a single iconic system (e.g., an iconic representation of a direction in space) may be used as a source domain for several metaphors (cf. Chapter Seven).

INTIMACY IS PROXIMITY

Another one-parameter metaphor is INTIMACY IS PROXIMITY (cf. Brennan 1990, for British Sign Language [BSL], Wilbur 1987). This metaphor gives

TABLE 7.3. Double Mapping for INTIMACY IS PROXIMITY

	ICONIC MAPPING	METAPHORICAL MAPPING
ARTICULATORS	SOURCE	TARGET
Two articulators (e.g., hands, fingers, body, spatial loci)	Two physical entities	Two referents (at least one is animate)
Degree of proximity of articulators	Degree of proximity of the entities	Degree of intimacy between the referents
Close articulators	Close entities	Strong intimacy between referents
Distant articulators	Distant entities	Little intimacy between referents
Movement of articulators together or apart	Movement of entities together or apart	Intimacy between referents becomes greater or lesser

significance to the relative locations of articulators in signing space. It partially motivates the physical forms of signs like LOVE, RESIST, FRIEND, CLOSE-FRIEND, MARRY, and DIVORCE.

This mapping is relatively simple; Table 7.3 spells it out. In brief, the degree of intimacy between two entities is given iconic and metaphorical representation by the degree of proximity between articulators: The closer the articulators, the stronger the intimacy and mutual affection between the entities (cf. Sweetser 1995 for a similar mapping in English).

As evidence for this metaphor, let us consider the forms of the signs that were listed above. First, many signs that refer to intimacy or affection involve closeness of articulators. In FRIEND and CLOSE-FRIEND, the index fingers of both hands intertwine; for CLOSE-FRIEND (Fig. 7.5), which describes a stronger emotional attachment, the fingers grasp each other more strongly and for a longer time. In MARRY, the two hands clasp each other. For LOVE (Fig. 7.6), both arms are held tightly against the body.

Second, the reverse is also true: Many signs that refer to dislike or emotional disapproval involve distance between referents. For RESIST (Fig. 7.7), the dominant arm is held rigidly away from the body, and for DIVORCE (Fig. 7.8), which refers to the breakup of a once-intimate relationship, the two D-shaped hands (index finger extended, thumb and middle finger touching, other fingers curled) start together and move apart.

Figure 7.5. CLOSE-FRIEND.

Figure 7.6. LOVE.

Figure 7.7. RESIST.

Figure 7.8. DIVORCE.

One other example deserves comment. ASL has a system for manually spelling English words using a succession of handshapes, one for each letter; these fingerspelled words are articulated in a special location, and their internal structure differs sharply from the structure of ASL signs. Sometimes, commonly used fingerspelled words are borrowed into ASL: Their internal structure simplifies to match the normal standards for ASL signs, and their movements, orientation, and place of articulation can change (Battison 1978). Two such fingerspelled "loan signs" are #OFF and #BACK.[4]

#OFF (variant *a*, as recorded by Battison) denotes the ending of a romantic relationship, and its movement pattern clearly draws on the INTIMACY IS PROXIMITY mapping: The two hands start together, both holding the O-shape, then move apart, opening to the F-shape. #BACK has become a motion verb meaning "to return"; its path through space indicates the starting and ending points of its referent. In combination with #OFF, it can be used metaphorically to refer to the resumption of a romantic relationship: The two hands, initially separate in signing space, move together while taking on the shapes *B, A,* and *K.* Generally, when used together, the two loan signs are repeated in rapid alternation: #OFF, #BACK, #OFF, #BACK. This sequence denotes an off-again, on-again relationship, where the two lovers repeatedly break up and reconcile; the movements of the hands apart and back together iconically and metaphorically represent the changing amounts of affection that the lovers feel for each other.

---

4 The symbol # has become standard in the ASL literature to indicate that a gloss represents a fingerspelled loan sign.

Finally, INTIMACY IS PROXIMITY affects signers' choices of where in signing space they establish loci to represent various referents. Users of Danish Sign Language put referents in different places depending on how they feel about them (Engberg-Pedersen 1993): In particular, people or institutions that are well liked will be placed close to the signer, whereas disliked people or institutions will be placed farther away. Engberg-Pedersen gives the example of a mother who sets up a locus for her daughter close to herself in signing space but sets up that for her daughter's kindergarten far away. For a similar ASL example, Engberg-Pedersen cites Padden (1986).

A few words on the evidence for INTIMACY IS PROXIMITY are in order. If we found only that signs referring to affectionate relationships involved closeness of articulators, we would not have full evidence for a consistent mapping between two conceptual domains. But in fact, we find that both ends of the proximity scale are used in consistent ways to refer to affection and dislike. This fact gives strong evidence for the existence in ASL of a consistent, conventional metaphorical mapping between the two domains.

It should be noted as well that a number of the signs described here involve more than just the INTIMACY IS PROXIMITY metaphor. In particular, LOVE, RESIST, and MARRY all incorporate body-for-body iconicity: LOVE presents an image of a hug, RESIST gives the image of keeping something at arm's length, MARRY shows hands clasping each other. One might question whether these signs should be considered metaphorical at all, because they all present vivid images of actions that are strongly associated with their meanings. Instead, these actions might be considered to be metonymic representations of the conceptual category.

But notice how each action includes both source- and target-domain aspects: A hug and a handclasp involve the physical closeness as well as the social intimacy of the two humans involved, whereas holding someone at arm's length shows that the person is not physically or emotionally close. These images invoke the *experiential basis* of the metaphor (Lakoff & Johnson 1980) – that is, the metaphor itself is no doubt based on the experience we all have of wanting people we like close to us and wanting to keep people we don't like far away. It is no coincidence that the signs involved draw on exactly these images; they are easily recognizable, familiar, and form the motivation for a deeply entrenched and typologically common conceptual metaphor.

INTENSITY IS QUANTITY

The third single-parameter metaphor that I will treat here can be called INTENSITY IS QUANTITY; it affects the handshapes of ASL signs. There are

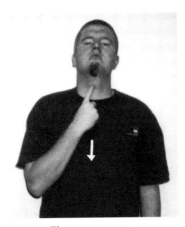

Figure 7.9. DESIRE.

a number of pairs of signs that differ only in the handshapes they use; in these pairs, one sign uses a 1-handshape, with index finger extended from a fist, and the other uses a 4- or 5-handshape, with all fingers extended. Moreover, the main difference in meaning between the signs is that the sign with all fingers extended denotes more intensity than does the sign with one finger extended.

The sign pairs that participate in this metaphor include COMPLICATED and VERY-COMPLICATED, MAKE-SINGLE-DIGRESSION (see Fig. 6.9) and MAKE-COMPLEX-DIGRESSION (see Fig. 6.10), and DESIRE (Fig. 7.9) and STRONG-DESIRE (Fig. 7.10). The last two are a typical pair: DESIRE is articulated by stroking the index finger down the front of the neck, whereas STRONG-DESIRE involves stroking all four fingers down the neck. The first sign

Figure 7.10. STRONG-DESIRE.

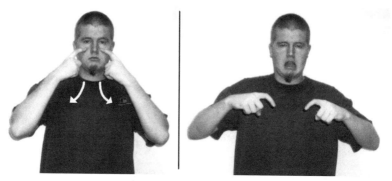

Figure 7.11. CRY.

refers to most desires and wants, whereas the second is reserved for intense desires, such as scoring the tie-breaking goal at the end of a football game.

All the sign pairs named so far refer to abstract concepts such as complexity, thinking, and desires. There are also sign pairs like CRY (Fig. 7.11) and WEEP (Fig. 7.12), which differ by handshape in the same way but refer to a concrete action. For CRY and WEEP, the handshapes iconically depict the amount of water coming from the eyes during painful emotion: The 1-handshape of CRY corresponds to moderate production of fluid and intensity of feeling, and the 4-handshape of WEEP corresponds to heavy fluid production and intensity of feeling. These two signs are frozen examples of element classifiers for the movement of water from the eyes, but they also participate in the INTENSITY IS QUANTITY metaphor: The images represented by these signs are part of the experiential basis for INTENSITY IS QUANTITY. This is analogous to the situation for LOVE, MARRY, and RESIST described above.

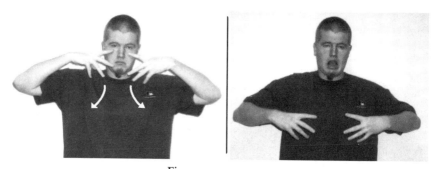

Figure 7.12. WEEP.

TABLE 7.4. Double Mapping for Intensity is Quantity

	ICONIC MAPPING	METAPHORICAL MAPPING
ARTICULATORS	SOURCE	TARGET
One finger	Small quantity	Low intensity
Four fingers	Large quantity	High intensity

The INTENSITY IS QUANTITY mapping is summarized in Table 7.4; it is quite simple (with only two correspondences) but deserves a few comments.

First, it is worth noticing that discrete quantity (*one* vs. *four*) is being used to represent continuous amount (*some* vs. *a lot*).

Second, note that the iconic representation of quantity (by number of fingers) is highly schematized: Use of one finger represents "small quantity," whereas use of four fingers represents "large quantity." No signs participating in this mapping make any finer distinctions than this: That is, no signs use two fingers to represent "medium quantity."

This differs from the classifier and number-incorporation uses of fingers to represent numbers of referents (Chapter Five); as we saw there, for those cases, each number of fingers (up to four or five) corresponded exactly to the number of referents.

MULTIPLE METAPHORICAL PARAMETERS IN A
SINGLE SIGN

We have seen that entire metaphors (albeit simple ones) can be represented by one parameter of a sign. But signs have many parameters. It should not be surprising, then, to learn that a single sign can incorporate more than one metaphorical–iconic parameter. In fact, there are signs whose handshape, movement, and location are all motivated by different metaphors (cf. Brennan 1990).

Let us take as a case study a number of signs for emotions: SAD, HAPPY, THRILL, and EXCITED. SAD (Fig. 7.13) consists of a downward motion of both spread-fingered hands, palm in, in front of the face. HAPPY (Fig. 7.14) involves a repeated upward brushing of the dominant flat B-hand, palm in, against the chest. THRILL (Fig. 7.15) has two open-8 hands (fingers spread, middle finger bent inward) whose middle fingers brush upward along the length of the abdomen and off the shoulders. Finally, in EXCITED (Fig. 7.16), the two open-8 hands alternate in short, rapid

Figure 7.13. SAD.

Figure 7.14. HAPPY.

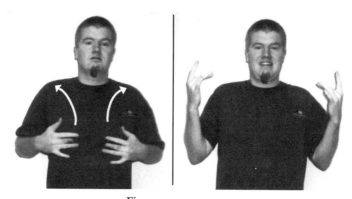

Figure 7.15. THRILL.

Figure 7.16. EXCITED.

brushes upward at the chest.[5] These signs form an interesting sequence in that SAD incorporates one iconic metaphor, HAPPY incorporates two, and THRILL and EXCITED incorporate three; moreover, THRILL and EXCITED bring in an iconic use of time.

As we go through the metaphors used in these signs, I will provide full mappings for each, along with additional signs that provide strong evidence for the mappings.

The first sign on our list is SAD; this sign builds an iconic metaphor into its *movement* parameter. The metaphor it uses is HAPPY EMOTIONS ARE UP, a simple mapping based on the up–down scale (noted for ASL by Holtemann 1990 and Wilbur 1987). (English has a similar metaphor, apparent from expressions such as *I'm feeling down today*; see Lakoff & Johnson 1980.) Table 7.5 summarizes the mapping. Many (though not all) emotion signs in ASL draw on this metaphor. The signs denoting positive feelings that have upward movement include INSPIRE and our other case-study signs HAPPY, THRILL, and EXCITED. Signs denoting negative feelings that have downward movement include SAD, DEPRESSED, and DISAPPOINTED.

Our second example is HAPPY; this sign uses two different metaphors, one motivating its direction of movement and another motivating its place of articulation. As just mentioned, HAPPY's upward movement comes from the metaphor HAPPY EMOTIONS ARE UP. The second metaphor can be called THE LOCUS OF EMOTION IS THE CHEST.

[5] The downward motions (indicated by dotted lines) do not contact the chest and are solely for the purpose of allowing the hands to make additional upward motions; they do not count in the metaphorical interpretation of the sign.

TABLE 7.5. Double Mapping for HAPPY EMOTIONS ARE UP

	ICONIC MAPPING	METAPHORICAL MAPPING
ARTICULATORS	SOURCE	TARGET
Upward movement	Top of the vertical scale	Happy emotions
Downward movement	Bottom of the vertical scale	Unhappy emotions

Many (but not all) ASL emotion signs are articulated at the chest: HAPPY, THRILL, EXCITED, DISAPPOINTED, DEPRESSED, ANGRY, INSPIRE, and CONCERN, to name a few. Some signs move to or from the chest in motivated ways: BE-TOUCHED, which moves inward and contacts the chest, denotes "being strongly emotionally affected by 'external' events," and EXPRESS-EMOTION (Fig. 7.17), which depicts objects being taken out of the chest and offered forward, denotes "sharing emotional experience with others."

Moreover, some signs take on an emotional meaning when articulated at the chest; the signs BOIL and BOIL-INSIDE are a good example of this. BOIL (Fig. 7.18) is articulated in a neutral area of signing space, with the non-dominant flat B-hand held palm down above the dominant spread 5-hand; the fingers of the 5-hand wiggle, as in the element classifier representing *fire*. This is clearly a frozen sign based on shape-for-shape and element classifiers; the meaning is *for liquid to boil*. In BOIL-INSIDE (Fig. 7.19), the same configuration of the hands is articulated at the signer's abdomen area; this sign means to "feel strong unexpressed anger."

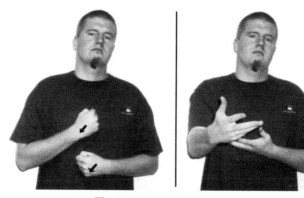

Figure 7.17. EXPRESS-EMOTION.

Figure 7.18. BOIL.

Table 7.6 gives the mapping for this metaphor.[6] Note that the final correspondence, *movement of object out of chest → emotional experience being communicated to others,* draws on the first metaphor we discussed, COMMUNICATING IS SENDING. Here the idea or topic being "sent" to others is a private emotional experience; it is metaphorically removed from the chest container and made accessible to other people.[7]

Figure 7.19. BOIL-INSIDE.

[6] Because this mapping links only one body part with one type of mental experience, it is reasonable to wonder whether we should properly consider it a metaphor, because metaphors consist of linkages between parallel structures in different domains. Another reasonable analysis is to consider this equation of the locus of emotion and the chest to be a conceptual metonymy, where one concept stands for a related concept. One could apply this analysis to the other one-body-part mappings in this chapter (e. g., head for locus of thought).

[7] This correspondence brings in other metaphors, namely KNOWING IS SEEING and PRIVATE IS HIDDEN, which we do not have space to discuss here. Sweetser (1995) discussed similar complexes of metaphors in English.

TABLE 7.6. Double Mapping for THE LOCUS OF EMOTION IS THE CHEST

	ICONIC MAPPING	METAPHORICAL MAPPING
ARTICULATORS	SOURCE	TARGET
Chest/abdomen	Chest region	Locus of emotional experience
Location at chest/abdomen	Location inside chest	Experience of emotion
Movement of object to chest/abdomen	Movement of object into chest	"External" events causing emotional experience
Movement of object away from chest/abdomen	Movement of object out of chest	Emotional experience being communicated to others

This mapping, THE LOCUS OF EMOTION IS THE CHEST, is part of a mapping of different parts of mental experience onto different parts of the body (cf. Johnson 1987, Sweetser 1990 for English counterparts). It contrasts with THE LOCUS OF THOUGHT IS THE HEAD, a metaphor that spatializes thought onto the head, and in particular, the forehead (Wilcox 1993). Thought-related signs located at the forehead include THINK (see Fig. 3.7A), KNOW (see Fig. 3.7B), UNDERSTAND, and FORGET; LEARN, which denotes the acquisition of new information, presents an object moving into the forehead, whereas INFORM (see Fig. 6.4), which denotes the sharing of information, presents an object moving out of the forehead.[8] In fact, the sign EXPRESS-EMOTION is practically a minimal pair for INFORM; both use instrument classifiers to represent the manipulation of mental experiences, and both show the "experiences" (i.e., thoughts or feelings) coming out of the appropriate body part and being sent to other people. Many cultures have similar pairs of metaphors, where the body and emotions are contrasted with the head and thought.

Our third example, THRILL, uses both of the metaphors we saw in SAD and HAPPY and adds a third: Its upward movement comes from HAPPY EMOTIONS ARE UP, its location at the chest comes from THE LOCUS OF EMOTIONS IS THE CHEST, and its open-8 handshape is motivated by the metaphor FEELING IS TOUCHING. In fact, THRILL's meaning is largely predictable from the metaphorical–iconic pairings that motivate its form.

---

[8] Wilcox (1993) gives evidence for this metaphor in ASL and shows that ASL signers spatialize unconscious thought onto the back of the head.

The open-8 handshape has a number of meanings in ASL; the one that concerns us here is *physical touch* or *contact*. An entire chapter could be written on the signs bearing this handshape and their semantic connections; space here allows me to list only a few of them, classifying them broadly into a group associated with physical contact and a group associated with emotions (cf. Frishberg 1979, Frishberg & Gough 1973). The central sign of the group is TOUCH (Fig. 7.20), where the extended middle finger of the dominant hand contacts the back of the palm-down nondominant hand. This sign is iconic: One basic way of *touching* is for the fingers to contact some object, and the sign TOUCH does in fact encode an image of a finger contacting an object. The iconicity is highly conventionalized, however; in ASL, it is crucially important that to represent the concept of *touching*, the middle finger must make the contact and not any other finger. Contact with, say, the index finger would be an excellent example of touching (and probably a more typical example), but in ASL, it would not serve to denote the concept of *touching*.

Other open-8 signs associated with physical contact include CONTACT, CONTACT-LENSES, and various iconic signs for sexual behavior (Woodward 1979).

The open-8 "touch" handshape has several metaphorical uses, but the primary one is to denote emotions or feelings. The mapping for this metaphor is given in Table 7.7. Here, a physical contact is used metaphorically to refer to an experience of an emotion.

Many ASL emotion signs use this metaphor, including THRILL, EXCITED, DISAPPOINTED, FEEL, TOUCHED, and CONCERN, which are located at the chest; and PITY (shown as I-PITY-HIM/HER/IT in Fig. 7.21) which is not. In some sense, the open-8 handshape has become an "emotion classifier"; it freely combines with other metaphorical–iconic pairings to

Figure 7.20. TOUCH.

TABLE 7.7. Double Mapping for FEELING IS TOUCHING

ICONIC MAPPING	METAPHORICAL MAPPING	
ARTICULATORS	SOURCE	TARGET
Open-8 handshape	Human hand	Human emotional capacity
Other articulators	Objects	Emotion-provoking stimuli
Open-8 touches other articulators	Human hand touches objects	Person feels emotions

designate any kind of emotion. Thus, THRILL and DISAPPOINTED have opposite directions of motion and basically opposite meanings: the sign with upward motion (THRILL) denotes a vivid, brief joyful experience, while the sign with downward motion (DISAPPOINTED) denotes a vivid, brief sorrowful experience. Klima and Bellugi (1979) in fact give an example of an invented sign that playfully draws on these metaphors: to represent feeling excited and sad at the same time, a signer simultaneously moved one open-8 upward along the chest, and the other open-8 downward along the chest. The meaning of this novel sign is completely transparent based on its form.

With this in mind, let us analyze our final example sign, EXCITED, and compare it to THRILL. EXCITED uses the same three metaphors as THRILL: With its upward motion, location at the chest, and open-8 handshape, it is virtually required to denote a positive emotion. Nonetheless, its mean-

Figure 7.21. I-PITY-HIM/HER/IT.

ing differs from THRILL's; whereas THRILL refers to a brief, vivid positive experience, EXCITED denotes a state of positive feeling and anticipation that can last for a long time.

Notice that EXCITED's form differs from THRILL's as well. In THRILL, both hands move upward in a single long, rapid stroke; in EXCITED, however, the two hands alternate making short upward movements at the chest. I claim that this difference of form comes from time-for-time iconicity. The temporal structure of THRILL's form, with its rapid, sharp movement, fits the temporal structure of THRILL's meaning (i.e., brief, vivid experience), whereas the temporal structure of EXCITED's form, with its repeated movements, fits the temporal structure of EXCITED's meaning (i.e., an ongoing state).

To summarize: Different aspects of ASL signs can be motivated by different iconic metaphors. Tables 7.8 through 7.11 lay out the metaphorical and iconic mappings for our four example signs. As we can see, the forms of some signs, such as SAD, are only partially motivated by metaphors, but the forms of other signs, such as EXCITED, are almost completely motivated by metaphor and iconicity.

These signs might well be described as metaphorical compounds. (Brennan [1990] used this term.) There are analogous cases in spontaneous gesture accompanying speech (Cienki 1998; Webb 1997). We can also compare these compounds to metaphorical compounds in spoken languages (e.g., English *black-hearted, cold-hearted*). These English compounds also each use two conceptual metaphors: THE LOCUS OF EMOTION IS THE HEART, along with GOOD IS WHITE and AFFECTION IS WARMTH. (All three of these metaphors can be justified with additional examples and the construction of a mapping; see Lakoff, Espenson, & Schwartz 1991 for details.) Thus, the words *cold* and *heart* and the *adjective-verb-participle* construction come together with these metaphors to produce the

TABLE 7.8. Double Mapping for SAD		
	ICONIC MAPPING	METAPHORICAL MAPPING
ARTICULATORS	SOURCE	TARGET

Handshape:
  Spread fingers
Location:
  Face
Movement direction:
  Downward
	Bottom of vertical scale	Unhappy emotions

TABLE 7.9. Double Mappings for HAPPY

ICONIC MAPPINGS	METAPHORICAL MAPPINGS	
ARTICULATORS	SOURCE	TARGET

Handshape:
  Flat B-shape
Location:
  Chest
	Chest region	Locus of emotional
		experience

Movement direction: Upward	Top of vertical scale	Happy emotions

meaning "having little capacity for affection." This productivity and compositionality is analogous to the situation for ASL emotion signs, but there are two major differences: The ASL signs express their metaphors *iconically* and *simultaneously,* rather than using *arbitrary* words in *sequence,* as spoken languages must do.[9]

TABLE 7.10. Double Mappings for THRILL

ICONIC MAPPINGS	METAPHORICAL MAPPINGS	
ARTICULATORS	SOURCE	TARGET
Handshape: Open-8	Physical contact	Emotional experience
Location: Chest	Chest region	Locus of emotional experience
Movement direction: Upward	Top of vertical scale	Happy emotions

Movement timing
  (iconic only):
  Single rapid movement
	Brief experience	

[9] The intertwining of discontinuous items such as *black* plus *-ed* with items such as *heart* is probably as close to simultaneous expression of metaphors as spoken languages can get.

TABLE 7.11. Double Mappings for EXCITED

	ICONIC MAPPINGS	METAPHORICAL MAPPINGS
ARTICULATORS	SOURCE	TARGET
Handshape:		
Open-8	Physical contact	Emotional experience
Location:		
Chest	Chest region	Locus of emotional experience
Movement direction:		
Upward	Top of vertical scale	Happy emotions
Movement timing (iconic only):		
Repeated movements	Ongoing state	

METAPHORICAL ICONICITY AND PURE ICONICITY
IN A SINGLE SIGN

Finally, we address a case in which two different types of iconicity combine with metaphorical iconicity in the structure of one sign. Our example is the sign TWO-WEEKS-IN-PAST, along with its relatives TWO-WEEKS-IN-FUTURE, THREE-WEEKS-IN-PAST, and so on.

Let us start with the basic sign, WEEK (Fig. 7.22), from which TWO-WEEKS-IN-PAST is derived. WEEK's form is already partially motivated by iconicity and metonymy. The nondominant hand is held palm-up in a flat B-shape, fingers together and thumb extended. The dominant hand takes on the 1-shape, index finger extended from a fist; it slides, palm-down, across the nondominant palm from the heel of the hand to the fingertips. The iconic image represented here is of a horizontal row on a calendar: The nondominant hand, in a typical flat-object form, represents the calendar page, whereas the sliding motion of the dominant *1* traces out one row on the calendar. As we know, the typical calendar is organized so that each row represents a week; this is a clever way to find a visual image to represent the temporal concept *week*.

WEEK is one of those signs that takes *number incorporation* (see Chapter Five); its basic handshape, the *1*, can be changed to any number handshape up to *9,* and its meaning then changes to indicate that number of weeks.[10] Figure 7.23 illustrates the sign TWO-WEEKS; that sign uses

---

[10] The numerals 6 through 9 are not strictly iconic; the number of fingers selected cannot directly correspond to the referent number, for obvious reasons.

Figure 7.22. WEEK.

two distinct kinds of iconicity: number incorporation and the representation of the calendar row.

Finally, WEEK and its number-incorporation derivatives can incorporate the metaphor THE FUTURE IS AHEAD. The movement pattern of the sign is altered: Instead of simply sweeping across the nondominant palm, the dominant hand sweeps across the palm and then either forward or backward to the dominant shoulder in an arc. The variant with the forward arc indicates a time in the future, and the variant with the backward arc indicates a time in the past.

Putting it all together, the sign TWO-WEEKS-IN-PAST (Fig. 7.24) is motivated by two different iconic mappings (in the dominant handshape, and in the nondominant handshape and initial configuration of the hands) and a metaphorical–iconic mapping (in the final backward movement).

Figure 7.23. TWO-WEEKS.

Figure 7.24. TWO-WEEKS-IN-PAST.

This situation is summarized in Table 7.12; note that the final two correspondences, which pick out a row on a calendar, refer to the concept *week* not directly but by metonymic association. The result is a sign meaning "a time two weeks in the past"; this meaning is predictable from its parts.

SUMMARY

We have seen in this chapter how metaphorical–iconic signs need not have all their aspects motivated by the same metaphor. Some signs (e.g., THINK–PENETRATE) are fully motivated by a single metaphor; other signs are only partially motivated (e.g., SAD); others are fully motivated by several metaphors at once (e.g., THRILL); and still others combine motivations by both metaphorical and pure iconicity (e.g., TWO-WEEKS-AGO).

TABLE 7.12. Mappings for TWO-WEEKS-IN-PAST

ICONIC MAPPINGS	METAPHORICAL MAPPINGS	
ARTICULATORS	SOURCE	TARGET
Movement backward	Area behind the signer	Earlier in time
Dominant 2-shape	The numeral 2	
Nondominant B-shape	Calendar page	
Dominant hand's sweep across B	Calendar row	

CHAPTER EIGHT

The Vertical Scale as Source Domain

MULTIPLE USES OF A SINGLE SOURCE DOMAIN

Conceptual metaphors are pairings of source and target conceptual domains. When discussing a metaphor, we must always specify both the source and the target domain, for a very good reason: A language may use the same source domain to describe many different target domains, and it may describe a single target domain using many different source domains. Each of these source–target pairings has a distinct mapping and should be treated as a separate conceptual metaphor. It makes little sense to talk about English's FIRE metaphors, for example, as a coherent group. English uses *fire* as a source domain for concepts such as *life, desire, destruction,* and *anger*; the target domains differ greatly, and each source–target pairing draws on different aspects of the *fire* domain.

In this section, we will go through several ASL metaphors that use the same source domain: the vertical up–down scale (cf. Sweetser 1995 for vertical-scale metaphors in English, Brennan 1990 for some BSL examples). As each source–target pairing is analyzed, we will see that they fall into two types: the "positive-end-up" type and the "positive-end-down" type. Moreover, each pairing's use of the vertical scale is different and is motivated by a different set of experiences in the world. The positive-end-up mappings are based on two different kinds of experience: the fact that piles of objects become taller when more objects are added, and the fact that height or high ground gives one an advantage in a physical confrontation. The positive-end-down mapping is related to the experience of digging into the ground to reach hidden objects.

We shall see as well that for each metaphor, the vertical scale is represented iconically in several different ways, using a number of interesting devices, and that these vertical-scale metaphors sometimes combine with other ASL metaphors, such as STATES ARE LOCATIONS.

A related study (Ogawa 1999) catalogues and compares vertical-scale metaphors in Japanese Sign Language (JSL) and spoken Japanese. Ogawa's results for JSL are similar to the ASL results: Many metaphors exist with the vertical scale as a source domain and various target domains; in addition, the source domain receives several different iconic representations. There is much overlap between the metaphors used in JSL and in the spoken language of Japan, as one might expect, but there are also a few vertical-scale metaphors unique to each language.

MORE IS UP

In our first metaphor, the vertical scale is mapped onto the domain of *quantity*. This metaphor can be called MORE IS UP because the high end of the vertical scale represents large amounts (cf. Lakoff & Johnson 1980 for English MORE IS UP and Wilbur 1987 for ASL). I will first give the metaphorical mapping by itself, in Table 8.1, because it shows up iconically in several different ways. We will discuss here two groups of signs that incorporate this metaphor: These can be called the "bent-B" group and the "H" group, after the handshapes they use.

The bent-B group is large and productive in that new signs of this class can be invented freely to fit the needs of the situation. In this group, both hands take on the bent-B shape: fingers together and bent at the first joint after the palm. The palms face each other, and the fingers are held parallel to the ground, defining a horizontal plane in signing space. For all members of this group, the nondominant hand's plane forms a *reference level* in signing space; the dominant hand's plane is to be compared to the reference level. (We will call this plane the *actual level*.) The double mapping for this group is given in Table 8.2.

TABLE 8.1. Metaphorical Mapping for MORE IS UP

SOURCE	TARGET
Up–down dimension	Scale of relative quantity
Higher locations	Larger amounts
Lower locations	Smaller amounts
Movement upward	Increasing amount
Movement downward	Decreasing amount

TABLE 8.2. Double Mapping for Bent-B Group

	ICONIC MAPPING	METAPHORICAL MAPPING
ARTICULATORS	SOURCE	TARGET
Vertical axis of signing space	Up–down dimension	Scale of relative quantity
Higher locations in signing space	Higher locations	Larger amounts
Lower locations in signing space	Lower locations	Smaller amounts
Nondominant bent-B's fingers	Reference level	Reference amount
Dominant bent-B's fingers	Actual level	Actual amount
Dominant and nondominant fingers on the same plane	Actual level equal in height to reference level	Actual amount equal to reference amount
Dominant fingers above nondominant fingers	Actual level above reference level	Actual amount greater than reference amount
Dominant fingers below nondominant fingers	Actual level below reference level	Actual amount less than reference amount
Dominant fingers move upward	Actual level rises	Actual amount increases
Dominant fingers move downward	Actual level falls	Actual amount decreases

Signs in the bent-B group include EQUAL, MORE-THAN, LESS-THAN, MIN-IMUM, and MAXIMUM. For EQUAL (Fig. 8.1), the fingers of both hands are on the same horizontal plane; this maps onto the meaning of "equal amount." MORE-THAN and LESS-THAN (Fig. 8.2) both start in the same configuration as EQUAL, but the dominant hand subsequently moves – to a higher position for MORE-THAN and to a lower position for LESS-THAN.[1] As one might expect, MORE-THAN is a predicate denoting "greater amount than the reference value" and LESS-THAN denotes "smaller amount than the reference value."

For EQUAL, MORE-THAN, and LESS-THAN, the reference level is approximately in the middle of signing space, but for MINIMUM and MAXIMUM,

---

[1] As we shall see, there are many pairs of signs like MORE-THAN and LESS-THAN that differ only in the direction of movement along the vertical scale. There is not enough space for me to illustrate both members of the pairs, but it is relatively easy to reconstruct the second member from the illustrated one.

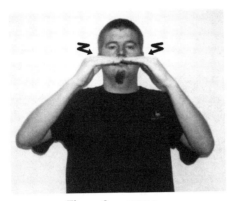

Figure 8.1. EQUAL.

the reference level is set at one endpoint of the vertical scale. In MINI-MUM, the nondominant fingers are fairly low in signing space; the dominant fingers touch the top of the nondominant fingers and move upward. Here, the nondominant fingers' reference level is set equal to the bottom of the vertical scale, which metaphorically corresponds to the minimum acceptable value. The dominant fingers sweep through a range of acceptable actual levels, which are all above the bottom of the scale and thus represent values greater than the minimum value. Similarly, in MAXIMUM (Fig. 8.3), the nondominant fingers are relatively high in signing space; the dominant fingers sweep upward and hit the bottom of the nondominant fingers. This time, the nondominant fingers represent the top of the vertical scale and thus the maximum allowable amount. The dominant fingers move upward through a range of acceptable levels but cannot go higher than the top of the scale; this shows that the actual amount is limited to be no more than the maximum amount.

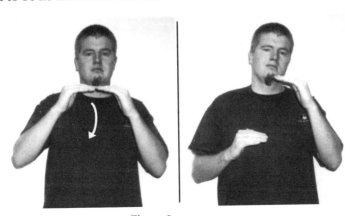

Figure 8.2. LESS-THAN.

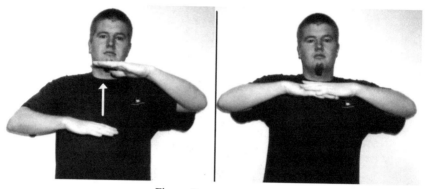

Figure 8.3. MAXIMUM.

The metaphorical–iconic pairing for the bent-B group is alive and well in ASL; signers are free to invent new signs of this type to fit the needs of the moment. Basically, what happens is that the signer shapes the hands into bent-B's and sets both fingers' planes on the same level in signing space; this has the effect of invoking the bent-B double mapping and establishing the reference level in space. Once this is done, the signer can move the dominant fingers to any level or series of levels that correspond to the amounts that he or she wishes to describe; this method provides a simple way to describe gradual or rapid increases or decreases in amounts.

The second group of signs connected with MORE IS UP is the H group, in which both hands take on the H-shape (index and middle fingers extended from a fist and touching each other). There are only two signs in this group: INCREASE-AMOUNT and DECREASE-AMOUNT.

The version of MORE IS UP that the H group uses is more detailed than the version used by the bent-B group; a better name for this version might be AMOUNT IS THE HEIGHT OF A PILE. We have all had experience in the world with objects stacked into a pile; we know that taller piles, on the whole, have more material in them, and shorter piles have less material; and we know that when we add material to the pile, the pile will get taller. This experience is probably the reason why metaphors like MORE IS UP exist, which map the vertical scale onto a scale of quantity; these metaphors use an abstract version of the source domain, in which only the vertical scale and not the pile itself is retained. The H group, however, still retains the vivid, detailed source domain; we can see in these signs the iconic representation of the top of a pile and of material being added to the top or taken away from it.

TABLE 8.3. Metaphorical Mapping for AMOUNT IS THE HEIGHT OF A PILE

SOURCE	TARGET
Pile of material	Quantity to be measured
Top of pile	Total amount
Material to be added or taken away	Amount to be added or taken away
Material being added to the pile	Amount being increased
Material being removed from the pile	Amount being decreased
Top of pile rising	Amount increasing
Top of pile falling	Amount decreasing
New top of pile	New total amount

The metaphorical mapping for AMOUNT IS THE HEIGHT OF A PILE is given in Table 8.3. Notice how the MORE IS UP metaphor preserves the structure of this mapping while using a more schematic source domain: In both metaphors, the vertical scale represents quantity, higher locations represent larger amounts, and lower locations represent smaller amounts.

The H group signs use H-handshapes to show the top of the metaphorical pile and the material being added to or removed from the pile. In INCREASE-AMOUNT, the nondominant H starts relatively low in signing space, fingers facing down and pointing forward and toward the dominant side. The dominant H's fingers begin faceup and are turned over and placed on top of the nondominant H's fingers; simultaneously, both hands rise in signing space. This sign means "for a quantity to increase." In DECREASE-AMOUNT (Fig. 8.4), the reverse happens: The dominant H's

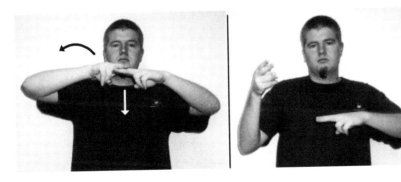

Figure 8.4. DECREASE-AMOUNT.

fingers start facedown on top of the nondominant H's fingers, and the entire configuration is relatively high in signing space. Next, the dominant H's fingers are removed from that position and turned faceup, and both hands move downward in space. As might be expected, this sign means "for a quantity to decrease." The movements of both signs can be repeated. These signs are used to describe increases and decreases in abstract quantities such as prices that cannot form piles; thus, their iconic depictions of piles' heights are metaphorical rather than purely iconic.

The double mapping for the H group signs is described in Table 8.4. The nondominant H's fingers define the level of the top of the pile, and the dominant H's fingers represent the material that is being placed onto or removed from the pile. At the same time, the height of the nondominant H's fingers in space represents the total amount of material in the pile; as the amount decreases, the pile becomes shorter and the nondominant H sinks lower (and vice versa for increases in amount). We can see that the meanings of the H group signs are strongly motivated by the iconic and metaphorical double mappings.

TABLE 8.4. Double Mapping for H Group

	ICONIC MAPPING	METAPHORICAL MAPPING
ARTICULATORS	SOURCE	TARGET
[Null]	Pile of material	Quantity to be measured
Nondominant H's fingers	Top of pile	Total amount
Dominant H's fingers	Material to be added or taken away	Amount to be added or taken away
Dominant H's fingers placed on top of nondominant H's fingers	Material being added to the pile	Amount being increased
Dominant H's fingers removed from top of nondominant H's fingers	Material being removed from the pile	Amount being decreased
Nondominant H's fingers rising	Top of pile rising	Total amount increasing
Nondominant H's fingers falling	Top of pile falling	Total amount decreasing
New level of nondominant H's fingers	New top of pile	New total amount

GOOD IS UP

Our second metaphor once again uses the schematic vertical scale, just as the bent-B group does. This time, the vertical scale represents the domain of progress and improvement; higher locations on the scale correspond to being better, and movement upward corresponds to improvement (cf. Wilbur 1987). It is interesting to note that in this metaphor, the ends of the vertical scale are given different social values: The high end has the most positive value and the low end has the least value. With MORE IS UP, on the other hand, neither the low end of the scale (representing small amount) nor the high end (representing large amount) is considered to be more valuable in and of itself.

The metaphorical mapping for GOOD IS UP is given in Table 8.5. This metaphor is given iconic representation in ASL in several different ways. We will discuss first a group of signs that use the nondominant palm as a landmark that iconically represents the vertical scale; I will refer to these signs as the "palm group." For this group, the nondominant hand articulates a B-shape (fingers straight and together), with fingers upward and palm facing the dominant side. The dominant hand also takes on the B-shape, with the thumb folded in and the edge of the index finger touching the nondominant palm. Once this configuration has been established, invoking the GOOD IS UP double mapping, the dominant hand's motion upward and downward represents improvement and deterioration in some condition. This double mapping has produced several frozen signs, including TOP, IMPROVE(1), WORSEN(1), and UP-AND-DOWN;[2] it can also be used to create new signs productively that fit the situation.

TABLE 8.5. Metaphorical Mapping for GOOD IS UP

SOURCE	TARGET
Up–down dimension	Scale of relative goodness
Higher locations	Better quality
Lower locations	Worse quality
Movement upward	Improvement
Movement downward	Deterioration

[2] The index *(1)* in these signs' glosses simply means that there are other signs that I want to gloss with the same English word. The index allows them to be distinguished: IMPROVE(1) versus IMPROVE(2).

The double mapping for the palm group is given in Table 8.6. The first sign of this group, IMPROVE(1), starts with the dominant hand touching low on the nondominant palm, fingers pointing upward; the dominant hand then slides upward a few inches along the nondominant palm. This sign can refer to one's state of mind, abilities, progress on a project, and many other areas that are subject to evaluation; in all areas, it means that the area being evaluated is *improving*. The second sign, WORSEN(1), begins just as IMPROVE(1) does, with a brief upward movement and orientation of the dominant fingers, but the fingers soon dip to point downward and then slide down to the lowest part of the nondominant palm. Predictably, WORSEN(1) means that the area of evaluation is *deteriorating*. Finally, UP-AND-DOWN(1) starts in the same way as IMPROVE(1) and WORSEN(1); the dominant hand slides up and down several times along the nondominant palm, and the dominant fingers orient themselves to point in the direction of motion. The meaning of this sign is that an area *repeatedly alternates getting better and getting worse*.

The next group of signs, which I will call the "space" group, is much like the palm group, except that there is no explicit landmark representing the vertical scale. That is, the dominant hand indicates relative quality by moving up and down in signing space, not by moving against a landmark such as the nondominant palm. I believe that this group is

TABLE 8.6. Double Mapping for Palm Group

ICONIC MAPPING	METAPHORICAL MAPPING	
ARTICULATORS	SOURCE	TARGET
Vertical axis of nondominant palm and fingers	Up–down dimension	Scale of relative goodness
Higher locations on nondominant palm and fingers	Higher locations	Better quality
Lower locations on nondominant palm and fingers	Lower locations	Worse quality
Movement upward along nondominant palm and fingers	Movement upward	Improvement
Movement downward along nondominant palm and fingers	Movement downward	Deterioration

derived from the palm group, because the iconic mapping is very similar: The only difference is that the nondominant palm landmark does not appear, and signers judge relative height on the basis of the vertical dimension of signing space itself.

Table 8.7 gives the iconic and metaphorical double mapping for the space group. There appear to be no frozen signs in the space group; instead, the movement of the dominant hand freely represents the "ups and downs" of the situation the signer wishes to describe. Thus, a person's fluctuating emotional state can be described by moving the hand up and down in signing space, with the fingers oriented in the direction of motion; this construction is demonstrated in Fig. 8.5.

The third set of signs that use GOOD IS UP can be called the "arm group": They use the nondominant arm as their landmark for judging relative height. The double mapping for the arm group is given in Table 8.8. The signs IMPROVE(2) and WORSEN(2) use this double mapping. IMPROVE(2), illustrated in Figure 8.6, begins with the dominant B-shape contacting the nondominant wrist; the contact is made on the outside edge of the B's little finger. Next, the B-shape makes an arc upward and contacts the nondominant biceps. The sign means "to improve." WORSEN(2) uses the same hand and arm configurations and contact points but with opposite movements: The dominant B-shape touches the nondominant arm first at the biceps and then at the wrist. Predictably, the sign means "to become worse." The movements and contact points of these signs can be changed, and the changes in meaning that result are predictable from Table 8.8; for example, it is common to start the dominant B at the nondominant wrist

TABLE 8.7. Double Mapping for Space Group

	ICONIC MAPPING	METAPHORICAL MAPPING
ARTICULATORS	SOURCE	TARGET
Vertical axis of signing space	Up–down dimension	Scale of relative goodness
Higher locations in signing space	Higher locations	Better quality
Lower locations in signing space	Lower locations	Worse quality
Movement upward in signing space	Movement upward	Improvement
Movement downward in signing space	Movement downward	Deterioration

Figure 8.5. Metaphorical–iconic description of a situation that goes from better to worse and back again.

and move slowly in several small arcs along the nondominant forearm, to indicate "slow, step-by-step improvement."

This group is particularly interesting for the following reason: the arm is mobile and changes its position with respect to true *up* and *down*. Imagine the arm hanging beside the body. The wrist is the lowest point on the arm and the shoulder is the highest point. This is the configuration that the arm group uses to determine its forms: When the arm hangs in this way, movement toward the shoulder is the same as movement upward. But what happens when the arm takes on different positions?

It turn out that for this group of signs, movement away from the wrist always counts as upward movement, no matter how the arm is positioned in space. It is in fact quite common for the nondominant forearm to be horizontal in signing space, because this configuration brings the hand and arm into the area where most signs are articulated. The movement pattern described above as meaning "slow, step-by-step improvement" is articulated on the forearm; more often than not, the dominant

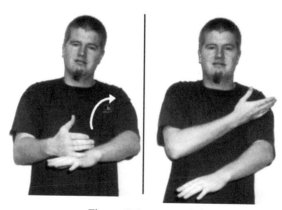

Figure 8.6. IMPROVE(2).

TABLE 8.8. Double Mapping for Arm Group

ARTICULATORS	ICONIC MAPPING SOURCE	METAPHORICAL MAPPING TARGET
Nondominant arm	Up–down dimension	Scale of relative goodness
Nondominant shoulder	Top of up–down scale	Best possible value
Nondominant wrist	Bottom of up–down scale	Worst possible value
Closer to shoulder on arm	Higher location	Better quality
Closer to wrist on arm	Lower location	Worse quality
Movement toward shoulder along arm	Movement upward	Improvement
Movement toward wrist along arm	Movement downward	Deterioration

hand will actually be moving *sideways* or perhaps even *downward* in space when it performs that movement. Nevertheless, the movement is toward the shoulder, in the direction defined as *upward* along the arm; and so the movement still denotes improvement rather than worsening. (Cf. Clark 1973 for a discussion of "canonical" body positions.)

POWERFUL IS UP

The third metaphor we will discuss can be named POWERFUL IS UP (cf. Sweetser 1995 for English and Holtemann 1990 for ASL). In this mapping, the vertical axis represents relative importance and social significance; higher locations are assigned to more important people, roles, institutions, and so on. This metaphor is partially based on the experience of physical confrontations: The person on the high ground has an advantage, and the taller person also in general has the advantage of weight and reach. Just as in GOOD IS UP, the top end of the vertical scale is given a positive value judgment: We feel that it is better to be powerful than to be without power. The metaphorical mapping is given in Table 8.9.

This metaphor gets represented iconically in ASL in at least two ways. The most straightforward way is for the vertical up–down axis of signing space to represent iconically the up–down dimension; this is the case for the signs ADVANCE(1) and BE-DEMOTED(1). Table 8.10 gives the double

TABLE 8.9. Metaphorical Mapping for POWERFUL IS UP

SOURCE	TARGET
Up–down dimension	Scale of relative power/importance
Higher locations	More important ranks
Lower locations	Less important ranks
Movement upward	Increasing power
Movement downward	Decreasing power

mapping shared by these two signs. In both of these signs, the hands articulate a bent-B shape, with fingers together and bent only at the first joint beyond the palm. The palms face each other, and the plane of the fingers defines a horizontal "level" in signing space. For ADVANCE(1), shown in Figure 8.7, the fingers start at a low level, then rise to a higher level; the sign means "to be promoted or to have high status." For BE-DEMOTED(1), the movement and meanings are reversed: The fingers start at a high level and descend to a lower level, denoting "to be demoted" or "to have low status."

The second iconic representation of POWERFUL IS UP is used by ADVANCE(2), BE-DEMOTED(2), and the signs for levels in school (FRESH-MAN, SOPHOMORE, JUNIOR, SENIOR); these signs draw on the device of using the nondominant hand as a "ranking" landmark (cf. Liddell 1990). In this use, the nondominant hand is held palm inward; the thumb points up, and the fingers are spread, so that the little finger angles toward the dominant side and downward. Each finger (or fin-

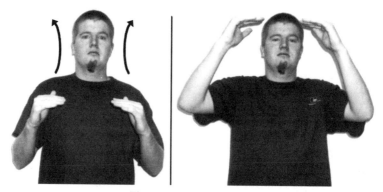

Figure 8.7. ADVANCE(1).

TABLE 8.10. Double Mapping for ADVANCE(1), BE-DEMOTED(1)

	ICONIC MAPPING	METAPHORICAL MAPPING
ARTICULATORS	SOURCE	TARGET
Vertical axis of signing space dimension	Up–down	Scale of relative importance
Higher locations in signing space	Higher locations	More important ranks
Lower locations in signing space	Lower locations	Less important ranks
Movement upward in signing space	Movement upward	Increasing power
Movement downward in signing space	Movement downward	Decreasing power

gertip) represents a "rank"; rank increases in order from the little finger (lowest rank) to the thumb (highest rank).[3] When the nondominant hand is held in this way, the relative heights of the fingers basically correspond to their ranks as predicted by POWERFUL IS UP; there is a slight deformation, as the thumb is not exactly above the other fingers. The metaphorical–iconic double mapping for this ordering device is given in Table 8.11.

TABLE 8.11. Double Mapping for Ranking Device

	ICONIC MAPPING	METAPHORICAL MAPPING
ARTICULATORS	SOURCE	TARGET
"Vertical" axis of nondominant spread hand's fingers	Up–down dimension	Scale of relative importance
Higher fingers on hand (starting with thumb)	Higher locations	More important ranks
Lower fingers on hand (starting with little finger)	Lower locations	Less important ranks

[3] There are ordinal uses of the nondominant hand where the counting begins with the thumb; compare Liddell (1990).

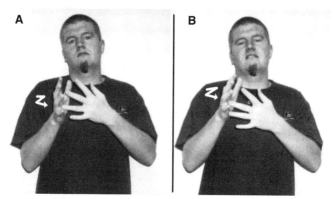

Figure 8.8. (A) FRESHMAN; (B) SOPHOMORE.

The signs for FRESHMAN, SOPHOMORE, JUNIOR, and SENIOR years in school are based on this metaphorical–iconic ranking device: For FRESHMAN (Fig. 8.8A); the dominant palm contacts the nondominant ring finger; for SOPHOMORE (Fig. 8.8B), it contacts the middle finger, and so on. It is clear from the use of the ranking device that FRESHMAN refers to a level that is fourth from the top, SOPHOMORE is third from the top, and so on.

Along with the ranking device, ADVANCE(2) and BE-DEMOTED(2) also incorporate a metaphorical use of the bent-V "legs" classifier, which has the handshape of index and middle fingers extended and slightly bent at all joints. This handshape, in its normal iconic classifier use, describes the movement of a two-legged creature (that is, a human) from one place to another. Here, the movement of this handshape is used metaphori-

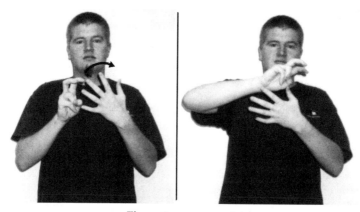

Figure 8.9. ADVANCE(2).

TABLE 8.12. Double Mapping for ADVANCE(2) and BE-DEMOTED(2)

	ICONIC MAPPING	METAPHORICAL MAPPING
ARTICULATORS	SOURCE	TARGET
Vertical axis of nondominant spread hand's fingers	Up–down dimension	Scale of relative importance
Higher fingers on hand (starting with thumb)	Higher locations	More important ranks
Lower fingers on hand (starting with little finger)	Lower locations	Less important ranks
Bent-V handshape	Referent person	Referent person
Bent-V moves to higher finger	Person moves to higher location	Person changes to more powerful rank
Bent-V moves to lower finger	Person moves to lower location	Person changes to less powerful rank

cally to represent a person changing from one rank to another.[4] Table 8.12 gives the complete iconic and metaphorical mappings for these two signs. For ADVANCE(2) (Fig. 8.9), the bent-V handshape begins at the little finger of the nondominant hand, then moves upward and to the side until it reaches the nondominant thumb. Conversely, for BE-DEMOTED(2), the bent-V begins at the thumb and moves sideways and downward along the "ranks" until it reaches the little finger. The meanings of these signs are completely predictable from the double mapping of Table 8.12: ADVANCE(2) means "for a person to change to a more powerful rank," and BE-DEMOTED(2) means "for a person to change to a less powerful rank."

ANALYSIS IS DIGGING

The final metaphor we will discuss in this chapter can be given the name ANALYSIS IS DIGGING; it uses the vertical scale to describe the domain of information and knowledge (cf. Lakoff & Johnson 1980, Sweetser 1995 for an English version). Some of the signs that partici-

---

4 This metaphor, STATES ARE LOCATIONS, exists in all the languages that metaphor analysts have looked at. Lakoff (1992) presented a detailed analysis of its structure in English. STATES ARE LOCATIONS has a long, detailed mapping in ASL as well as in English; space does not permit its presentation here.

TABLE 8.13. Metaphorical Mapping for ANALYSIS IS DIGGING

SOURCE	TARGET
Surface	Simplest, most summarized information
Area below surface	Information that requires effort to figure out
Digging or descending below surface	Figuring out more details
Scale of depth below surface	Scale of degree of detail
Closer to surface (= higher)	Less detail
Deeper below surface (= lower)	More detail

pate in this metaphor are SURFACE, DEEP, and ANALYZE. As we shall see, this mapping is different from the others we have looked at: The vertical scale is seen as a measure of *depth,* not of *height.* That is, for this metaphor, the vertical scale begins in the middle of signing space and proceeds downward.

The metaphorical mapping for these signs is not based on the experience of stacking up objects to make a tall pile; instead, it is based on the experience of digging downward into the earth to find buried objects. Table 8.13 lists the source–target correspondences for this metaphor.

As we can see, in this mapping, people work hard to get to *lower* levels, not to *higher* levels; there is a positive value to being lower on the depth scale. Also, though *descending* corresponds to "figuring out more details," *rising* does not correspond to the opposite, "forgetting more details." This comes from our knowledge about digging for hidden objects: Once we have excavated deeply enough to find the object, the object is *found*; we still know where and what it is when we return to the surface. In the source domain, *rising* does not function as the opposite of *descending*; therefore, *rising* cannot be mapped as the opposite of "figuring out details" in the target domain.

The signs SURFACE and DEEP have essentially opposite meanings; the first denotes a brief, summarized, even superficial analysis, whereas the second denotes a long, involved, detailed analysis. These signs partially share a metaphorical–iconic mapping: Both use the nondominant B-hand, palm down, as a landmark representing the metaphorical "surface." This surface acts as a "reference level"; the dominant hand's vertical location, which represents the actual level of detail being described, is compared to the vertical location of the reference level. This double mapping is given in Table 8.14.

TABLE 8.14. Double Mapping for SURFACE and DEEP

	ICONIC MAPPING	METAPHORICAL MAPPING
ARTICULATORS	SOURCE	TARGET
Nondominant B-hand	Surface as reference level	Simplest, most summarized information
Locations below nondominant B-hand	Area below surface	Detailed information requiring effort to figure out
Level of dominant hand	Actual depth level being described	Amount of detail in the current information
Dominant B-hand co-located with nondominant B-hand	Actual depth level located at the surface	Current information has minimal detail
Dominant 1-shape descends below surface	Actual depth level descends below surface	Current information contains more and more detail

For SURFACE (Fig. 8.10), the dominant B-hand, palm down, rubs the top of the nondominant B-hand, which is also palm down. Here, the dominant and nondominant hands are co-located at the level that iconically represents the "surface" of the depth scale; this level metaphorically corresponds to the least possible amount of detail. For DEEP (Fig. 8.11), the dominant 1-shape, index finger extended downward from a fist,

Figure 8.10. SURFACE.

Figure 8.11. DEEP.

starts at the nondominant B-hand and moves downward with a slight wiggle. (The wiggle is part of the iconic resources of ASL and represents "movement over a long distance.") Thus, in DEEP, the dominant hand's depth level, and therefore the amount of detail in the information, is portrayed as very large.

The third example of ANALYSIS IS DIGGING, ANALYZE (Fig. 8.12), uses a different iconic mapping. Here, the metaphorical surface is not given an explicit representation with a flat-object classifier; instead, the hands portray the digging and separating movement necessary for penetrating downward beneath the surface. The double mapping is given in Table 8.15.

To articulate the sign ANALYZE, both hands take on the bent-V shape: index and middle finger extended from the fist and bent slightly at every joint. The bent-V's are held, palm down and forward, at a high level in signing space; this level represents the metaphorical "surface." Next, the fingers of the bent-V's contract at every joint as the hands descend slightly in signing space; this movement is repeated twice. The effect of this movement is to iconically represent the digging process, where suc-

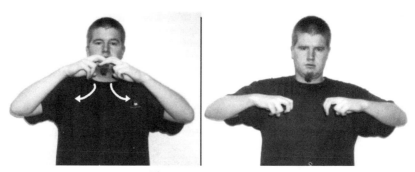

Figure 8.12. ANALYZE.

TABLE 8.15. Double Mapping for ANALYZE

	ICONIC MAPPING	METAPHORICAL MAPPING
ARTICULATORS	SOURCE	TARGET
Bent-V hands' initial position in signing space	Surface	Simplest, most summarized information
Regions in signing space below hands' initial position	Area below surface	Information that requires effort to figure out
Bent-V hands contract and descend in space	Person digs and descends below surface	Person figures out more details

cessive layers of dirt are stripped away. Metaphorically, this represents the process of figuring out more and more details of information; as we might predict, this process is exactly what the sign ANALYZE denotes.

DIFFERENT MOTIVATIONS FOR DIFFERENT USES

We have now seen four different iconic metaphors in ASL that all use the vertical scale as a part of their source domain. It is clear, however, that the four mappings use the vertical scale in different ways. Some discussion of the "positive-end-up" type and the "positive-end-down" type is in order (and see also Sweetser 1995, Ogawa 1999 for more details).

The positive-end-up type derives (at least in part) from the basic metaphor MORE IS UP. This mapping is widespread and deeply entrenched in the languages of the world. MORE IS UP is based on the universal experience of adding objects to a pile and noticing that the top of the pile gets higher; this experience naturally associates greater quantity with higher levels on the vertical scale.

Metaphors like POWERFUL IS UP are partially based on MORE IS UP, in that *more* power or status is mapped as being *higher* on the vertical scale. Other experiences contribute to this metaphor as well, including (as noted above) the benefit of height and high ground in a physical fight.

Because we value power and status, in POWERFUL IS UP we view the higher end of the vertical scale as being better than the lower end of the vertical scale. This kind of metaphor, which puts together the notion of MORE IS UP with some desired quality like POWER, is also extremely common in the languages of the world. Because these metaphors value the high end of the scale over the low end of the scale, they naturally lead to the next metaphor, GOOD IS UP.

GOOD IS UP, another common metaphor, is indirectly based on MORE IS UP, and more directly based on groups of metaphors that define *more* of some *good quality* as *up*. When enough of these metaphors exist, the high end of the vertical scale itself become strongly associated with good qualities. Thus, *good* in general comes to be seen as *up*, and *improvement* as *movement upward*.

The positive-end-up metaphors derive, directly or indirectly, from MORE IS UP. ANALYSIS IS DIGGING, a positive-end-down metaphor, comes from another lineage altogether. It is not in any way based on the experience of piling up objects; instead, it is based on the experience of digging down below some surface to find hidden objects. Though the vertical up–down dimension is crucial to this metaphor, it is used in a very different way: The valued end of the continuum is at the bottom, and *movement upward* does not even participate in the mapping.

The moral of this story is that it is not enough to simply talk about "vertical scale" metaphors. Metaphors that use what seems to be the "same" source domain can be very different from each other. They may be based on different kinds of experiences and produce different valuings and interpretations of the elements of the source domain. It is crucial to treat each metaphor on its own terms, carefully gathering examples and constructing individual, self-consistent mappings; one cannot lump metaphors together and assume that their details will be the same.

CHAPTER NINE

Verb Agreement Paths in American Sign Language[1]

AMERICAN SIGN LANGUAGE VERB AGREEMENT

Now that we understand how iconicity and conceptual metaphor function, and how they work together in signed languages, we are ready to tackle a core issue of ASL's grammar: *verb agreement*. We touched on this topic briefly in Chapter Five, while discussing space-for-space iconicity; it concerns how some ASL verbs move in space from an area representing one referent to an area representing another referent.[2]

Most linguists talk about this phenomenon as if the two endpoints of the movement were all that mattered; they refer to it as "incorporation" of the referents' spatial locations into the verbs' movement patterns. I prefer to discuss it in terms of the verb's entire movement: In my analysis, the verb traces a path from one referent to the other that is specified by the verb's semantics.[3]

In this discussion we will limit ourselves to frozen or lexicalized ASL verbs, and not examine classifier forms (which have their own iconic principles for incorporating movement). There are several different "systems" within ASL for determining how verbs move; all are highly iconic, and some are metaphorical as well. Some are based on the verb's seman-

---

[1] An earlier version of this chapter appeared as Taub (1998).
[2] We are concerned only with person–number agreement here, not movements that result from aspectual inflections or "distributional" inflections (cf. Padden 1988).
[3] Some verbs that are considered to be of this type do not actually *move* from one referent to the other. Instead, they *orient* their handshapes so that the palm and fingers face one referent and the back of the hand faces the other referent. Most treatments of verb agreement class these verbs together with verbs that move without further comment; for lack of space, I will do the same here. They are equally difficult for treatments based on locus incorporation as for my path-based treatment. We can think of them as indicating the direction of their paths by which way they "point" their fingers and palms.

tics in a clear and obvious way, and others have taken on layers of conventionalized structure on top of the direct semantic motivation.

Earlier linguists (e.g., Friedman 1975, Gee & Kegl 1982) tried to put forward semantically based theories of verb agreement, but the complexities of the system were too difficult to handle at that time (cf. Padden's 1988 rebuttal to Friedman). Yet ASL verb movement *is* deeply rooted in semantics. With the understanding of iconicity and metaphor outlined in this book, and with the tools of cognitive linguistics (especially frame semantics and prototype theory), we are fully prepared to give a semantic account of verb agreement.

THE SEMANTICS OF VERBS

Let us start with some background on the semantics of verbs. As many cognitive scientists have noted (e.g., Fillmore 1982, Lakoff 1987; Schank & Abelson 1977), our information about the world comes in bundles or "frames" that are basically self-contained (see also Chapter Two). The meanings of words can be set out most clearly by referring to one of these frames. For example, to understand the English phrase *third base,* one needs to know about the game of baseball, its rules, and its equipment; without that frame, the concept cannot be easily defined. Frames can be extremely complex, including long scenarios with many characters (e.g., *baseball, dining at a restaurant, the U.S. government*); or they can be quite simple, involving only a scale or other simple relation (e.g., *size, color, distance*).

Verbs (for the most part) refer to frames in which there is a relationship that either is ongoing or changes over time; in the frame's scenario, some entity does something or exists in some state, affecting either only itself or one or more other entities. The verb refers to the scenario and picks out one or more of the entities to which it pays special attention. These entities are called the "arguments" of the verb. For example, in the frame of *hitting,* one entity forcefully contacts another entity; the English verb *hit* takes both entities as arguments, as in the sentence *John hit the wall.* In the frame of *restaurants,* which contains *waiters, customers, menus, tables, food,* and so on, the verb *order* takes *customers* and *food* as arguments, as in *Lucy ordered a sandwich.*

As we can see from the restaurant example, the verb need not involve as arguments all the entities in the frame. Verbs pick out certain aspects of the frame to focus on (Langacker [1987] would say they *profile* those aspects); only the profiled entities are chosen as arguments. Thus, the verb *order* (in the restaurant scenario) profiles the customers and the food while treating the cooks and menus as "backgrounded" information, important for comprehension yet not specifically mentioned.

Different verbs can highlight variations on a scenario. For example, there is a frame of *transferring objects,* in which an object begins with one person and ends up with another person. Many English verbs refer to that frame, and many of them refer to particular variations of the basic scenario. The verb *give* treats the original owner as the active party in the transfer, whereas the new owner is a passive recipient; conversely, the verb *take* treats the new owner as active and the original owner as passive.

Though semantic frames describe many different kinds of actions and states, there are some types of structure that many frames share. For example, many frames have one entity that acts so as to affect another entity. In the frame of *hitting,* the "hitter" is that actor; in the frame of *digging,* it is the "digger"; and so on. Linguists have found it useful to give a name to that kind of actor; they call it an *agent* (abbreviated *AGT*) and refer to it as a *semantic role* or *role archetype* that appears in many frames (cf. Fillmore 1968, Langacker 1991b, and the analogous *theta-roles* of Chomksy [1981]).

There are a number of semantic roles that frames share. The ones that concern us here are *agent* (AGT), the intentional causer of some change; *patient* (PAT), an entity that undergoes a change of state; *theme,* an entity that moves, is located, or is the subject of perception; *experiencer* (EXP), a person who perceives or feels some stimulus; *source,* the location from which some literal or metaphorical object moves; and *goal,* the location to which some literal or metaphorical object moves.[4]

The following English sentences briefly exemplify these roles. In *Alice hit Betsy, Alice* is an AGT and *Betsy* is a PAT. In *The ball rolled from the table to the door,* the *ball* is a THEME, the *table* is a SOURCE, and *door* is a GOAL. In *Lucy hates ice cream, Lucy* is an EXP and *ice cream* is a THEME.

The use of semantic roles in this chapter follows that of Langacker 1991b (and cf. Fried 1995). Many linguists (e.g., Fillmore 1968) assign exactly one role to each argument of a verb; this is useful for certain kinds of linguistic theories, as they use this principle to constrain the number of elements that can appear in sentences (e.g., the *theta-criterion* of Principles and Parameters Theory, Chomsky 1981). Thus, for the English verb *give,* the "giver" would be considered to be an AGT but not a SOURCE, even though the "giver" fits the definition of this other role

---

4 I will follow the convention of putting the names of the roles in capital letters.

as well. Yet semantically, the AGT/PAT, SOURCE/GOAL, and EXP/THEME pairs of roles draw on different cognitive structures or schemas; there is no reason why a verb's meaning should not incorporate more than one of these structures. AGT and PAT have to do with the schema of *willful action and its effects,* SOURCE and GOAL have to do with *movement from place to place*; and EXP and THEME have to do with *mental experience due to some stimulus.* The English verb *give,* in its prototypical sense of object transfer, uses at least two of these structures; the "giver" is thus AGT and SOURCE at once. The two schemas for these roles are not correlated in any necessary way and can recombine in other patterns; thus, *take* has an AGT–GOAL argument.[5]

In this chapter, we will find it useful sometimes to talk in terms of the generic semantic roles (AGT, PAT, etc.) and sometimes in terms of the roles that are specific to each frame (*giver, mover,* etc.). We will see that ASL's verb agreement structures draw on patterns from both levels. As we discuss each verb, its frame and scenario will be briefly described, along with its arguments, roles, and the point of view it imposes.

HOW AMERICAN SIGN LANGUAGE VERBS MOVE
THROUGH SIGNING SPACE

It is well established that verbs in ASL (and other signed languages) fall into three major categories, and these have been given the names *plain, spatial,* and *agreement verbs* (Padden 1988). Plain verbs do not change their movement patterns except to express aspectual or temporal information, whereas the other two types incorporate meaningful spatial locations into their structure.

Differences between spatial and agreement verbs' use of signing space have been widely noted (e.g., Padden 1988); it has also been noted that classifiers pattern with spatial verbs, and pronouns pattern with agreement verbs. It has been argued (e.g., Klima & Bellugi 1979; Poizner, Klima, & Bellugi 1987) that classifiers and spatial verbs use space in a semantically motivated way to show relative locations of referents (*locative* use), whereas agreement verbs and pronouns simply use spatial locations as syntactic placeholders for referents (*pronominal* use). In most theories that incorporate this view, the manner in which a lexical item uses space (i.e., locative or pronominal) must be marked as an arbitrary feature of that item.

---

[5] I also follow Langacker (1991b) in treating the "receiver" in the *giving* frame as an EXP: This captures the change in the receiver's internal mental state as she or he gains a new possession. The receiver is thus SOURCE/EXP. (Compare the later section on EXP/THEME verbs.)

I argue throughout this chapter that both patterns are semantic in nature and involve mappings of envisioned mental spaces onto signing space; moreover, we can predict which pattern an item will use based on its meaning. Spatial verbs and classifiers, as fits their focus on precise descriptions of spatial relations, draw on a detailed, highly iconic mapping of an envisioned mental space onto signing space. Pronouns and agreement verbs, on the other hand, make use of a highly schematic and often metaphorical mapping of mental space elements onto signing space; this matches their concern with more abstract interactions.

With this approach, we would expect to find no strict boundary between the two types of uses of space but instead a continuum based on how relevant spatial precision is to the context; we would also expect to find that lexical items might draw on both patterns, depending on what the signer wishes to focus on. We shall see below that this is in fact the case. Engberg-Pedersen (1993) has also argued against a strict separation of this sort.

In the first pattern, verbs iconically trace out the path of some "mover" object, or THEME, from one place (SOURCE) to another (GOAL). This strategy motivates the movement patterns of spatial verbs such as RUN or TRAVEL: The verb starts at a locus in signing space that represents the THEME's initial location in some mental space and moves to another locus representing the THEME's stopping place in the mental space. In general, spatial verbs have their THEME argument as their syntactic subject (except for a subset that has an AGT argument as subject; e.g., THROW or PUT). Verbs that use this strategy map the mental space onto every point along the verb's path. We could say that their mapping of the mental space onto the signing space is *complete:* It faithfully represents relative distances and locations.

This theory of how spatial verbs function is supported by Padden's (1988) observation of the semantic consequences of small modifications in spatial verb's paths. She noted that small differences in the path taken by a spatial verb create small changes in the verb's meaning.[6]

For example, consider the verb RUN (Fig. 9.1). If the signer has already established loci in signing space for his or her home and a store, RUN can move from the first locus to the second, with the meaning "run from home to the store." But the verb can also move *partway* along this path, with meanings such as "run from home halfway to the store" or "run from home almost all the way to the store"; the distance along the path in signing space corresponds directly to the distance of running that the verb asserts.

---

[6] Padden did not attribute this fact to semantic factors.

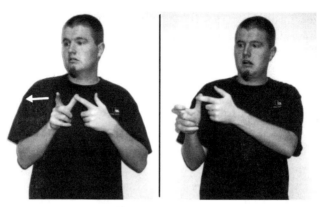

Figure 9.1. RUN.

This is exactly the pattern that we expect if the verb draws on a detailed mapping from a mental space onto signing space. Small changes in the envisioned mental-space path, corresponding to small changes in meaning, would lead directly to small changes in the verb's path through signing space.[7]

In the second or "pronominal" use of space, verbs also incorporate meaningful locations, but there is a significant difference: Small changes in the verb's path do not have semantic consequences. That is, a verb that moves part of the way to an argument's locus will have the same meaning as a verb that moves all the way to that locus. Moreover, the initial and final loci correspond to the syntactic subject and direct or indirect object of the sentence. Verbs like DEFEAT (see Fig. 9.2) and BOTHER are in this category.

As an example of how this pattern works, consider the agreement verb GIVE (see Fig. 9.5). If the signer has set up loci for two people (let us call them Alice and Betsy), movement of the verb from Alice's locus to Betsy's locus would mean *Alice gives (something) to Betsy*. Yet movement of the verb *partway* along this path does not change the verb's meaning (conceivably to something like *Alice partially gives [something] to Betsy*); instead, the verb will mean *Alice gives (something) to Betsy* regardless of what percentage of the distance along the path has been covered.

Accounting for this movement pattern is somewhat more challenging than accounting for spatial verbs' movement, and linguists have attempted the task in a number of different ways. Padden's (1988) approach was based on grammatical functions: Agreement verbs move

---

7 This analysis owes a debt to Liddell's (1998) analysis of classifier predicates as drawing on a blend of signing space and some mental space.

Figure 9.2. I-DEFEAT-HIM/HER/IT.

from their subject's locus to their object's locus. Because nearly all ASL agreement verbs with AGT arguments have the AGT as subject, this is roughly equivalent to the semantics-based claim that agreement verbs move from AGT locus to PAT or other locus.[8] Both of these formulations account for the majority of agreement verbs' movements. They both fail, however, to account for a small class of agreement verbs in ASL (and most other signed languages; cf. Meir 1998) that move in the reverse pattern (i.e., from object or PAT to subject or AGT). Padden referred to these as "backwards" verbs and handled them theoretically by marking them with a special syntactic feature.

Padden's solution – to mark backwards verbs as anomalous – is unsatisfactory because scrutiny of the class of backwards verbs shows that they have a semantic commonality. A large number of them (e.g., STEAL, BORROW, TAKE) have a THEME object that moves from SOURCE to GOAL; in addition, the GOAL argument is the verb's AGT. These verbs can thus be described as following the THEME's path from SOURCE to GOAL.

If one notes as well that many "forward" agreement verbs (e.g., GIVE, SEND, in some dialects LEND) also follow the path of a THEME object from SOURCE to GOAL, and that the same is true (as stated above) for all spatial verbs, it seems natural to formulate another theory that covers both types: ASL verbs that involve space move from SOURCE to GOAL.

---

[8] Padden argued extensively against stating the generalization in terms of roles such as AGT or PAT. Her main objection is that many verbs' subject argument is not an AGT but instead an EXP or even a RECIPIENT, and thus any statement of verb agreement using roles would need to generalize over several roles. It turns out, however, that making the generalization in terms of "heads" and "tails" on the action chain rather than specific roles solves this problem. See the analysis below.

This is essentially the approach of Friedman (1975) (cf. also Gee & Kegl 1982).

Such an approach is desirable in that it unifies the treatment of spatial and agreement verbs. Yet Friedman's theory was inadequate in a number of respects: It did not account for differences between spatial and agreement verbs nor for agreement verbs that do not have obvious THEME, SOURCE, and GOAL arguments (e.g., BOTHER, DEFEAT, HATE, INFLUENCE). Finally, as we shall see in detail below, there are a number of verbs with more than one path in their semantics (e.g., SUMMON, INVITE, SELL), and Friedman's theory does not tell us which path the verb will select.[9]

Meir (1998), using Jackendoff's (e.g., 1990) formalist theory of Conceptual Semantics rather than a cognitivist approach, created a unified model of spatial and agreement verbs. For her, both types of verbs contain a PATH predicate and the endpoints of the verb's movement are identified with the endpoints of the PATH. In addition, agreement verbs contain a TRANSFER predicate, which affects the assignment of syntactic subject and object and the direction in which the verb "faces." Meir's model solves nearly all of the problems inherent in Friedman's approach and accounts neatly for the differences between the two types of verbs; indeed, it bears certain resemblances to the present model (first presented as Taub 1997). But it does not explain the behavior of verbs with multiple paths, nor does it explicitly show how to account for verbs without literal paths.[10]

The analysis presented here claims that both types of verbs involve conceptual mapping of elements from their semantic frames onto signing space. For spatial verbs, the mapping is iconic and detailed. For agreement verbs, the mapping is still iconic but more schematic and often metaphorical. Moreover, there are cognitive principles that motivate which path is selected in verbs with multiple conflicting conceptual paths. In sum, all spatial properties of ASL verbs can be predicted on semantic grounds. The next sections set forth the analysis in more detail.

---

[9] Padden (1988) raised another problem with this approach: One locus (and only one) can optionally be deleted from agreement verbs' paths. Comparison of normal and backwards verbs shows that we cannot state the rule for locus deletion in terms of SOURCE and GOAL arguments; instead, Padden argued, it is the subject's locus that is deleted. One could also state this generalization in terms of heads and tails on the action chain; compare the previous footnote.

[10] A detailed analysis of the relative merits of the cognitivist and formalist approaches will be the topic of a future article.

SEMANTIC AND PHONOLOGICAL BASIS FOR AMERICAN SIGN LANGUAGE'S VERB CLASSES

The first part of the puzzle concerns verbs' membership in the three classes: How do we know whether a verb will move at all? And if it moves, will it map space completely (as a spatial verb) or incompletely (as an agreement verb)? In answering these questions, I draw on work by Janis (1995) on ASL and Meir (1998) on Israeli Sign Language (ISL). I have reframed their insights in terms of cognitivist concepts.[11]

According to Janis, verbs will follow the spatial pattern "…whenever the location of [an argument] influences how the action (or state) expressed by the verb is characterized" (p. 216). In other words, let us say that a verb refers to exact locations in some mental space; in ASL, that verb will map those locations *and their relationship to each other* onto signing space. This produces the pattern noted above: Small variations in the paths of spatial verbs, or verbs concerned with exact locations, create small variations in the verbs' meanings. We can look at this as a principle of iconic primacy: The verbs with the most concrete, specific envisioning of space are exactly those verbs which map space most completely.

Meir has worked out a semantic motivation for agreement verbs for ISL: in her terms, agreement verbs are verbs of "transfer" – that is, something passes from one entity to another. In my terms, these verbs have paths in their semantics, just as do spatial verbs, but they are not concerned with exact physical location; instead, the paths lead from one significant entity to another, and the verbs focus on the moving object's transfer from the influence of one entity to the influence of another. The paths and objects can be either literal or metaphorical.

Meir shows that all such verbs manifest as agreement verbs in ISL, unless their phonological characteristics (e.g., being anchored to a specific location on the body) block movement through space. A similar proposal could be made to work for ASL, though it is beyond the scope of this chapter. Thus, we find that in the absence of phonological interference, those verbs with paths that focus on spatial relations manifest as spatial verbs; those with paths that focus on interactions between entities manifest as agreement verbs; and all others manifest as plain verbs.

---

[11] For example, Janis made her explanation in terms of theoretical constructs such as *locative case* and *direct case*; I am reframing her work without these constructs, drawing instead on our understanding of iconicity, metaphor, and conceptual mappings. In her terms, *nominals with locative case impose locative agreement*; in my terms, *arguments concerned with location impose a full iconic mapping onto signing space*. In her terms, *nominals with direct case can impose direct-case agreement*; in my terms, *arguments that are not concerned with location can impose a partial iconic mapping onto signing space*.

This position is supported by evidence noted by Janis (1995). Certain ASL verbs can change their spatial patterning depending on the signer's intended meaning. We will take SIT and STEAL as our examples.

Signers can use SIT to focus on the exact location where a person sits down; at those times, SIT acts like a spatial verb, moving to the locus representing the specific seat. But signers can also use SIT *without* focusing on the exact location, simply using it to report a change in posture; at those times, SIT acts like a plain verb, articulated in the "neutral space" in front of the signer. Similarly, STEAL can incorporate the locus where the stolen object was located (e.g., a place in a house that has been set up in signing space); in this use, it functions as a spatial verb. But it can also incorporate the locus of the person from whom the object was taken; at these times it functions as an agreement verb.

It seems that exact location can be important to the signer at some times but not at other times. When the signer wishes to focus on exact spatial relations, the verb will take the spatial pattern; when the signer focuses on interpersonal interactions, the verb will take the agreement pattern; and when neither is in focus, the verb will not incorporate space at all.

Yet not all verbs are flexible as to category. We can divide verbs into several types. Verbs like RUN, which *always* consider exact location to be important, will always be spatial verbs, imposing a fully metric mapping of signing space. Verbs like HATE, which *never* consider exact location to be important, will never be spatial verbs. Finally, verbs like SIT and STEAL can take on two distinct patterns.

To summarize: ASL has conventionalized some verbs as always indicating exact location; these verbs always impose a metric mapping onto signing space. Other verbs are conventionalized as never indicating exact locations. And some verbs, as we see with SIT and STEAL, are allowed to indicate exact location or not, depending on the specific meaning the signer wishes to convey.

There is also some evidence that the distinction between the two patterns is a matter of degree, not of absolute difference. Padden herself introduced data (see also Engberg-Pedersen 1993 and Liddell 1990, among others) suggesting that the two are not strictly separable. When a referent is established at one locus in signing space and then is shown (via the spatial description system) to have moved, agreement verbs will then agree with the new location, not the old one, showing that they can draw on the spatial description system as well. Thus, for this situation, a single locus can control grammatical agreement *and* take part in a more comprehensive mapping between signing space and a mental space.

It should not be surprising to find all variations along the continuum, from highly schematic mappings that involve perhaps only a single entity's location in signing space, to intermediate mappings involving perhaps only the general spatial relations between several entities, to strongly iconic uses of loci that participate in a comprehensive mapping between signing space and a mental scene. If classes of verbs need to be distinguished, we might do better to base the distinction on how the verbs are used most conventionally: Do they *tend* to focus on exact spatial relations or is their tendency to show more abstract interactions?

DIRECTION OF MOVEMENT: PATHS IN SIGNING SPACE

We have established the semantic basis for the type of spatial mapping used by ASL verbs. Our analysis of spatial and plain verbs is essentially complete; now we must look more closely at agreement verbs. As noted above, some move from syntactic subject to object, and others (the backwards verbs) move from object to subject. The main contribution of this chapter is to establish semantic criteria for the direction of motion.

The reason why backwards verbs move as they do is easy to see intuitively: They are iconic, and they trace the path of some object in a mental space. For example, STEAL traces the path of the stolen object from EXP/SOURCE (the victim) to AGT (the thief).[12] But we need some sophistication to make this approach work, particularly with backwards verbs such as COPY and TAKE-ADVANTAGE-OF, which do not involve the movement of any concrete object in physical space. We need to know the conditions for when an "objectless" verb will move from AGT to PAT, as with DEFEAT, and when it will move from PAT to AGT, as in TAKE-ADVANTAGE-OF.

The following discussion shows that there is a delicate balance for agreement-type verbs that determines the direction of their movement. I claim that *all* agreement verbs trace out a literal or metaphorical path from their semantic frame. A number of verbs, including the backwards ones, have two or more paths in their frames; I provide a semantic hierarchy that can predict which path the verb will follow. This discussion completes our account of metaphorical–iconic paths in ASL verbs: We will be able to predict on semantic grounds whether a verb will incorporate an iconic path movement, whether it will be of the "spatial" or

---

[12] As noted above, STEAL has two different agreement patterns: moving from "victim" to "thief" and from "stolen object's initial location" to "thief." Verbs like TAKE and BORROW show the same two patterns, sometimes originating at the EXP/SOURCE's location and sometimes at the THEME's initial location. In the rest of this chapter, I treat only the first pattern, but the second pattern is equally if not more strongly motivated by the verb's semantics and poses no problems for my analysis.

"agreement" types (i.e., how much of an iconic mapping it will impose on signing space), and which direction the verb will move (i.e., which path it will take if two possibilities are in conflict).

DEFEAT: *The Action-Chain Path*

We will structure our discussion of movement direction by going through a series of verbs whose frames are more and more complex. The entire discussion is summarized in Table 9.14, which lists all the verbs and their path directions, and Table 9.15, which gives the principles for determining path direction in case of a conflict. But let us start slowly by considering the simplest cases first.

The verb DEFEAT is shown in Figure 9.2, in the inflected form I-DEFEAT-HIM/HER/IT. The verb has an AGT and a PAT argument and means "for one person [the AGT] to defeat another person [the PAT] in some contest or battle."[13] As Janis would predict, DEFEAT is an agreement verb; it moves from AGT's locus toward PAT's locus.

If we are to claim that all agreement verbs move along the path of some object in the verb's semantics, we are immediately faced with a challenge: Where is the path in the semantics of DEFEAT? No object literally changes hands in the frame of *defeating*, and we would be hard pressed even to find a metaphorical object (e.g., an *idea*, as in IDEAS ARE OBJECTS, Chapter Six; *respect*; *status*) moving from victor to loser. Yet we are rescued by one fact: For DEFEAT, an AGT acts in a way that strongly affects a PAT. Recall the widespread metaphor, mentioned earlier, that treats *effects* as *objects that move from agent to affected one.* Though the frame of *defeating* doesn't supply its own literal or metaphorical object, it shares with all other AGT/PAT frames the metaphorical "effects" object, which "moves" from AGT to PAT. Thus, DEFEAT does have a path available in its semantics, and it traces that path, moving from its AGT's locus to its PAT's locus. This situation is summarized in Table 9.1.

I will refer to the victor-to-loser path as the *action-chain* path, in reference to a cognitive model of causation that bears that name. For DEFEAT, this path leads from AGT to PAT, but that is not the only possibility.

---

[13] In describing the verbs' meanings in this chapter, I formulate them in terms of a proto-typical case in which all the participants (except the literal or metaphorical mover) are "people" or animate beings. The participants can of course be nonhumans as well: institutions, organizations, and so on.

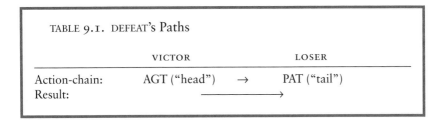

TABLE 9.1. DEFEAT's Paths

	VICTOR		LOSER
Action-chain:	AGT ("head")	→	PAT ("tail")
Result:		——————→	

Cognitive linguists (notably Croft 1991, Langacker 1991b) have found it useful to develop a model of how we conceptualize events. Typically, when we perceive a network of interrelated changes, movements, and other occurrences, we figure out some story about why those events took place; in general, we trace events back to some original cause effected by some particular entity.

For example, the breaking of a windowpane can be seen as caused by the impact of a baseball, which was caused by the movement of the ball in a particular trajectory, which was caused by the impact of a bat against the ball, which was caused by the actions of a girl named Jane. In this scenario, *Jane* is conceived of as the original cause of the window's breaking. She is the "head" (to use Langacker's terms) of a chain of caused events that ends with the window's breaking; because the window does not affect any other entity, it is the "tail" of the chain. This chain is diagrammed in Figure 9.3. Each of the double arrows indicates that one entity is affecting the next; the single arrow at the end indicates that the window's breaking is not conceived of as affecting any other entity.

In general, any event (particularly physical, concrete events) can be broken down into an *action chain* of one or more entities each affecting the next, the first entity being the *head* and the last entity being the *tail*. Because, metaphorically, effects are conceived of as objects, we can speak of "effects objects" moving from entity to entity along the chain from head to tail. Thus, a metaphorical path exists from head to tail along the action chain, and it is always accessible to motivate the meaning of a verb.

Figure 9.3. Action chain for a complex event.

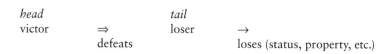

head		tail	
victor	⇒	loser	→
defeats		loses (status, property, etc.)	

Figure 9.4. Action chain for DEFEAT.

Our current example, DEFEAT, has a very short action chain (shown in Fig. 9.4). The victor is the head, the loser is the tail, and there are no intermediate entities. The same is true for many verbs with AGT–PAT arguments (though often there is an intermediate entity on the chain, an *instrument* by which the AGT affects the PAT); for this type of verb, the AGT is always the head and the PAT is the tail of the action chain. We shall see in the next section that the situation is more complex for verbs like GIVE and TAKE, but the head and the tail are still readily identified.

To summarize: For verbs like DEFEAT, with an AGT argument and a PAT argument, the verb traces the action-chain path from AGT/head to PAT/tail.

GIVE: *Literal and Action-Chain Paths Aligned*

If every verb only had one path in its semantics, ASL verb agreement would be simple and regular. But that is not the case; many verbs have two paths or even more, and these paths often run in conflicting directions.

Our next case hardly poses a problem, however. The verb GIVE, shown in Figure 9.5 as I-GIVE-(TO)-HIM/HER/IT, has two paths, but they

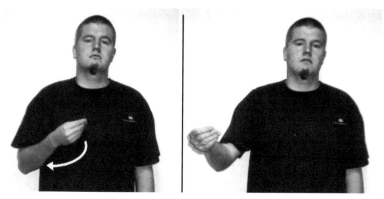

Figure 9.5. I-GIVE-(TO)-HIM/HER/IT.

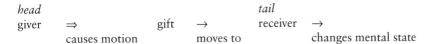

head   *tail*
giver   ⇒   gift   →   receiver   →
      causes motion   moves to   changes mental state

Figure 9.6. Action chain for GIVE.

lead in the same direction. The verb means "for someone to give an item to another person"; it has as arguments a *giver*, who is both an active AGT and a SOURCE of the object; a *receiver*, who is GOAL and EXP; and a *gift object* or THEME that passes from the giver to the receiver. In the prototypical case, the gift is a concrete object that is literally passed from giver to receiver; it is this case that determines the verb's agreement pattern.

The first path in GIVE's semantics is the literal path of the gift from the giver to the receiver. The second path is the metaphorical action-chain path. This requires a bit of discussion. Figure 9.6 summarizes the action chain for GIVE. The head of this chain is the giver, who causes the object to move to the receiver. When the object arrives, it causes the receiver to experience a change in mental state: She or he is now the owner of a new object. Following Langacker (1991b), I capture this change in state by giving the receiver the role of EXP, not PAT, but regardless of role, the receiver is still the tail of the action chain. The metaphorical action-chain path leads from head (giver/AGT) to tail (receiver/EXP).

For GIVE, then, the action-chain path and the literal path (giver to recipient) lead in the same direction. This situation is summarized in Table 9.2. There is no conflict, and predictably, the verb form moves from giver's locus to receiver's locus.

We should note here that the gift object and its path are not necessarily physical; GIVE can denote the transfer of some nonphysical object like an idea or a story, or even some physical object that is too large to be literally passed from hand to hand. In these cases, we can understand the path as metaphorical. Wilcox (1993) has a lengthy discussion of GIVE's

TABLE 9.2. GIVE's Paths			
	GIVER		RECEIVER
Action-chain:	Head	→	Tail
Literal:	SOURCE	→	GOAL
Result:		———————→	

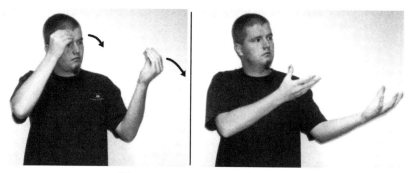

Figure 9.7. I-INFORM-HIM/HER/IT.

meanings, based on extensions from the prototypical case of physical transfer by hand.

INFORM: *Metaphorical and Action-Chain Paths Aligned*

The situation for INFORM (illustrated in Fig. 9.7 as I-INFORM-HIM/HER/IT) is much like that of GIVE: The verb's semantic frame has two paths that do not conflict. In INFORM's scenario, one person (the informer) tells another person (the learner) some information. As we have seen (Chapter Six), in ASL information can be metaphorically and iconically represented as an object that moves from informer to learner. The path of this metaphorical object is the first path in INFORM's semantics. The second path is once again the action-chain path of "effects," summarized in Figure 9.8. The informer's direct action is to express the information; the learner's perception of that information is conceptualized as an effect the information has on the learner. Thus, the AGT/informer is the chain's head and the EXP/learner is the tail.

Both paths lead from informer to learner, and naturally enough, this is the direction in which INFORM moves. The situation is summarized in Table 9.3. We should notice that *both* of INFORM's paths are metaphorical – based on COMMUNICATING IS SENDING, for the SOURCE–GOAL path, and on CAUSING IS GIVING, for the action-chain path – but the first path is more specific to the frame of communication. This fact will become important when we start dealing with path conflicts. (In the rest of this

head				*tail*	
informer	⇒	information	⇒	learner	→
	expresses		impinges on		changes mental state

Figure 9.8. Action chain for INFORM.

TABLE 9.3. INFORM's Paths

	INFORMER		LEARNER
Action-chain:	Head	→	Tail
Metaphorical:	SOURCE	→	GOAL
Result:		——————→	

chapter, we will abbreviate "specific metaphorical path" to "metaphorical path" and "action-chain metaphorical path" to "action-chain path"; this is for ease of reading and writing and is not intended to imply that the action-chain path is not metaphorical.)

TAKE: *Literal and Action-Chain Paths in Conflict*

At last we begin to look at those verbs which have been called backwards. We shall see that the movement of these verbs is by no means anomalous but is the result of a sensible resolution of path conflicts.

The verb TAKE, illustrated in Figure 9.9 as I-TAKE-(FROM)-HIM/HER/IT, means "for someone [the 'taker'] to take an item from another person [the 'previous owner']." Here, the AGT/taker is a GOAL, not a SOURCE, and the previous owner is a SOURCE, not a GOAL. This is because the taken object moves from previous owner to taker, whereas the taker is seen as the active cause of the movement.

The action chain for TAKE is diagrammed in Figure 9.10. Just as for GIVE, the head of the path is an AGT causing the movement of the item; and once again, the movement causes a mental experience for the previous owner or SOURCE/EXP; the only difference is that this time the experience is the loss rather than the acquisition of a possession.

Figure 9.9. I-TAKE-(FROM)-HIM/HER/IT.

head   *tail*
taker ⇒   item ⇒   previous owner →
       causes motion   moves from   changes mental state

Figure 9.10. Action chain for TAKE.

TABLE 9.4. TAKE's Paths			
	TAKER		PREVIOUS OWNER
Action-chain:	Head	→	Tail
Literal:	GOAL	←	SOURCE
Result:	←		

The two paths in TAKE's semantics are aligned in opposite directions. The literal path of the taken object leads from previous owner (SOURCE) to taker (GOAL), but the action-chain path leads from taker (head) to previous owner (tail). This situation is summarized in Table 9.4. How does ASL resolve this conflict? We could imagine several possibilities: For example, ASL could have a rule that both paths are represented, or that the action-chain path always "wins." Neither of these is the case: As we can see from Figure 9.9 and Table 9.4, TAKE follows the path of the literal object from affected party to agent. This is our first data point in figuring out the criteria for resolving path conflict: When a literal path and the action-chain path conflict, the literal path "wins." Other verbs of this type, with a literal path and the action chain in conflict, include STEAL and QUIT-FROM; both of these verbs move from tail to head in terms of the action chain.

QUOTE: *Metaphorical and Action-Chain Paths in Conflict*

The verb QUOTE is illustrated in Figure 9.11 as the inflected form I-QUOTE-HIM/HER/IT. This verb means "for one person to say/sign/write what another person said/signed/wrote," and it emphasizes the fact that the first person (or "quoter") knows that the other person made the comment first. QUOTE's arguments include the quoter (AGT/GOAL); the quoted material (THEME); and the originator of the material (SOURCE). In some sense, the quoter is "taking control" of the quoted material by using it for his or her purposes; before the event of quoting, the originator was the only "controller" of the material.

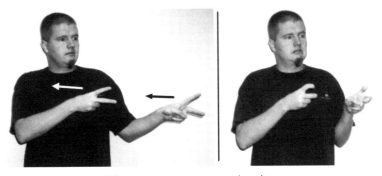

Figure 9.11. I-QUOTE-HIM/HER/IT.

The action-chain path runs from the quoter to the originator, as shown in Figure 9.12. The quoter's primary effect is on the material that she or he reuses; the effect of the reuse on the originator is admittedly indirect or subtle, but it still can be conceptualized as causing a mental experience for the originator (i.e., the experience of being quoted).

There is a second path here as well: The quoted material is understood as a metaphorical THEME object that "moves" from the originator to the quoter. (The COMMUNICATING IS SENDING data in Chapter Six provide independent evidence for this claim.) A new metaphor is used here as well: *being located near an entity* is used to represent *being controlled by an entity*. As the quoted material "moves" from originator to quoter, it comes under the control of the quoter.

Both the path of the "effects" object and the path of the "quoted material" object are metaphorical; they differ, however, in their degree of specificity. The action-chain path is part of the semantics of causation and the structure of events; this conceptual structure is highly generic and has few vivid details. The quoted material's metaphorical path, on the other hand, is much more specific to this particular verb's frame. Table 9.5 summarizes these paths.

As we can see from Figure 9.12 and Table 9.5, the verb QUOTE follows the vivid, specific metaphorical path and moves from originator to quoter, rather than from head to tail along the action chain. We can

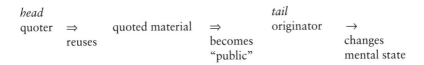

head				*tail*	
quoter	⇒	quoted material	⇒	originator	→
	reuses	becomes		changes	
		"public"		mental state	

Figure 9.12. Action chain for QUOTE.

TABLE 9.5. QUOTE's Paths

	QUOTER		ORIGINATOR
Action-chain	Head	→	Tail
Metaphorical:	GOAL	←	SOURCE
Result:		←	

hypothesize from this example that *specific* metaphorical paths "beat" the generic action-chain path. And indeed, we find that other two-path verbs with conflicting action-chain and metaphorical paths do follow the metaphorical path: The verbs COPY and TAKE-ADVANTAGE-OF both move toward their AGT/head arguments, as the result of specific metaphorical paths in their semantics.

So far, our situation is still fairly simple: For two-path verbs, when the action-chain path conflicts with a frame-specific path, either literal or metaphorical, the action-chain path loses. But two-path verbs are not the limit of complexity. We will now move on to cases with *three* paths in the verb's semantics: the action-chain path and two others (the *frame-specific* paths).

On the basis of what we have already seen, there are a number of logical possibilities of path types. The two frame-specific paths can be both literal, as in BORROW, where an object goes from owner to borrower and is expected to return back again; both metaphorical, as in ASK, where asker metaphorically "sends" words to answerer, and answerer is requested to "send" other words back; or one of each, as in INVITE, where an invitation metaphorically "travels" from host to guest in the hope that the guest will literally travel in the reverse direction. We will find as well that one of these paths is often treated as the *profiled* path (i.e., the one to which the verb directs our attention) and the other is "backgrounded" (i.e., presupposed, suggested but unrealized, or in some other way a backdrop for the profiled path). With these three factors – metaphorical versus literal, profiled versus backgrounded, and frame-specific versus action-chain – we will be able to predict in all cases the direction of the verb's path motion.

BORROW: *Two Literal Paths*

I will begin by noting that there are at least sixteen different possible combinations of profiled, backgrounded, and action-chain paths, if both specific paths can be either literal or metaphorical and can move either with or against the action-chain path. I have not found examples of all these possibilities in ASL; indeed, some of these possibilities (e.g., two literal paths that move in the same direction) are likely to manifest as reduplicated or compounded forms of simpler verbs rather than as verbs in their own right. (For example, a situation in which a person gives a gift to the same person twice would be represented by two occurrences of the verb GIVE, not by some other verb meaning "give twice.") Others of the missing possibilities may be accidental gaps in the lexicon of ASL or in my ASL data collection. Luckily, however, it is not necessary to examine every possible combination of parameters to figure out the principles behind the choice of path direction in ASL verbs, and the examples we do have are the right ones for that task.

We first consider a verb with two literal paths plus the action-chain path. This verb is BORROW, illustrated in Figure 9.13 as the inflected form I-BORROW-(FROM)-HIM/HER/IT. The frame of BORROW is complex: In this frame, an item is owned by one person; another person temporarily takes that item with the expectation that it will be returned to the owner. For BORROW, the second person (or *borrower*) is viewed as active and the owner (or *lender*) is viewed as a passive affected party. (English *borrow* is the same way, but for *lend* the owner is viewed as active.)

The verb asserts that the item does move into the borrower's control, but it does not assert that the item actually is returned to the lender; the expectation of return is part of BORROW's background information. Therefore, BORROW profiles the path from lender to borrower and backgrounds the reverse path.

Figure 9.14 shows the action chain for BORROW; because this verb asserts only one path, I will assume that the action chain should deal

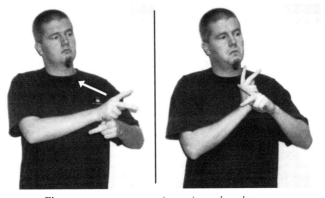

Figure 9.13. I-BORROW-(FROM)-HIM/HER/IT.

head				*tail*	
borrower	⇒	item	⇒	lender	→
causes		moves		changes mental	
motion		from		state	

Figure 9.14. Action chain for BORROW.

TABLE 9.6. BORROW's Paths

	BORROWER		LENDER
Action-chain:	Head	→	Tail
Literal:	GOAL	←	SOURCE (loan)
[Literal:	SOURCE	→	GOAL] (return)
Result:		←	

only with that path. As we can see, the borrower is the head of the chain and the lender is the tail.

The three paths line up as follows: The action-chain path leads from borrower to lender; the profiled path (or actual path of the item) leads from lender to borrower; and the backgrounded path leads from borrower to lender. This situation is summarized in Table 9.6. The brackets around the second literal path indicate that it is a backgrounded path.

As we can see from Figure 9.13 and Table 9.6, BORROW moves in the direction of the literal profiled path, not in the direction of the literal backgrounded path or the action-chain path.[14]

ASK: *Two Metaphorical Paths*

The profiled path "beats" the backgrounded path when both paths are literal; now we must ask whether the same is true when both paths are metaphorical. Signs like ASK provide us with the answer to that question.

Figure 9.15 shows the sign I-ASK-HIM/HER/IT. The semantic frame of ASK involves two participants (the "asker" and the "answerer") and a piece of information that the answerer is likely to know. The asker makes a request of the answerer, that the answerer would tell him or her that

---

[14] If we had an example of two literal paths where the profiled path aligned with the action-chain path, it would be discussed here. The expectation is that the profiled path would still "win" (because it "won" when both the background *and* the action-chain paths aligned against it), and the verb would move from lender to borrower. Some dialects of ASL do have a sign LEND, similar in hand configuration to BORROW, which moves in exactly the manner predicted.

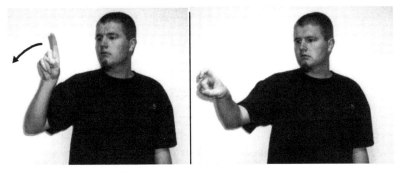

Figure 9.15. I-ASK-HIM/HER/IT.

head				*tail*	
asker	⇒	question	⇒	answerer	→
expresses		impinges on		changes mental state	

Figure 9.16. Action chain for ASK.

information. The verb ASK treats the asker as AGT and the answerer as affected party; it asserts that the asker is making the request, but it does not assert that the answerer provides the information.

The action chain for ASK is shown in Figure 9.16; again, I have selected only the asserted portion of ASK's frame. As we can see, the action-chain path runs from asker to answerer.

The other two paths involve metaphorical movement of linguistic material (i.e., questions and answers). Because the question is asserted, its path (also from asker to answerer) is profiled. The path of the answer, which leads in the opposite direction, is not asserted and is thus backgrounded. This situation is summarized in Table 9.7. As we can see, when both frame-specific paths are metaphorical, once again the profiled path "wins."

TABLE 9.7. ASK's Paths

	ASKER		ANSWERER
Action-chain:	Head	→	Tail
Metaphorical:	SOURCE	→	GOAL (question)
[Metaphorical:	GOAL	←	SOURCE] (answer)
Result:		———————→	

Other verbs of this type include ANSWER and DRILL-ANSWER-OUT; they also follow a profiled metaphorical path from AGT to PAT, not a backgrounded metaphorical path from PAT to AGT.

INVITE: *Profiled Metaphorical Path, Backgrounded Literal Path*

When the frame-specific paths are both literal or both metaphorical, the verb follows the profiled path. This suggests that profiled paths should be ranked above backgrounded paths in some "verb path hierarchy." Does this hypothesis hold true when one frame-specific path is literal and one is metaphorical? There are two verbs that give the data we need for an answer: INVITE and SUMMON both have profiled metaphorical paths and backgrounded literal paths.

Figure 9.17 illustrates the verb I-INVITE-HIM/HER/IT. The frame of INVITE has two participants: an "inviter" and a "guest." Prototypically, the two are at different locations. The inviter tells the guest that his or her presence with the inviter (usually at some event) would be welcome; the guest is then free to decide whether to join the inviter.

The inviter is regarded as the AGT and the guest as the affected one. The invitation that the inviter extends to the guest is, like all linguistic material, a metaphorical object moving from inviter to guest; and the potential movement of the guest to the inviter's location is of course a literal movement through space. INVITE asserts that the invitation has been made, but it says nothing about whether the guest accepts the invitation; thus, the guest's path is backgrounded and the invitation's path is profiled. Figure 9.18 gives the action chain for INVITE's asserted path.

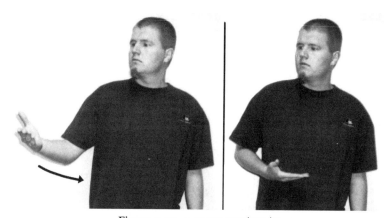

Figure 9.17. I-INVITE-HIM/HER/IT.

head   *tail*

inviter ⇒   invitation ⇒   guest   →

     expresses   impinges on   changes mental state

Figure 9.18. Action chain for INVITE.

TABLE 9.8. INVITE's Paths

	INVITER		GUEST
Action-chain:	Head	→	Tail
Metaphorical:	SOURCE	→	GOAL (invitation)
[Literal:	GOAL	←	SOURCE] (guest's movement)
Result:	←		

For INVITE, then, the action-chain path leads from inviter to guest, as does the metaphorical profiled path. The backgrounded path is literal and runs from guest to inviter. Table 9.8 summarizes this situation. As we can see, contrary to what we might have expected, the profiled path does not "win" here. Instead, the verb follows the backgrounded path.

We can explain this data by hypothesizing that verbs will follow literal rather than metaphorical paths and that although profiled paths are preferred to backgrounded paths, it is important enough for the path to be literal that the "profiled" preference can be overridden.[15]

---

[15] Padden (1988) argued against a semantic path-based analysis of verbs like INVITE because of the following fact: If the *event* to which the guest is being invited is set up in space at a locus different from the inviter's locus, the verb INVITE still moves from guest's locus to inviter's locus, not guest's locus to event's locus.

It is not clear that for these cases, the inviter and the guest will not become co-located at the event: That is, the inviter will likely meet the guest at the event. The situation in which the inviter asks the guest to an event that he or she will not actually attend him- or herself is so unusual that language users see it as a strange use of the verb INVITE.

Thus, the inviter and the guest will likely both move to the event's location. Why, then, does the verb move to the inviter's current locus and not to the event's locus? This is not a major problem for path-based analyses. The *prototypical* invitation is a situation in which the inviter asks the guest to join him or her. Thus, the guest's *prototypical* path is to the inviter, regardless of where the event takes place. The direction of the verb's movement is computed on the basis not of the actual situation at hand but of the prototypical situation; the movement direction then becomes a conventional yet motivated property of the verb.

PAY *and* SELL: *Two Equally Asserted Literal Paths*

We are almost done figuring out the principles for path direction in agreement verbs; there are just a few more cases that we must consider. The first of these involves a situation with two paths that are equally asserted by the verb.

The verbs PAY and SELL (Fig. 9.19, I-PAY-(TO)-HIM/HER/IT; Fig. 9.20, I-SELL-(TO)-HIM/HER/IT) both draw on the same semantic frame. In this frame, one person (the buyer) has money and another person (the seller) has an item that the buyer wants. The buyer gives money to the seller and the seller gives the item to the buyer; these transfers are understood as happening simultaneously, so one is not more asserted than the other. Also, both buyer and seller have active roles.

PAY and SELL both refer to this frame, and they both assert that the two transfers have taken place. They differ, however, as to which participant they profile: PAY draws our attention to the buyer and his or her action, whereas SELL draws attention to the seller and his or her action. Though both the buyer and the seller affect each other, each verb profiles only one set of effects.

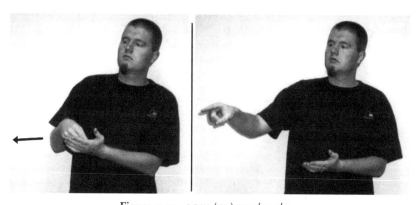

Figure 9.19. I-PAY-(TO)-HIM/HER/IT.

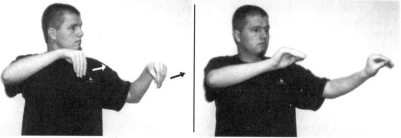

Figure 9.20. I-SELL-(TO)-HIM/HER/IT.

A note about the action chain for these verbs is necessary. As verbs' scenarios become more and more complex, with actions by different participants, agreements between participants about what actions to take, and so on, the action chain becomes less prototypical and harder to work out. For BORROW, ASK, and INVITE, which assert only one (literal or metaphorical) transfer, I adopted the solution of choosing the action chain for that asserted transfer; it seemed reasonable to compute the chain for only the events that are assumed to take place.

This solution will not work for our next examples, PAY and SELL, because they assert *two* paths. What is the "head" or original cause of a transaction in which a goat is exchanged for thirty dollars? What is the "tail"? Are the participants both heads and tails to each other? Does it depend on the specifics of the situation? We could adopt the solution of computing the action chain for only the *profiled* path, but that seems unsatisfactory.

Luckily, we do not need to answer these questions. As we shall see, in these cases we can always pick the correct path direction on other grounds (i.e., by making a principled choice between the two frame-specific paths). Thus, I will resort to marking the action-chain path of verbs like PAY, SELL, EARN, and BRIBE (to name a few other examples) as "indeterminate."

The paths for these verbs lead in the following directions: Both PAY and SELL have literal asserted paths running from buyer to seller (with the money) and from seller to buyer (with the item), but each verb profiles only one of these paths. For PAY, the profiled path runs from buyer to seller, and for SELL, it runs in the opposite direction. This situation is summarized in Tables 9.9 and 9.10. We can see from these tables that although the two frame-specific paths are completely balanced in how literal and asserted they are, the profiled path once more wins the day. As we might expect, the verb moves in the direction of the profiled object-transfer.

TABLE 9.9. PAY's Paths

	BUYER		SELLER
Action-chain:		Indeterminate	
Literal:	SOURCE	→	GOAL (money)
[Literal:	GOAL	←	SOURCE] (item)
Result:		——————→	

TABLE 9.10. SELL's Paths

	SELLER		BUYER
Action-chain:	Indeterminate		
Literal:	SOURCE	→	GOAL (item)
[Literal:	GOAL	←	SOURCE] (money)
Result:			
	——————→		

DISCUSS: *Completely Balanced Paths*

Let us now consider a group of verbs whose scenarios are basically reciprocal in nature: They involve two (or more) participants, each essentially performing the same action and affecting the other person(s) in the same way. Verbs of this type include DISCUSS, EXCHANGE, and COMMUNICATE.[16]

We will use DISCUSS as our main example; it is illustrated in Figure 9.21 as I-DISCUSS-(WITH)-HIM/HER/IT. In this verb's frame, two (or more) participants (the "discussants") take turns telling each other their thoughts and opinions on some topic. Via the COMMUNICATING IS SENDING metaphor, each act of telling is understood as the movement of an object from teller to addressee. Because the verb asserts that the two participants alternate roles, there are metaphorical paths leading in both

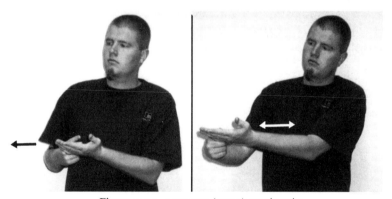

Figure 9.21. I-DISCUSS-(WITH)-HIM/HER/IT.

---

[16] These verbs are not prototypical agreement verbs. They can be "plain" (i.e., not incorporating spatial loci into their forms) *or* their paths can be modified for at least the loci of first person and one more locus. Their lack of prototypicality in form can be ascribed to their unusual semantics and their completely balanced paths; more typical agreement verbs will choose one path over the others (in form as well as in meaning).

TABLE 9.11. DISCUSS's Paths

	DISCUSSANT		DISCUSSANT
Action-chain:		Indeterminate	
Metaphorical:	SOURCE	→	GOAL
Metaphorical:	GOAL	←	SOURCE
Result:		←——————→	

directions, and neither direction is more "asserted" than the other. Moreover, this verb does not profile one path over the other; it draws attention to both paths equally.

This situation is summarized in Table 9.11. Once again, I have considered the direction of the action-chain path, in this complex situation, to be "indeterminate."

So what does ASL do when all the paths in the verb are fully balanced with identical paths taking the opposite direction? It turns out that because there are no grounds for a decision, ASL essentially "refuses" to decide: In verbs of this type, ASL represents *both* paths. Thus, for DISCUSS, the two hands move back and forth together between the discussants' loci.

Verbs of this type are somewhat idiosyncratic about how they represent the two paths: EXCHANGE uses a vertical circling motion in which the hands switch places twice, and COMMUNICATE has the hands moving back and forth in an alternating manner along parallel paths. But in all cases, both paths are represented.

LOOK and PERCEIVE-BY-EYES: EXP and THEME Arguments

There is one final puzzle that we need to address: the agreement patterns of verbs like HATE, PITY, LOOK, PERCEIVE-BY-EYES, and PERCEIVE-BY-EARS. These verbs each have two participants in their semantic frames; one participant is a sentient being who has a mental experience (a thought, perception, emotion, etc.) and the other participant is the subject, content, or trigger of that mental experience. The participants have the semantic roles of EXP and THEME, respectively.

The puzzle is that the EXP/THEME verbs do not display a consistent agreement pattern: HATE, PITY, and LOOK move from EXP's locus to THEME's locus, whereas PERCEIVE-BY-EYES and PERCEIVE-BY-EARS move in the reverse direction. In this section, I show that the EXP–THEME relationship intrinsically has two metaphorical paths. The individual verbs each profile one of those paths; as usual, it is the profiled path that the verb traces.

Let us begin with a discussion of the structure of mental experiences. The action-chain model of causation, which works well for physical events, is less appropriate for experiences. Though we can usually tell the direction of causation in physical interactions (e.g., the ball breaks the window, not vice versa), mental events of perception and emotion are less clear-cut (Croft 1991, Langacker 1991b, Sweetser 1980). Neither EXP nor THEME is a prototypical head or tail of an action chain.

An example will clarify this point. If we perceive a rose blossom and experience it as beautiful, in some sense that rose has affected us. Because we are affected, we are the receiver of a metaphorical "effects" object and should come later on the action chain than the rose. Yet the rose certainly did not *do* anything to cause our perception and experience; it was in no way active and thus makes an odd head or "causer" for an action chain.

On the other hand, if we perceive the rose and delight in its beauty, in some sense we are directing our energy – our senses, our thoughts, our emotions – toward the rose. By directing energy toward the rose, we are behaving much like the prototypical head of an action chain; the direction of this energy forms another metaphorical path leading from us to the rose. But of course, the rose is not itself affected by this mental energy; thus, it is not a prototypical tail for the action chain.

Thus, we can apply the action chain model to EXP/THEME verbs in two different ways – but neither is a particularly good fit. Figure 9.22 diagrams the possibilities. In Figure 9.22A, the head does nothing to cause the tail's experience, and in Figure 9.22B, the head has no effect on the tail.

As we can see from the preceding discussion, there are good reasons to look at either EXP or THEME as the head of the chain; in other words, there are generic-level metaphorical paths that lead in both directions. Once again, we have a situation of path conflict – and once again, it is resolved in a principled way.

We will take the verbs LOOK and PERCEIVE-BY-EYES for examples, as their meanings are extremely similar; they are illustrated in Figure 9.23, I-LOOK-(AT)-HIM/HER/IT, and Figure 9.24, I-PERCEIVE-BY-EYES-HIM/HER/IT. Both verbs draw on the frame of *vision*; this frame has as participants a being with eyes (the EXP, or "viewer") and a physical object (the THEME, or "picture"). If the picture is positioned in front of the viewer's eyes, the viewer will have a visual experience of the picture.

The verbs profile slightly different parts of the frame, however. LOOK profiles the energy that the viewer directs at the picture; it means,

A.   *head*   *tail*
      THEME   ⇒   EXP   →
                   [null]   mental experience

B.   *head*   *tail*
      EXP   ⇒   THEME   →
                   directs energy   [null]

Figure 9.22 Two action chains for EXP/THEME verbs.

Figure 9.23. I-LOOK-(AT)-HIM/HER/IT.

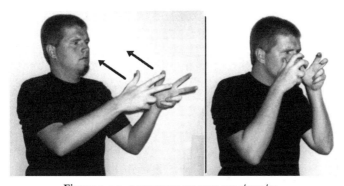

Figure 9.24. I-PERCEIVE-BY-EYES-HIM/HER/IT.

roughly, "for a viewer to direct the eyes toward [and thus perceive] a picture." PERCEIVE-BY-EYES, on the other hand, profiles the experience that the viewer "gets from" the picture; it means "for a viewer to visually perceive a picture [by directing the eyes toward it]."

Clearly, these verbs each profile a different action chain in the two EXP/THEME possibilities. In metaphorical terms, for LOOK the EXP sends a metaphorical object toward the THEME, whereas for PERCEIVE-

TABLE 9.12. LOOK's Paths

	VIEWER/EXP		PICTURE/THEME
[Action-chain (1):	Tail	←	Head] (information)
Action-chain (2):	Head	→	Tail (attention)
Result:		————————→	

TABLE 9.13. Paths for PERCEIVE-BY-EYES

	VIEWER/EXP		PICTURE/THEME
Action-chain (1):	Tail	←	Head (information)
[Action-chain (2):	Head	→	Tail] (attention)
Result:	←————————		

BY-EYES, the EXP receives a metaphorical object from the THEME. Once again, we have a situation with two metaphorical paths, one of which is profiled and the other of which is backgrounded. Tables 9.12 and 9.13 show the paths for LOOK and PERCEIVE-BY-EYES, respectively.

As we can see from the tables and the photographs, LOOK's path is directed from viewer to picture, whereas PERCEIVE-BY-EYES moves from picture to viewer.[17] Both verbs trace out the profiled path in their semantics. Other EXP/THEME verbs in ASL such as HATE, PITY, and PERCEIVE-BY-EARS work in the same way; they, too, profile one of the two EXP–THEME action-chain paths, and they move in the direction of their profiled path.

There are other ways to think about mental experiences than by applying the action chain model, but the action chain is a strong proto-type model, and language users attempt to apply it, even when it is not quite appropriate. The result is that across languages, EXP/THEME verbs display mixed patterns: They sometimes treat the EXP like an AGT or action-chain head and sometimes like a PAT, or action-chain tail. Linguists have found (as with ASL) that these choices are made in princi-

---

[17] In the form shown here, LOOK does not actually move along its path; the path's direction is indicated by the palm and fingers' orientation toward the picture and away from the viewer (cf. footnote 2 this chapter). In forms inflected for repetitive and continuative aspect, this verb does in fact move repeatedly a short distance along its path in the direction indicated.

pled ways, based on the verbs' semantics (e.g., Croft 1991, Langacker 1991b, Sweetser 1980).

A MODEL OF VERB AGREEMENT PATHS

Our survey of the ASL verb agreement path data is now complete; Table 9.14 gives a summary of the verbs and their directions. Happily, we can represent all these complex data with a simple model, summarized in

TABLE 9.14. Agreement Verbs and Their Path Directions

GLOSS	PATHS		"WINNER"
DEFEAT	→	Action-chain	→ Action-chain
GIVE	→	Action-chain	→ Action-chain and literal
	→	Literal	
INFORM	→	Action-chain	→ Action-chain and
	→	Metaphorical	metaphorical
TAKE	→	Action-chain	← Literal
	←	Literal	
QUOTE	→	Action-chain	← Metaphorical
	←	Metaphorical	
BORROW	→	Action-chain	← Literal profiled
	←	Literal profiled	
	→	Literal backgrounded	
ASK	→	Action-chain	→ Action-chain and
	→	Metaphorical profiled	metaphorical profiled
	←	Metaphorical backgrounded	
INVITE	→	Action-chain	← Literal backgrounded
	→	Metaphorical profiled	
	←	Literal backgrounded	
PAY		Indeterminate action-chain	→ Literal profiled
	→	Literal profiled	
	←	Literal backgrounded	
DISCUSS		Indeterminate action-chain	↔ Both directions
	→	Metaphorical profiled	
	←	Metaphorical profiled	
LOOK	→	Action-chain profiled	→ Action-chain profiled
	←	Action-chain backgrounded	

Table 9.15. The model uses three criteria to rank paths. The first is *literalness*, or whether a path is literal or metaphorical; this distinguishes a literal path from both the metaphorical and the action-chain paths. The second is *specificity*, or whether a path is frame-specific or generic; this distinguishes metaphorical and literal paths from the action-chain path. Finally, the third is *profiling*, which distinguishes profiled paths from backgrounded paths.

This model selects the correct path direction for all the verbs in Table 9.14. For the one-path verb DEFEAT, there is no path conflict, so rule 1 selects the action-chain path. Our two-path verbs are also straightforward. GIVE, TAKE, INFORM, and QUOTE all select their frame-specific paths over the action-chain path, by rule 2.

BORROW and ASK are slightly more complex. Their two frame-specific paths are tied for specificity (rule 2) and literalness (rule 3), but rule 4 correctly selects the profiled path in both cases. Other sets of rules could have handled BORROW and ASK, but INVITE's path shows us that literalness must override specificity. For INVITE, the two frame-specific paths are tied at rule 2, but rule 3 correctly chooses the literal background path over the metaphorical profiled path.

For PAY, once again rules 2 and 3 produce a tie between the two literal frame-specific paths, and rule 4 correctly selects the profiled path. DISCUSS's two balanced metaphorical profiled paths are tied all the way down to rule 5, which correctly predicts that both path directions will be represented. And finally, LOOK's two action-chain paths are tied until rule 4 chooses the profiled path.

The set of rankings and rules in Table 9.15, as we can see, successfully predicts the choice of path direction in the ASL verbs we have discussed.

TABLE 9.15. Selection of Verb Agreement Path

Rankings
  Specificity: [literal, metaphorical] > action-chain
  Literalness: literal > [metaphorical, action-chain]
  Profiling: profiled > backgrounded

Rules (in order)
  1. Choose a path in the verb's semantic frame.
  2. If there is a tie, choose the most specific path.
  3. If there is a tie, choose the most literal path.
  4. If there is a tie, choose the most profiled path.
  5. If there is a tie, represent both paths.

But, we must note, this model does not *explain* the path direction; it simply provides an accurate description.

Like Langacker (1987), I believe that a good grammar of a language should not include rules; elements of the grammar should either be actual forms of the language or "schemas" that generalize over forms of the language. The model in Table 9.15 does not fit my standards of a good grammatical model. We can regard it, however, as a sort of short-hand for a full cognitive model that has not yet been worked out. The rule systems and hierarchies are useful in that they do accurately describe the facts of the language, but it is unlikely that they actually "exist" within an ASL user's grammar. I do not believe, for example, that language users go through a series of ordered rules to derive correct linguistic structures.

It is heartening to see, however, as we look at the model in Table 9.15, that the rankings and rules are well motivated on semantic grounds. They are not unreasonable or arbitrary, and they clearly will lend themselves well to a cognitive-grammar-style analysis. In general, the paths that are more cognitively basic and the paths that have more attention drawn to them are the paths that are selected.

Let us first discuss the rankings. The *literalness* ranking tells us that a literal path is to be chosen over a metaphorical path. Literal paths (i.e., movements of objects through space) are more conceptually basic than metaphorical paths; we can directly perceive literal paths with our senses, whereas metaphorical paths "exist" only when we map a literal, concrete path onto an abstract conceptual domain. Thus, for this dimension, ASL chooses a basic path over a conceptually "manufactured" path.

The *specificity* ranking tells us that a frame-specific path is to be chosen over the generic action-chain path. Although there are reasonable conceptual motivations in either direction, it is not surprising that the specific path is chosen. The specific paths (e.g., the path of the borrowed item for BORROW, the path of the quotation for QUOTE) are based on vivid details of the verbs' frames; portraying them gives a more direct representation of the verbs' meanings. Though the action-chain path also contains useful information about the verbs' semantic roles, it is unlikely (though possible) that a signed language would prefer this path; I find it hard to imagine, for example, a sign meaning *take* that would move from the taker to the previous owner.

Finally, the *profiling* ranking tells us that a profiled path is to be chosen over a backgrounded path. The profiled path is the one on which the verb focuses our attention; it is the most salient path in the verb's semantics. If this is the path to which our attention should be drawn, what better way than to have the verb trace it out for us?

All three of these rankings are highly motivated; the more basic, vivid, or focused paths are chosen over the alternatives. But what happens when the rankings are pitted against each other? Is a literal path "more basic" than a frame-specific path? Is profiling "more important" than literalness? We have seen that for ASL verbs like INVITE, when a literal backgrounded path meets a metaphorical profiled path, the literal backgrounded path "wins." That is, in ASL, literalness is a more powerful criterion than profiling. The other rankings do not collide with each other in our data set. We cannot pit literalness and specificity against each other, for example, because that would require a verb with a literal action-chain path, which is a contradiction in terms.

To pit specificity against profiling, we would need a verb with an asserted action-chain path and a literal or metaphorical backgrounded path that lead in opposite directions. A verb of that type might have a meaning like that of English *extort*, or "threaten so as to get money" (though *threatening* arguably involves a metaphorical communication path from AGT to PAT/EXP); other possibilities would be something like "defeat in order to get money" or "defeat in order to get praise." I have not found ASL verbs with these meanings. If such verbs exist, my model predicts that the frame-specific path would be selected over the asserted path, via either rule 2 or rule 3. Thus, verbs with meanings like "extort" or "defeat in order to get something" would move from PAT to the "extorter" or "defeater," which seems reasonable.

How motivated is it for literalness and specificity to be more powerful than profiling? This is an area in which languages could differ from each other. The individual rankings seem fairly universal, but it is possible to imagine a signed language in which profiling "wins" over literalness and the verb meaning "invite" moves from host to guest. This is not a problem for motivation-based linguistic theories; when two opposite choices have equal (and different) motivations, this is an area in which we predict cross-linguistic variation. (See Croft 1990 for a discussion of how linguistic theory can handle cross-linguistic variation in terms of competing motivations.)

VERB AGREEMENT IS PREDICTABLE

The data and discussion in this chapter have shown that verb agreement in ASL is thoroughly iconic in nature and that the movement patterns of individual verbs can be predicted from their semantics.

The distinctions between plain, spatial, and agreement verbs are semantic in nature: Spatial verbs refer to exact spatial locations and agreement verbs are concerned with entities' interactions (e.g., transfers) rather than exact locations. These two kinds of verbs impose mappings of mental spaces onto signing space. Plain verbs impose no such mappings onto signing space; their semantics involves no spatial concepts. Phonological factors such as body anchoring may cause verbs with spatial semantics to manifest as plain verbs.

Both spatial and agreement verbs trace out paths in their semantic frames from SOURCE to GOAL arguments; differences in the nature of those paths can be explained by differences in the spatial mappings they impose. A single lexical verb can impose different kinds of mappings; indeed, rather than being two sharply distinct types, there is evidence that spatial and agreement verbs' uses of space form a continuum of mapping types from richly detailed to highly schematic.

Our model of ASL verb agreement shows why verbs like TAKE, QUOTE, and INVITE have been regarded as backward: the prototypical model of causation, the *action chain,* would predict that they should move *away* from their AGT argument, but instead, they move *toward* that argument. But of course, this movement direction is not backward or odd at all; it is a result of a highly motivated system of principles that selects one path from a verb's semantic frame.

It should also now be clear that iconicity and metaphor are not limited to the lexicons of languages nor are they in any way superficial or easily dismissed. Agreement verbs, with their complex and conflicting literal and metaphorical paths, show that metaphor and iconicity are deeply intertwined in the core grammar of ASL.

CHAPTER TEN

Complex Superposition of Metaphors in an American Sign Language Poem[1]

METAPHOR AND POETRY

Poetic language draws on the same linguistic resources that we use in everyday language. Undoubtedly, most users of language strive for beauty in their linguistic output, and there are ample possibilities for such devices as wordplay, echoing/repetition, symmetrical structure, and joint creation of metaphor in normal conversation (cf. Ferrara 1994, Silverstein 1984). But the poet specifically focuses effort on fitting together linguistic structures to make a pleasing, coherent, and compelling whole. As we shall see, the linkage of metaphor and iconicity in signed languages provides the poet with rich resources for linguistic art.

A skilled poet can combine a number of usually distinct metaphors to form a coherent whole. In particular, the poet can create a scenario that contains the source domains of several metaphors – via the mappings, this scenario's concrete events evoke the corresponding abstract events. Using the terminology of Fauconnier and Turner (1996), we can describe the scenario as a *blend* of the metaphors.

In our chosen text, "The Treasure," poet Ella Mae Lentz crafts a story that, on one level, describes a person digging down to discover buried treasure, and the reactions to her discovery – but on another level, describes the person's linguistic analysis of ASL, and the reactions to *that* discovery.[2] The poem weaves together many different conventional

---

[1] This chapter appeared in an earlier form as Taub (2001). I thank Linda Coleman, Joseph Grady, George Lakoff, Scott Liddell, Eve Sweetser, Mark Turner, and an anonymous reviewer for their comments on this research project; special thanks are due to Ella Mae Lentz for permission to work with her poetry.

[2] The poem was published in *The Treasure: Poems by Ella Mae Lentz*. VHS videotape. Berkeley, CA: In Motion Press.

metaphors into a compelling appeal to viewers to cherish and respect ASL.

There is not space here for a complete analysis of all the poetic devices that Lentz employs; nor can a true sense of the poem be conveyed through glosses or through English paraphrases. This chapter limits itself to a summary of the poem's scenario, a catalogue of the major conceptual metaphors used at each stage of the scenario (with additional evidence from ASL lexical items for each metaphor, where possible), and an analysis of how Lentz blends the metaphors together into a coherent whole that forcefully conveys the message that ASL is precious, endangered, and in need of rescue. Appendix Two gives an English translation of the poem.

Lentz's poem metaphorically defines ASL as a valuable treasure that has been buried underground. She frames linguistic analysis of ASL as uncovering the treasure, and the common disregard for ASL as reburying the treasure. Table 10.1 shows the basic structure of the poem: It opens with signing described as "under a layer of earth" (stage 1) and follows Lentz in her efforts to analyze ASL, metaphorically portrayed as digging into the ground (stage 2). At the poem's central scene, Lentz

---

TABLE 10.1. Stages of "The Treasure"

1. Introduction: signing is "underground"
2. Poet begins her analysis
   Digging
   First discovery
   Digging
   Second discovery
   Digging
   Third discovery
   Extended digging
3. Gleaming treasure uncovered
   Poet is inspired
4. Poet attempts to communicate with those on the surface
   First conversation
   Dirt shoveled onto poet and treasure
   Second conversation
   Dirt shoveled onto poet and treasure
   Third conversation
   Dirt shoveled onto poet and treasure
5. Treasure completely reburied
6. Coda: Treasure is still alive
   Poet offers treasure to viewer

makes a major discovery, shown as a box of glowing treasure (stage 3). Lentz attempts to communicate her discovery and excitement to others but is rebuffed (stage 4) – they show their disdain by shoveling dirt down onto her. Eventually, the treasure is reburied (stage 5). At the end of the poem, Lentz makes one final appeal, this time to the viewer (stage 6).

As we shall see, much of the power of this poem comes from Lentz's evocation of two familiar cultural frames: The frame of *archeology*, in which researchers carefully unearth valuable artifacts, structures stage 2 of the poem, whereas the frame of *burial*, in which dead bodies are covered with earth, structures stage 4. Because these frames share many particulars – for example, dirt, shovels, underground objects – they are easily combined into a blended scenario. The combination adds much to each half of the poem: ASL is seen both as a treasure and as a living thing, reburied while still alive; Lentz, in digging up the treasure, is both scientist and rescuer; the rejecters of ASL are both willfully ignorant and murderers, in that they rebury the living treasure.

The analysis of the poem is based on three types of data: non-metaphorical signs, which simply belong to the overall target domain of ASL and linguistics; lexicalized metaphorical signs, which iconically present some source domain yet have become conventionalized as part of the lexicon of the target domain; and free metaphorical signs, which give a novel, classifier-based representation of the source domain that is interpretable in context as referring to the target domain. For example, in the second stage of the poem, Lentz uses the nonmetaphorical signs DEAF and SIGN; the lexicalized metaphorical sign ANALYZE (see Fig. 8.12); and many metaphorical classifiers, including a representation of a shovel blade scraping away dirt (see Fig. 10.1).

In the following sections, we will go through the poem step-by-step. We will see how Lentz constructs her two major metaphorical framings from the conventional resources of ASL, using both lexicalized metaphorical signs and metaphorical applications of classifier signs. Though her two framings (LINGUISTIC ANALYSIS IS ARCHEOLOGY and OPPRESSION IS BURIAL) are not conventional metaphors in general use in ASL, they are built up from ASL's conventional metaphors.

STAGES OF "THE TREASURE"

Let us now consider the stages of the poem. For each stage, I summarize the major events and list the relevant metaphors. I also include glosses of pertinent passages (see Appendix One for glossing conventions and Appendix Two for a full, idiomatic translation). Extended evidence for

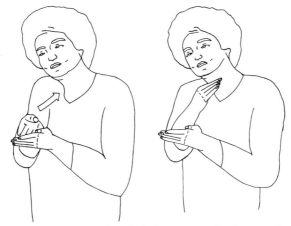

Figure 10.1. CL:BB_R "shovel blade removes dirt from surface"

each metaphor follow in the next section of the chapter; in this section I will simply give the metaphor a TARGET IS SOURCE name.[3]

1. Introduction: Signing Is "Underground"

At the start of the poem, Lentz describes Deaf people's signing as "underground," trivialized, and devalued. She uses classifiers to show signing as an object covered by a layer of earth, as we see in excerpt 1. (Throughout this chapter, *rh* means "right hand," *both* means "both hands," and *lh* means "left hand." See Appendix One for a full description of glossing conventions.)

(1)
rh:
both: CL:Flat-OO "hold flat object in front of self"
lh:

rh:
both: DIRT CL:55 "flat surface" DEMOTE TRIVIAL.
lh:

"It (i.e., *signing*) has been covered with dirt, devalued, trivialized."

---

3 Note that the name is meant simply to be a useful label; the metaphor actually consists of the cross-domain mapping. The name is probably about as accurate and helpful as the average English gloss for an ASL sign.

In this section, nonmetaphorical items such as SIGN, TELL-STORY, and EXPERIENCE allow us to deduce the actual topic, or overall target domain, of the story: Deaf people's signing. The metaphorical items treat signs as objects that can be passed from person to person or hidden underground. We have evidence in this passage for the conventional metaphors SIGNS ARE OBJECTS, POWERFUL IS UP, and KNOWING IS SEEING. Lentz has laid the metaphorical groundwork for her two framings: KNOWING IS SEEING will combine with other metaphors to form the *archeology* framing, whereas POWERFUL IS UP will form the basis of the *burial* framing.

2. Poet Begins Her Analysis

In stage 2, after "looking over" the situation, Lentz undertakes her analysis of ASL. She describes herself both as "analyzing" and as digging into the earth, using both classifiers and lexical signs, as we see in excerpt 2.

(2)
rh: PRO-I LOOK-AT$_R$ LOOK-AT$_L$
both: ANALYZE$_L$ ANALYZE$_R$
lh:

rh:
both: CL:BB$_R$ "shovel blade removes dirt from surface"
lh:

rh:
both: CL:BB$_L$ "shovel blade removes dirt from surface"
lh:

"I look at this, look at that; I analyze this, analyze that; my shovel digs there, digs here."

Figure 8.12 gives the sign ANALYZE, a metaphorical lexical item; the classifier form CL:BB$_R$ "shovel blade removes dirt from surface" is given in Figure 10.1.

This section of the poem consists of digging interspersed with three discoveries of signs. Almost immediately on beginning the digging, Lentz makes a discovery. She "uncovers" two signs, holds them side-by-side, and notices that though they look alike, they have different movements and different meanings. Excerpt 3 shows this event.

(3)
rh:
both: CL:Flat-OO "hold two objects side-by-side"
lh:

rh: FACE + $_R$SAME-AS$_L$ POSS-PRO-$_{3R}$
both:
lh: CL:Flat-O "continue holding object"   POSS-PRO-$_{3L}$

rh:
both: MOVEMENT DIFFERENT DIFFERENT MEAN
lh:

"I hold them next to each other. They look alike, but their movements are different, and they have different meanings."

Lentz's next discovery is a sign with an English word "pasted" to its surface. She peels away the label and can now see the sign's true meaning for Deaf people, as we see in excerpt 4.

(4)
rh:
both: SIGN ENGLISH WORD CL:HB "strip across front of surface"
lh:

rh: CL:F "pull strip off surface and drop it"
both:
lh: CL:B "surface" ————————————

rh: $_1$LOOK-AT$_{surface, then downward}$
both: MEAN DEEP
lh: CL:B "surface" ————————————

                      (gaze to CL:B)
rh: BELONGING-TO$_{far R}$ DEAF   WOW
both:
lh: CL:B "surface" ————————————

"[It's] a sign with an English word pasted across the front. I pull the word off and drop it. I look into the sign. Its meaning is profound and belongs to the Deaf world. How impressive!"

Finally, Lentz uncovers and picks up two more signs with English words labeling them. She pulls off the labels and holds the signs side-by-side. Then she decides that they are in the wrong order and reverses them. She also notices that they have facial expressions associated with them – eyebrows rising and falling above the signs. These manipulations are described in excerpt 5.

(5)
rh: CL:B "flat surface moves to L ctr" ——— BETTER
both: (wrists cross)
lh: CL:B "flat surface moves to R ctr" ————

rh:
both: EXPRESSION CL:XX$_R$ "brows wiggle over right surface"
lh:

rh: FINE$_{wg}$
both: CL:XX$_L$ "brows wiggle over left surface"
lh:

"I reverse [the signs'] order – that's better. Facial expressions dance over the first sign and the second sign – how lovely!"

In stage 2, Lentz develops her *archeologist* framing of ASL research. There is evidence in this passage for the metaphors ANALYSIS IS DIGGING, SIGNS ARE OBJECTS, KNOWING IS SEEING, and UNDERSTANDING IS MANIPULATING. As we shall see, these metaphors combine into a compound metaphor we could call LINGUISTIC ANALYSIS IS ARCHEOLOGY.

3. Gleaming Treasure Uncovered

Lentz continues to dig and now hits a large object: a box, whose contents glitter and glow up at her. Lentz is inspired, as we see in excerpt 6.

(6)
rh:
both: BOX CL:BB "lid opens"
lh:

rh: CL:Open-8$_{CTR}$ "shiny"   CL:Flat-O/5$_R$ "glow" ———
both:
lh: CL:Open-8$_{CTR}$ "shiny"   CL:Flat-O/5$_L$ ——— "glow"

rh:
both: INSPIRE EXCITED
lh:

"I open the lid of the box. The contents glitter and glow. I am inspired and excited."

This passage forms the center of the poem and marks the transition from the *archeology* framing to the *burial* framing. The archeology framing is "capped" with the addition of the metaphor VALUE IS MONETARY VALUE: Lentz as archeologist has not merely made an important discovery but has found a valuable treasure. Lentz is inspired and "uplifted" by her discovery; the addition of the HAPPY IS UP metaphor shows that the vertical dimension is now taking different metaphorical significance.

4. Poet Attempts to Communicate with Those on the Surface

Lentz now tries, from down in her trench, to get the attention of people up on the surface, as described in excerpt 7.

(7)

```
        gaze up/right ————————————————————
rh:                     "wave for attention"UP/R
both:
lh:

        gaze up/left ————————————————
rh:                             UP/RLOOK-ATDOWN/CTR.imper.trill+
both:
lh:     "wave for attention"UP/L    UP/LLOOK-ATDOWN/CTR.imper.trill+
```

"I look up and wave to both sides. 'Look down here, everyone!'"

She engages three different people in conversation but is unsuccessful in persuading them of the value of ASL. (From Lentz's introduction to the poem, we can gather that all three are deaf.) Notably, none of the three mention or even notice the treasure, although Lentz frequently points to it. At the end of each conversation, the interlocutor shovels dirt down onto Lentz, and the dirt smears down her face and body. Excerpt 8 is from the first conversation.

(8)
```
rh:
both: CL:SS "shovel dirt from R to down/L"
lh:

rh: CL:O/5 "dirt falls from R to down/L"
both:
lh:

rh:                 CL:O/5 "dirt falls from up/R across face
                    and chest"
both: RS (narrator):<                                          >
lh:
```

"S/he shovels dirt down into the trench. The dirt falls down. It falls onto my face and body."

Figures 10.2 and 10.3 illustrate some of the classifiers and referential shifts from this excerpt. In Figure 10.2, Lentz has taken on the first interlocutor's persona, as we can see from her nasty facial expression; her right hand performs the classifier form CL:O/5 "dirt falls from R to down/L" while her left hand retains the S-fist shape used in the previous classifier form. Immediately thereafter, as shown in Figure 10.3, Lentz returns to her "narrator" persona, gazing upward with a dismayed look; her right hand again traces the dirt's path, this time from the narrator's perspective, with the form CL:O/5 "dirt falls from up/R across face and chest."

The first person to look down expresses a belief that analyzing ASL is for hearing people and that Deaf people already know how to sign, so further analysis is not needed. Lentz contradicts this opinion, but the person has no time to listen to her.

The second person states that ASL is only for fun and that it lacks many grammatical structures when compared to English, which is an advanced, exact language suited for serious endeavors. Lentz responds that ASL is of equal status to English, possessing many structures that English lacks. This person accuses her of lying.

The last person uses Signing Exact English (SEE) to communicate instead of ASL. She tells Lentz to accept the "fact" that signed English is easier for hearing parents of deaf children. Lentz counters that if the par-

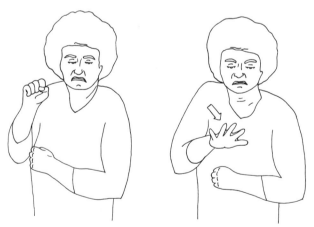

Figure 10.2. CL:O/5 "dirt falls from R to down/L"

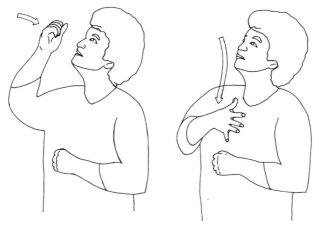

Figure 10.3. CL:O/5 "dirt falls from up/R across face and chest"

ents saw the treasure, they'd be eager to learn ASL. The SEE signer responds that having a Ph.D. makes her the authority on this issue.

This section develops an entirely different framing of the situation. Here, the metaphors POWERFUL IS UP, COMMUNICATING IS SENDING, and BAD IS DIRTY combine to create the metaphor EXPRESSING DISRESPECT TO SOMEONE LESS POWERFUL IS BURYING HIM/HER. Lentz herself still holds to the *archeology* framing, continually pointing to the treasure she sees in front of her, as we see in excerpt 9, from the third conversation.

(9)
rh: SUPPOSE++ MOTHER+FATHER
both: RS (narrator):< "no, no"
lh:

rh: SEE$_{down/ctr}$ RESPECT-PRO-3$_{down/ctr}$
both:
lh:

rh: WILL   #ASL WILL
both: EXCITE EAGER LEARN++   "what" >
lh:

"I reply, 'No, no – if parents see what's down here, they'll get excited and eager, and learn ASL.'"

But in refusing to see the treasure, the three people refuse to give any support to this framing or any value to ASL and Lentz's work.

5. Treasure Completely Reburied

Dirt continues to fall on Lentz and the treasure (presumably from the shovels of many other disdainful people), until the box is completely reburied. She frames this second burial as an act of oppression. Excerpt 10 shows how she does this: Her classifiers for dirt rising to cover the box merge into the metaphorical lexical item OPPRESS, with its fist-shaped nondominant hand and its downward-pressing 5-shaped dominant hand.

(10)
rh: CL:5 "level rises to top of container and over top"
both:
lh: CL:C "container" —————— CL:S "container"

rh:
both: OPPRESS
lh:

"Dirt rises, covers the box, and pushes it down – oppression."

Figures 10.4 through 10.6 illustrate this passage as well. Figure 10.4 shows the right-hand 5-CL (indicating the level of the dirt) rising past the left-hand C-CL (indicating the container).

In Figure 10.5, the 5-CL circles the top of the left hand, indicating that the dirt has covered the box, as the left hand begins to close into a fist. Finally, Figure 10.6 shows the lexical sign OPPRESS, where the right 5-

Figure 10.4. CL:5C "dirt rises to top of container"

Figure 10.5. CL:5C "dirt covers top of container"

hand pushes down forcefully on the left fist; this sign can also be read as a continuation of the classifier construction, with the meaning "dirt pushes down on the box."

Stage 5 continues to develop the *burial* framing, with the addition of the metaphor OPPRESSION IS DOWNWARD PRESSURE. The entire framing might now be called OPPRESSION IS BURIAL. Meanwhile, a consequence of the reburial for the *archeology* framing is that the treasure is now hidden again – no longer accessible, no longer available for study, no longer usable to enrich the lives of Deaf people.

Figure 10.6. OPPRESS or CL:5S "dirt pushes down on container"

6. Coda: Treasure is Still-Alive

Though the treasure is buried, Lentz tells us that those glowing lights are still alive. She offers the box to the viewers, urging us to consider what should be done. Excerpt 11 gives the final lines of the poem.

(11)

	gaze to camera, nod
rh:	
both:	STILL LIVE STILL LIVE
lh:	

rh:	THINK + SELF$_{camera}$
both:	CL:55 "hold box out toward camera"
lh:	CL:5 "hold box"

"[It's] still alive – still alive. Here it is – you decide what to do."

This last stage is a coda, a final comment on what the viewers have seen. The assertion that the treasure is "still alive" brings in the metaphor EXIS-TENCE IS LIFE, and it forces us to see the buriers as murderers because we know that a living creature cannot survive buried underground.

At the end, Lentz's offering of the box to the viewers brings in the metaphor CONTROL IS PHYSICAL CONTROL. This final act serves as a comment on all that has gone before. Lentz uses the box to bring in the framing of ASL as a treasure one last time, but she abandons the careful, consistent source–domain structure that she has built up throughout the poem: We are no longer down in the trench and ASL is no longer buried – we are now exhorted to think on what she has told us and to act appropriately.

METAPHORICAL COMPOSITES IN "THE TREASURE"

In this section, we will look at the two major metaphorical framings: LIN-GUISTIC ANALYSIS IS ARCHEOLOGY and OPPRESSION IS BURIAL. Each of these framings is made up of several less-complex metaphors; we will go through each of the component metaphors and review the evidence for it both in the poem and in the lexicon of ASL. Then we will see how the metaphors fit together to create the composite framings.

We will also see how the central episode of the poem causes a slight shift in the first metaphorical framing and how the addition of EXISTENCE IS LIFE in the coda sharpens the second framing. We do not have space to address all the metaphors in the poem – only the ones that participate in the major framings.

The First Framing: LINGUISTIC ANALYSIS IS ARCHEOLOGY

The first major framing in the poem, LINGUISTIC ANALYSIS IS ARCHEOLOGY, is made up of the components ANALYSIS IS DIGGING, SIGNS ARE OBJECTS, KNOWING IS SEEING, and UNDERSTANDING IS MANIPULATING. Let us go through each in turn.

ANALYSIS IS DIGGING As we saw in Chapter Eight, in ANALYSIS IS DIGGING the domain of digging down below a surface is mapped onto the domain of finding out more and more about a topic. Table 10.2 reviews the exact mapping from source to target domain.

Lentz uses this metaphor again and again; if one metaphor could be chosen as the basis of her poem, this is the one. She explicitly introduces it with the lexical item ANALYZE, in stage 2; the form of ANALYZE, with two bent-V handshapes, resembles the act of scraping away a surface to reveal what lies beneath. She immediately follows up this lexicalized image with several classifier representations of digging: B-handshapes show the blade of the shovel pushing away dirt, and S-handshapes show her wielding the shovel.

The interesting thing about this metaphor is that conventionally, only the downward direction is mapped. There is no conventional sign showing upward movement or reburial of objects that has a meaning like "ignore" or "cover up facts." The poem, of course, uses the upward direction as well; this is Lentz's poetic elaboration.

SIGNS ARE OBJECTS The next important metaphor, and the first one to appear in the poem, might be called SIGNS ARE OBJECTS. Here signs are described as if they were physical objects that can be examined,

---

TABLE 10.2. ANALYSIS IS DIGGING

SOURCE	TARGET
Surface	Simplest, most superficial information
Area below surface	Information that requires effort to figure out
Digging or descending below surface	Figuring out a more complete account
Scale of depth below surface	Scale of degree of completeness
Closer to surface (= higher)	Less information known
Deeper below surface (= lower)	More information known

TABLE 10.3. SIGNS ARE OBJECTS

SOURCE	TARGET
Physical objects	Signs
Manipulating and examining objects	Analyzing signs
Passing signs to others .	Teaching signs

manipulated, passed to others, and stored in a box. This mapping is probably a special case of a more general metaphor where any abstract entity can be described as if it were a physical object.[4]

The mapping for SIGNS ARE OBJECTS is given in Table 10.3. This metaphor occurs throughout the poem, but particularly in stages 1 through 3. Lentz first brings it in via the lexical signs GIVE-TO$_{each.other}$ "we have given signing to each other" and PASS-DOWN-THROUGH-GENERATIONS "we have passed down signing for many years"; both signs have the flat-O handshape, which is a classifier for handling flat objects, and both refer to signs in this case.

Lentz also freely and repeatedly uses flat-O and B classifiers to describe how she "picked up" signs from her excavation trench, held them up for examination, and later set them aside. The use of these classifiers shows that Lentz is envisioning signs as flat objects.

Finally, though Lentz never explicitly says so, the treasure box is understood to be full of signs that glitter and glow.

KNOWING IS SEEING The third major metaphor in the *archeology* framing can be called KNOWING IS SEEING (cf. Lakoff & Johnson 1980 for English examples); in this metaphor, the domain of receiving visual information is mapped onto the domain of understanding information in general. This metaphor is conventional in ASL; evidence for the mapping can be found in signs such as PERSPECTIVE, in which an understanding of a situation is shown as a way of "looking at" a referent; BLURRY, in which difficulty in understanding is shown as visual blur; and CLEAR/OBVIOUS, in which ease in understanding is shown as visual clarity. Table 10.4 gives the mapping.

An important corollary of this mapping might be given the name UNKNOWN IS HIDDEN: That is, facts that are not accessible to our intelli-

---

4 Neither of these metaphors has been documented in ASL outside this poem, and this chapter makes no claim as to whether they are conventional.

TABLE 10.4. KNOWING IS SEEING

SOURCE	TARGET
Visible objects	Facts or ideas
Looking at something	Directing attention at some fact or idea
Receiving visual information	Understanding
Difficulties in receiving visual information	Difficulties in understanding

gences are described as if they were hidden from view. This corollary is especially important for "The Treasure."

Lentz uses this mapping throughout her poem. At the beginning and at the end, ASL is described as covered up by a thick layer of dirt; this entails that the truth about ASL is unknown, inaccessible to most people's understanding. As Lentz uncovers signs, she makes them visually accessible – and, in fact, she examines them with her eyes (as shown by lexical items such as LOOK-AT and classifier representations of looking). Part of her analysis involves removing English "coverings" from the signs and looking at what is revealed; via this mapping, the English labels serve as barriers to true understanding of ASL signs. When she discovers the treasure, the signs are described as glittering and glowing – visually beautiful, and by the metaphor, intellectually pleasing.

In the second half of the poem, Lentz continually tries to get others to look at the signs, but they refuse; metaphorically speaking, they refuse to consider the facts. When they throw dirt down on Lentz and the treasure, reburying it, they are making it impossible for themselves and others to learn about ASL's structure, because the facts are no longer accessible.

UNDERSTANDING IS MANIPULATING The final metaphor in the *archeology* complex, UNDERSTANDING IS MANIPULATING, also focuses on the target domain of knowledge and understanding; here the domain of physical handling and arranging of objects is mapped onto the domain of receiving and organizing information about a topic.[5] Wilcox (1993) presented many examples in which ASL classifiers for showing how objects are handled were used to describe collection, selection, and organization of ideas. The cross-domain mapping is given in Table 10.5.

---

[5] There is no significance to the two different names for the target domain.

TABLE 10.5. UNDERSTANDING IS MANIPULATING

SOURCE	TARGET
Tangible objects	Ideas or facts
Manipulating objects	Analyzing information
Arranging objects	Organizing information
Gathering objects	Collecting information

Lentz makes repeated use of this mapping in stage 2 of the poem: As we see from her use of flat-O, B, and F classifiers, she picks up signs, turns them over in her hands, pulls off labels from them, and arranges them in what she feels is the proper order. Metaphorically, she is collecting, analyzing, and arranging data to yield a satisfying analysis of ASL's linguistic structure.

THE COMPOSITE The four metaphors described here are separate conceptual mappings: There is clear independent evidence for each of them (except perhaps SIGNS ARE OBJECTS) in ASL's lexical items and metaphorical classifiers. Yet the four fit together naturally into a single framing or scenario.

Quite often in our lives, there is an object we wish to understand. We pick it up, turn it over, and receive at the same time both visual and kinesthetic information about it. Experiences such as this one bring together a number of conceptual domains in what Grady and Johnson (in press) call a *primary scene*. This particular scene involves tight correlations among the domains of visual perception, object manipulation, and information gathering. The correlation between visual perception and information gathering provides the experiential basis for the metaphor KNOWING IS SEEING; a similar correlation provides the basis for UNDERSTANDING IS MANIPULATING and for a general metaphor that might be called CONCEPTS ARE PHYSICAL OBJECTS.

In this poem, Lentz tells us clearly in stage 1 that the metaphorical objects under consideration are ASL signs; once that has been established, it is perfectly natural to reconstruct the rest of the primary scene and to show investigation of the signs as handling, arranging, and visually examining the objects.

The poem adds one more metaphor that fills in more details of the scenario. The combination of SIGNS ARE OBJECTS, KNOWING IS SEEING, and UNDERSTANDING IS MANIPULATING gives information about how the objects are treated but not about where they came from. The additional metaphor, ANALYSIS IS DIGGING, provides those details along with a specific setting for the scenario.

In ANALYSIS IS DIGGING as conventionalized in the lexicon of ASL, found objects are not mapped. That is, the lexical items that draw on this metaphor, SURFACE, DEEP, and ANALYZE, do not depict found objects in any way; they simply draw attention to the depth of the excavation, or to the digging process. Yet we know that in the domain of digging, one usually is digging to find something. There is an obvious "slot" in the source domain for extension and elaboration: the found objects.

The four metaphors thus fit neatly together to form a coherent scenario, outlined in Table 10.6. Each stage of the scenario is listed, along with the metaphors that apply to it. As we can see, this scenario matches the basic modus operandi for the science of archeology. Because the sign ANALYZE, used repeatedly by Lentz, suggests a scientific endeavor of some sort, the scenario evokes archeology as an overall source domain. Taken together, then, the four metaphors create a composite that can be given the name LINGUISTIC ANALYSIS IS ARCHEOLOGY.

TABLE 10.6. Scenario for Archeology Framing

SOURCE SCENARIO	TARGET SCENARIO
There is a interesting, undisturbed site.	There is an interesting topic about which little is known (in this case, ASL signs).
(ANALYSIS IS DIGGING, KNOWING IS SEEING)	
Person digs down into earth.	Person starts to investigate topic.
(ANALYSIS IS DIGGING)	
Person finds objects.	Person discovers interesting data about signs.
(ANALYSIS IS DIGGING, SIGNS ARE OBJECTS)	
Person picks up objects, manipulates, and arranges them.	Person collects, organizes, and gets information about signs.
(UNDERSTANDING IS MANIPULATING, SIGNS ARE OBJECTS)	
Person looks carefully at objects.	Person thinks carefully about signs.
(KNOWING IS SEEING, SIGNS ARE OBJECTS)	
Result: person knows much more about objects and site.	Result: person knows much more about signs and ASL.
(Composite of all four metaphors)	

There is a major consequence to this evocation of archeology. Linguistics is not a particularly well known field; moreover, many nonlinguists believe that they know as much about language as any expert could. Archeology, on the other hand, has piqued the popular imagination; its methods are easily understandable to anyone who has ever imagined digging up strange and ancient artifacts. By linking linguistic analysis to archeology, and by using the stages of archeological research to explain the stages of linguistic research, Lentz strengthens the framing of linguistics as a science – indeed, as an adventurous, exciting field of research.

Through this composite metaphor, then, Lentz informs the viewers that she as a linguist is an expert and that her analysis of ASL is valuable scientific research. When Lentz's interlocutors rebury the treasure in stage 5, this metaphor frames them as "know-nothing" ignorers of science; the effect of their actions is to make the facts about ASL once more unknown and inaccessible.

The Central Episode: Discovering the Treasure

VALUE IS MONETARY VALUE   Stage 3 of the poem adds one more detail to the already-completed *archeology* framing: Lentz "strikes it rich" by discovering a box full of treasure. This event does a number of things: It adds the metaphor VALUE IS MONETARY VALUE to the composite, it subtly shifts the framing from a scientific excavation to a treasure hunt, and it metaphorically defines ASL as a treasure of great worth.

In this metaphor, the domain of money and financial riches is mapped onto the domain of worth in general.[6] The mapping is given in Table 10.7. Lentz uses this metaphor in two ways. First, during stage 4 Lentz uses the lexical item RICH to refer to ASL and its grammatical structure. Second, and more significantly, she describes ASL as a box full of glitter-

TABLE 10.7. VALUE IS MONETARY VALUE

SOURCE	TARGET
Financial worth	Worth
Worth a large amount of money	Extremely valuable
Worth a small amount of money	Not valuable

---

[6] This metaphor is widespread in English (cf. Lakoff, Espenson, & Schwartz 1991) but has not been previously documented in ASL; this chapter makes no claim as to whether it is part of ASL's conventional resources.

ing, gleaming objects, using open-8 ("shining") and 5/O ("light-emitting") classifiers. In the poem, she never explicitly states what is in the box, but the context of the excavation, the buried box, the reflected light, and Lentz's ensuing excitement, along with the poem's English title ("The Treasure") all lead us to conclude that the box must be full of precious objects such as jewels, gold, and silver.

The addition of this metaphor to the scenario in Table 10.6 creates a shift of emphasis in the framing. Up to this point, Lentz's analysis of ASL has been described in a way consistent with a scientific venture: She has been examining objects to figure out their nature. Now, however, she has found gold and jewels, a discovery that strongly evokes a frame of adventure and exploration. The two frames are not mutually exclusive, of course: The best scientific endeavors have an element of the treasure hunt in them, and major scientific discoveries are at least as rewarding as gold and jewels. (This very point is emphasized in the poem by the overlapping of the two frames.) At the end of the poem, when Lentz's interlocutors rebury the treasure, they are understood as squandering vast riches as well as ignoring scientific facts.

The Second Framing: OPPRESSION IS BURIAL

The second framing in the poem, OPPRESSION IS BURIAL, is developed in stages 4 and 5. Throughout these stages, it is a composite of the metaphors POWERFUL IS UP, OPPRESSION IS DOWNWARD PRESSURE, COMMUNICATING IS SENDING, and BAD IS DIRTY. At stage 6, Lentz adds the metaphor EXISTENCE IS LIFE, which gives additional power and urgency to the *burial* framing. Let us first consider the metaphors in the earlier composite.

POWERFUL IS UP Chapter Eight established the existence in ASL of POWERFUL IS UP, which maps the vertical scale onto the domain of social standing and power. Table 10.8 restates the mapping. Lentz invokes this

TABLE 10.8. POWERFUL IS UP	
SOURCE	TARGET
Up–down dimension	Scale of relative power/importance
Higher locations	More important ranks
Lower locations	Less important ranks
Movement upward	Increasing power
Movement downward	Decreasing power

metaphor at the beginning of the poem, describing ASL with the signs DEMOTE and TRIVIAL; moreover, Deaf people's signing is beneath the ground (as described with the sign EARTH and spread-5 "surface" classifiers). Through the rest of the first half, as she develops her *archeology* framing, the POWERFUL IS UP mapping is in the background but at some level still accessible. Though Lentz at this stage is framing her actions as scientific research, we can also use POWERFUL IS UP to see her as a "rescuer of the downtrodden," a visitor from the world of power who decides to visit the world of the powerless.

As soon as Lentz tries to communicate her discovery to the people on the surface, this metaphor comes back into the foreground. Her interlocutors are high up, and she is underground with the treasure. The interlocutors clearly have the power to ignore and suppress her findings; she and the treasure are framed as powerless. She tries in vain, using signs such as ADVANCE and EQUAL (which themselves incorporate the POWERFUL IS UP mapping), to persuade them that the treasure has value, but to no avail. By reburying her and the treasure, they ensure that ASL will continue to be stuck at a "low" status.

OPPRESSION IS DOWNWARD PRESSURE The next metaphor in this group, OPPRESSION IS DOWNWARD PRESSURE, is also well established for English but not documented in ASL. This mapping could be considered an elaboration of POWERFUL IS UP, in which pressure exerted downward by those above is mapped onto oppressive actions by those more powerful. There are at least two signs that give evidence for this elaboration in the lexicon of ASL: the sign OPPRESS, in which the dominant B-hand presses down on the nondominant S-hand, and the sign FORCE, which has a downward movement of the dominant C-hand.

Table 10.9 gives a mapping for OPPRESSION IS DOWNWARD PRESSURE. Lentz uses this metaphor in stage 5 of the poem: With a 5-CL for the dirt's level and a C-CL for the box, she shows how the dirt thrown down on the treasure accumulates until it reburies the treasure. As her domi-

TABLE 10.9. OPPRESSION IS DOWNWARD PRESSURE

SOURCE	TARGET
Up–down dimension	Scale of relative power
Higher locations	More powerful status
Lower locations	Less powerful status
Downward pressure	Oppressive action

nant hand shows the dirt rising to cover the treasure, her classifiers merge into the lexical sign OPPRESS. In this way, she indicates that the weight of the dirt pressing down on the treasure should be understood as oppression directed toward ASL.

COMMUNICATING IS SENDING and BAD IS DIRTY The last two metaphors in this composite function together in the poem, so I will treat them together.

The metaphor COMMUNICATING IS SENDING was extensively discussed in Chapter Six; Table 10.10 restates the mapping. Lentz uses a novel elaboration of this metaphor, analyzed here as a compound with a mapping called BAD IS DIRTY: in communicating with Lentz, her interlocutors throw dirt at her.

The metaphor BAD IS DIRTY, though well documented in Western cultures (cf. expressions such as *unclean, pure,* and *filthy* to refer to moral states), has not yet been established as conventional in ASL. There is some evidence supporting its existence: The sign DIRTY can be used to mean "bad" or "immoral", and the sign CLEAN is most likely related to the sign NICE. Whether or not the metaphor is conventional in ASL, Lentz would likely have access to it through the American culture in which she lives.

BAD IS DIRTY maps the scale of cleanliness onto a scale of moral goodness. Table 10.11 gives a mapping. If we combine this mapping with COMMUNICATING IS SENDING, we get the entailments that good messages are clean objects, whereas bad messages are dirty objects. The interlocutors' action of shoveling dirt is shown through S-shaped "handling" classifiers, and the dirt itself is shown with an O that opens to a 5. In throwing this dirt, then, they are sending Lentz the worst possible message. We might give this combination of metaphors the name EXPRESSING DISRESPECT IS THROWING DIRT.

TABLE 10.10. COMMUNICATING IS SENDING

SOURCE	TARGET
Objects	Ideas
Sending object	Articulating idea in language
Catching object (and putting it in head)	Understanding idea
Sender	Communicator
Receiver	Addressee
Difficulties in sending or catching	Difficulties in communication

TABLE 10.11. BAD IS DIRTY	
SOURCE	TARGET
Clean	Good
Dirty	Bad
Clean objects	Good things
Dirty objects	Bad things

THE FIRST COMPOSITE We have already seen how COMMUNICATING IS SENDING and BAD IS DIRTY combine to form EXPRESSING DISRESPECT IS THROWING DIRT. The addition of the vertical dimension, with the metaphors POWERFUL IS UP and OPPRESSION IS DOWNWARD PRESSURE, leads us to a composite scenario in which disdainful, dismissive actions by people in power are understood as acts of burying.

In the first framing, three of the four component metaphors fit together into a scene that every human experiences starting from early childhood (i.e., picking up objects and examining them). This is not the case for the second framing. Instead, the component metaphors combine to create a scenario that happens rarely if ever in our experience.

COMMUNICATING IS SENDING forms the basic framework, in which messages are understood as objects that move from communicator to addressee. BAD IS DIRTY specifies the nature of the objects: Because they are negative messages, they are represented as dirt. POWERFUL IS UP now gives us the relative locations of the communicator and addressee: Because the communicators are framed as more powerful, they are located above the addressee. Finally, OPPRESSION IS DOWNWARD PRESSURE adds detail to the effects of the messages: They have an oppressive effect, and so the dirt settles on top of the addressee with a heavy weight.

Taken together, the source domains of these metaphors create a scenario of burying. Table 10.12 outlines the scenario.

Thus, through this framing, Lentz's interlocutors are powerful and dismissive; Lentz is powerless to stop them; and ASL falls under a heavy weight of oppression. As we have seen, the interlocutors never accept Lentz's *archeology* framing; they never even look at the treasure. In their own minds, they are simply burying Lentz – and this is reflected in the fact that the dirt falls first onto Lentz. But the end result is the burial of the treasure.

TABLE 10.12. Scenario for *Burial* Framing

SOURCE SCENARIO	TARGET SCENARIO
One person shovels dirt down onto another person.	A powerful entity says disrespectful, dismissive things to a less-powerful entity.
(POWERFUL IS UP, COMMUNICATING IS SENDING, BAD IS DIRTY)	
The process of shoveling dirt continues until the person is fully buried.	The process of disrespect from powerful sources continues until the entity is completely powerless.
(POWERFUL IS UP, COMMUNICATING IS SENDING, BAD IS DIRTY, OPPRESSION IS DOWNWARD PRESSURE)	
The dirt weighs heavily on the buried person.	The situation is extremely oppressive to the disrespected entity.
(POWERFUL IS UP, OPPRESSION IS DOWNWARD PRESSURE)	

EXISTENCE IS LIFE In stage 6, Lentz adds one more metaphor to the mix: EXISTENCE IS LIFE, where the concept of continued life is used to understand the concept of continued existence. This metaphor is highly productive in English (e.g., *That idea is dead in the water*; *His business is barely alive*, etc.) but not documented in ASL.

Table 10.13 gives a mapping for the metaphor as it is used in English and as it functions in Lentz's poem.

At stage 6 of the poem, once the treasure has been buried, Lentz describes it as "still alive." That is, though it is no longer easily accessi-

TABLE 10.13. EXISTENCE IS LIFE

SOURCE	TARGET
Alive	Existent
Dead	Nonexistent
Remaining alive	Persisting
Dying	Ceasing to exist

TABLE 10.14. Final Stage of Burial Framing

SOURCE	TARGET
The buried person eventually dies under the weight of the dirt.	The oppression eventually causes the entity to cease to exist.

ble, and though it has been ridiculed, ASL and its beautiful structure still exist. This new metaphor adds a twist to the existing "burial" composite.[7]

The New Composite Up until stage 6, the *burial* framing has claimed that ASL is under heavy oppression by those who dismiss its importance. The addition of EXISTENCE IS LIFE gives the implication that ASL's very existence is in danger.

We know that one main function of underground burial is to dispose of dead bodies; similarly, we know that any live creature buried underground cannot survive there for long. Table 10.14 gives one final stage that we must add to the OPPRESSION IS BURIAL scenario: The eventual effect of heavy oppression is extirpation. Thus, in the final framing of the situation, ASL is an endangered being, Lentz is a would-be rescuer, and her interlocutors are not just oppressors but murderers.

SUMMARY

A close analysis of "The Treasure" has shown how a skilled poet can take the conventional resources of her language and elaborate them into a work of art. In this poem, Lentz has blended together many conventional metaphors of ASL and of American culture in a dramatic statement of the importance of ASL linguistics to deaf people and Deaf culture. Starting from a scenario of digging up and reburying artifacts, she crafts two framings of the state of ASL research: LINGUISTIC ANALYSIS IS ARCHEOLOGY and OPPRESSION IS BURIAL.

Her message draws much of its power from the salience of these framings to our everyday experiences; we may be unfamiliar with linguistic

---

[7] An anonymous reviewer suggests a different view of this passage. In this view, Lentz does not add to the *burial* framing in stage 6; instead, she drops it for a new framing. She now stands in a different place with the treasure in hand; ASL is not buried or endangered but rather still alive and accessible to us.

research, but we certainly know about archeology, treasure hunts, and death. Taken together, these framings tell us that ASL is an important artifact, a treasure chest, a living thing; that linguists are scientists, lucky adventurers, rescuers; that people who "put down" ASL are willful disregarders of science, wasters of valuable resources, and murderers. This poem clearly shows the power of conceptual metaphor to influence our understanding and framing of complex issues such as the linguistic analysis of ASL.

CHAPTER ELEVEN

The Future of Signed-Language Research

OUR PAST

Since Stokoe's (1960) first bold article proclaiming that signing had linguistic structure, the field of sign language research has grown immensely and gone through a number of stages. Following Newport (1996),[1] I wish to summarize our progression and list some key issues that we as a group have not been addressing. I believe that truly addressing these issues will transform sign linguistics, and the field of linguistics as a whole, by requiring us to handle linguistic motivation, iconicity, and metaphor.

The earliest signed-language research focused on proving that ASL (and soon thereafter, other signed languages) was a true language, with the same types of structure to be found in spoken languages. Researchers sought to counter the myths that signing is a single, universally understood system, or that it is "just pictures" on the hands; that it is "broken English," or not capable of describing abstractions.

Some linguists, particularly the earliest ones, marveled at the differences between ASL and spoken languages. For example, Stokoe's first description of ASL's form component was called *cherology*, after the Greek word *cheir*, or "hand." It emphasized the simultaneous nature of signs, in which the formational components of handshape, location, and movement occur in a simultaneous package; by contrast, spoken-language components – vowels, consonants, glides, and so on – occur in a sequence.

[1] Some of the framing of this chapter draws on Elissa Newport's keynote lecture, "Sign Language Research in the Third Millenium," at the Fifth International Conference on Theoretical Issues in Sign Language Research, University of Quebec at Montreal and McGill University, September 19–22, 1996.

Later sign linguists sought to minimize those differences. The term *cherology* was quickly abandoned in favor of the term *phonology* (from the Greek *phon-*, meaning "sound"); which is used for spoken languages' form component. The point of this change was to emphasize the similarities between signed and spoken languages. A number of other terms have been imported from spoken language research, including *syllable* and *classifier*; debates are still ongoing as to whether these terms are appropriate for signed languages. The "hold/movement" model of sign structure (Liddell & Johnson 1989) was widely acclaimed by many not just for its merits but also because it was a *sequential* model rather than Stokoe's simultaneous model; it made signs appear more like spoken-language words with their sequences of consonants and vowels. And of course, as we have seen, ASL's iconicity was treated as minor or unimportant.

One reason for emphasizing similarities between signed and spoken languages was political, aimed at convincing skeptics that ASL was a true language "like any other language." But another, deeper reason came from the desire to understand what is universal about language itself, about the human capacity to develop productive and flexible communication systems. Tantalized by the new awareness of language in more than one modality, researchers began to look for universals of *language,* rather than universals of *spoken language.*

Since the 1980s, linguistic analyses of more and more signed languages have been carried out, including languages from South Africa, Nigeria, Sweden, Belgium, Holland, France, Spain, Italy, England, Quebec, Mexico, Venezuela, Nicaragua, Brazil, Argentina, Japan, Taiwan, Bali, Australia, New Zealand, India/Pakistan, and Israel.[2] As that information comes in, little by little we can begin to get a picture of what *signed language* looks like and to compare language in the signed and spoken modalities. As expected, there are many similarities between the two – but we are also finding differences.

OUR CHALLENGE

Along with Armstrong (1988) and Newport (1996), I believe that it is time to turn our attention to the areas in which signed languages are *different* from spoken languages. One area in which the differences become particularly obvious is the "mutual intelligibility" of languages.

---

[2] The Sixth International Conference on Theoretical Issues in Sign Language Research, November 12–15, 1998, at Gallaudet University in Washington, DC, had papers on signed languages from these countries; other signed languages have been analyzed as well.

For spoken languages, it is a truism that speakers of different languages will not be able to understand each other. A person who speaks only English and a person who speaks only Thai, or Swahili, or French will not be able to carry on any kind of conversation with each other. By pictures and gesturing, some communication may be established, but it will be sharply limited and laborious. Only if the two languages are closely related will their speakers be able to communicate well; language pairs of this sort, such as Spanish and Portuguese (to some extent), or Low German and High German, share a common ancestor language and are sometimes considered to be dialects of a single language rather than separate languages in their own right. The fact that spoken languages are not, on the whole, mutually intelligible, is used as evidence for their lack of iconicity: If sounds and meanings were connected in a motivated way, people would do better at figuring out each others' languages.

The situation is different for signed languages. We know that many signed languages are not historically related to each other; for example, the signed languages of France and Great Britain do not share a common ancestor, and the brand-new signed language of Nicaragua appears to have no linguistic ancestors at all (Kegl, Senghas, & Coppola 1995; Senghas 1995). These languages' vocabularies are very different from each other. Yet, when Deaf people from different language groups get together, they are able to establish easy communication in a surprisingly brief period of time (Rutherford, personal communication).[3]

As linguists, we must ask: What causes this difference? Some part of it must be attributed to the remarkable communication skills of Deaf people, who have had to function their entire lives in a community of hearing people who do not sign; Deaf people have had to become expert in communicating across a language barrier. Yet we must also ask: Is there more? Is there a structural difference between signed and spoken languages that makes signed languages mutually intelligible? The answer to that question appears to be yes.

Spoken languages, considered as a group, are quite diverse in their structural types. There is hardly space to summarize the diversity here, but a few examples will help. Word order within a normal declarative clause, for example, is extremely variable: Some languages put the subject (S) first, then the verb (V), then the object (O) (SVO ordering); others have the orders SOV or VSO (Greenberg 1966a). Grammatical

---

[3] During her twenty years of fieldwork on Deaf culture, many Deaf people have reported this experience to Dr. Susan Rutherford; the Deaf people in question came from many countries, including the United States, Canada (in particular, Quebec), Sweden, Austria, Spain, the Netherlands, England, France, Finland, Brazil, and Taiwan.

inflections are also quite variable: Some languages inflect their nouns, some inflect their verbs, some inflect adjectives and even prepositions (e.g., Irish), whereas other languages do not use inflections at all (e.g., Mandarin). The field of *linguistic typology* (e.g., Comrie 1985; Croft 1990; Talmy 1985a, 1985b, 1987) is devoted to cataloguing the differences and noting the similarities among languages; the related field of *language universals* (e.g., Greenberg 1966a, 1966b) looks at what all spoken languages seem to share and postulates that those shared properties result from the shared language "machinery" of the human brain.

Signed languages, on the other hand, are remarkably *similar* in their structural types. Linguists have not emphasized this fact, perhaps because it appears to reinforce the common myth that "sign language" is a single universal system understood all over the world. There is no such universal system; different signed languages differ considerably in their vocabulary and parts of their grammatical structure. But as more and more sign linguists begin to study languages other than ASL, as the data begin to come in from Asia, Africa, Europe, and Latin America, we cannot help but notice that all signed languages seem to share certain grammatical structures.

To the best of our knowledge, all signed languages have *classifiers*: systems of iconically motivated forms for representing shapes, locations, and movements. All signed languages establish *referential loci* in space – special locations in signing space that represent people, places, and so on – and have pronouns and verbs that change their movement patterns to "agree" with those loci. Finally, all signed languages inflect their verbs for *temporal aspect.*

These structures are not unique to established signed languages. Whenever humans are required to communicate using gestures of the hands, face, and body, structures of this type emerge. We see them in *homesign* (e.g., Singleton, Goldin-Meadow, & McNeill 1995): Deaf children who are raised without exposure to signing of any kind typically create their own personal gestural communication systems. These systems are rudimentary, lacking much vocabulary and structure; in families where there are several deaf children, the systems become far more complex and languagelike, which shows how the flow of communication encourages the invention of language. But we find that even the systems used by only a single child have the basic structures: classifier-like forms, referential loci, and agreement with the loci. When a critical mass of homesigning deaf children is brought together, the children together meld their individual systems into a new language. This phenomenon is still occurring today; in Nicaragua, the first school for deaf children was established in 1980, and a new signed language has been developing there ever since (Kegl et al. 1995, Senghas 1995). This new language, like its homesign forebears and like other signed languages, uses iconic classifiers and spatial agreement morphology.

Deaf children with hearing parents are often brought up to use a manual code for English, instead of ASL. There are several such codes (SEE I, SEE II, LOVE, and so on); the codes are created by a radical restructuring of ASL vocabulary. For each English word and common inflection (e.g., -tion, -ness, -s), a sign equivalent is invented, borrowed from ASL, or created by changing an ASL sign. These sign equivalents are then strung together in English word order, without any of ASL's grammatical structure or spatial mappings. The result is not a natural language but a "code" or representation of English on the hands. Recent research by S. Supalla (1991) has shown that Deaf children, when given this unnatural system, tend to "reinvent" some of the characteristics of ASL; in particular, they introduce referential loci, and pronoun–verb agreement with those loci.

The children who create these innovations are using visual/gestural communication systems every day; they have plenty of time to develop changes. But even on a much shorter time scale, people adopt classifier-like and locilike structures. In some experiments, researchers have brought hearing, nonsigning adults into the laboratory and asked them to communicate without talking. One study (Morford, Singleton, & Goldin-Meadow 1995) asked people to describe some animated video clips of objects moving across landscapes; the subjects all used their hands, movements, and space in classifier-like ways to convey the images they saw. Another, more anecdotal study (Bloom 1979, cited in McNeill 1992) asked a college student to tell the story of "Sleeping Beauty" without speaking; over the next twenty minutes, the student developed a system of spatial loci, "pronouns" and "verbs" referring to them, and a set of iconic classifier-like forms for describing shapes and movements.

Even the gestures that accompany hearing people's speech, though they do not encode all the information in the speech, are influenced by spatial mapping (McNeill 1992). The gestures of the hands and head are often aimed toward specific spots when referring to specific people or things, and they can also show the shape or movement of objects in space, or the repetition or continuity of events over time.

All these data, from signed languages, homesign systems, modifications of manual codes for English, hearing people's gestures without speech, and gestures accompanying speech suggest the same conclusion: Communication systems in the visual/gestural modality will naturally develop classifiers, referential loci, and aspectual marking. Why does this happen? Newport suggested we look toward the neural structures for language in the brain, and that is a useful and fruitful direction to take. But I think that even before we collect new brain data, we can give an answer. That answer is *motivation,* and in particular, motivation by *iconicity* and *conceptual metaphor.*

THE IMPORTANCE OF ICONICITY AND METAPHOR

We have seen how ASL's referential loci are fundamentally iconic and how ASL's verb agreement system is deeply iconic and metaphorical. The classifier system as well is iconic, and we have also seen how signs for abstract concepts can develop from that iconic system. There has also been an example of how ASL's aspectual system uses time in an iconic way (i.e., the repetitive inflection), and the remaining aspectual inflections are equally iconic. All of these parts of ASL are strongly motivated by universal properties of human cognition: the ability to establish concepts, associate them with visual and kinesthetic images (some of which are universal), simplify the images, and choose body parts and movements to encode these images.

These motivations are part of being human, of having the kinds of brains, bodies, and experiences that we do. Thus, humans all over the world are capable of making the same kinds of iconic representations – first as mime, and later, through repetition, memorization, and reanalysis, as a linguistic system.[4] These representations are so powerful and so well motivated that whenever meaning must be communicated in the gestural modality, humans reinvent them. We reinvent shape- and interaction-based classifiers, reinvent referential loci, and reinvent time-based aspectual inflections, rederiving all three types from our basic human understanding of space, time, experience, and similarity. All over the world, in isolated homes, laboratories, and Deaf schools, children are remaking the underpinnings of gestural languages using their natural human abilities.

This is the reason why signed languages share so much structure, why signed languages with separate origins are mutually intelligible, why Deaf children and hearing adults create the same kinds of gestural com-

---

4 Research with connectionist computing networks (e.g., Elman & McClelland 1984; Regier 1996; Rumelhart, McClelland, & the PDP Research Group 1986) gives some clues as to how this process might happen. The topic is too large to address here but will be taken up in future work.

munication systems. The universal motivations of iconicity and conceptual metaphor, combined with the special resources of the visual/gestural modality, naturally lead to languages of this sort.[5]

A NOTE ON "LOSS OF ICONICITY"

There has been much research showing how signed languages "lose their iconicity" over time (e.g., Frishberg 1979); this deserves some comment.

Signed languages are young languages. Because most Deaf children are born to hearing parents, it is through the Deaf schools and the Deaf community that the language develops and is passed on. In many countries, Deaf schools were established only a few centuries or even a few decades ago; because of the recent establishment of these institutions, signed languages are mostly less than a few centuries old. The discussion in this book of iconicity and metaphor has focused on the *creation* of iconic signs, not what happens to them after they are created.

There is some evidence that change in ASL over time reduces iconicity (cf. discussion in Chapter Four). For example, Frishberg (1979) noted that signs tend to move from their original locations toward the center of signing space. This process may make the sign easier to perceive, by moving closer to where the eyes fixate, but it would reduce a sign's iconicity by moving it from the iconically appropriate location. This is, as claimed, a true loss of iconicity.

Inflection of signs, another process that has been claimed to reduce iconicity, actually increases it. The common example is the sign SLOW, made with the dominant flat hand slowly stroking toward the wrist along the nondominant hand's back, combined with the inflection for intensity, which is a rapid, tense movement. When these two combine, the resulting sign VERY-SLOW is articulated with a rapid movement. The claim (Klima & Bellugi 1979) is that VERY-SLOW is less iconic than its

---

[5] Related claims have been made by Armstrong (1988), Brennan (1990), Liddell (1995), and Meir (1998).

S. Wilcox (1998) made additional specific predictions based on this line of reasoning. To give one example, he applied Langacker's (1991b) definitions of *objective* ("on-stage" or perceived) versus *subjective* (part of the perceiver or conceptualizer) to the articulators of ASL. He argued that the hands are "on-stage" or visible to the conceptualizer, and as such should iconically represent objective concepts, whereas the face is necessarily subjective and part of the conceptualizer, and thus should represent subjective concepts. Because, in his view, lexical signs tend to have objective meanings and morphology tends to have more subjective meanings, he predicted that all sign languages will tend to code lexical material with the hands and not the face; facial morphemes, when present, will tend to be bound rather than free.

component parts, and so their combination has less iconicity. In fact, the combination is *more* iconic; the two iconic mappings simply do not combine into a consistent picture. VERY-SLOW resembles the highly iconic and metaphorical emotion signs in Chapter Seven; these signs combine several metaphorical and iconic mappings in their structures, though they do not present a unified iconically represented image.

We do not yet know what an older signed language will look like; the signed languages of today have not had much time to diverge from their highly motivated origins, if indeed they will diverge.[6] Perhaps in older signed languages, many of the fully imagistic frozen signs will be modified, their origins covered over in layers and layers of conventionalized changes. But on the other hand, there are some core iconic/metaphorical areas that will probably never lose their profound iconicity.

We have evidence that iconicity can overwhelm systematic change in highly motivated cases: As described in Chapter Four, English *peep* (for high-pitched bird sounds) should have changed to *pipe* as the Great Vowel Shift took place, but the older, iconic form survived as well. *Peep* is a highly motivated iconic word, yet I doubt it is more motivated than the core iconic structures that appear in signed language after signed language, in homesign and in hearing people's gestures.

I do not believe that signed languages will ever lose their iconic classifier systems. The classifiers may change slightly in nature; Morford et al. (1995) suggested that as homesign systems develop, classifier-like gestures start as strict representations of an object's shape but later represent an entire semantic category regardless of each member's shape (e.g., all vehicles would eventually get the same classifier, as in today's ASL).[7] Yet this would not change the essential iconicity of the system; classifiers would still be chosen based on the shape of the category prototype.

Similarly, Senghas (1995) noted that in Nicaraguan Sign Language, some classifier constructions based on the movements of handling objects are replaced by constructions that represent the shape and size of the object; this may be a move away from "mimetic enactment," as she claimed, but it is certainly not a loss of iconicity itself. Boyes-Braem (1981) noted a similar distinction between motor-based and shape-based

---

[6] We might gain insight by looking at parallels between signed languages and creoles: The youngest spoken languages are quite transparent semantically (though not nearly as iconic as signed languages). One form is reliably associated with a single unified meaning. In contrast, in an old language like English, a single form (e.g., *over, back, just*) can have dozens of historically related meanings, some acquired by principle and some by chance. For an overview of this issue, see McWhorter (1997).

[7] This change could also be based on the child's development of semantic categories, rather than a change in the iconic system itself.

iconicity in ASL. She described this as *de-iconicization*, in which the new form is less pantomimic and more "sign-like" than the old, but once again, the two forms are equally iconic.

Moreover, the system of referential loci will never lose its iconicity, nor will the inflections for verb agreement and temporal aspect – they are already highly abstract and fully motivated. The changes in frozen signs may remove some small portion of signed languages' iconicity, but the core iconic grammatical structures that appear in language after language will never disappear.

OUR FUTURE

One major challenge for the future of signed-language research is thus to investigate and describe linguistic iconicity and to incorporate it into linguistic theories. This book demonstrates how this may be done in the cognitive linguistics framework, using the tools of *conceptual mappings, frame semantics, prototype theory*, and *conceptual metaphor theory*. The cognitive linguistics approach treats form and meaning as integrated on every level of linguistic structure; this makes it well suited for treating issues of linguistic motivation. In particular, the intimate form–meaning connections in iconicity demand this kind of approach. Conceptual metaphor, with its complex connections between conceptual domains, is best treated in this framework.

In this book, we have seen major differences between signed and spoken languages in how iconic they can be and in how easily they can connect metaphor and iconicity. Signed languages are easily, beautifully, naturally iconic – they describe space and movement iconically, use iconicity and metaphor in their grammar, and connect metaphor to iconicity to describe abstract concepts. The iconicity and metaphor are so pervasive and so motivated that signers familiar with one language's system can quickly master the basics of another language's system. Spoken languages have much less iconicity and rarely (if at all) connect it to their own rich and beautiful metaphorical systems.

Yet we must remember that these differences, though seemingly deep, are a direct consequence of the languages' modalities. We have seen that the process of creating iconic forms is identical in both signed and spoken languages and that metaphorical mappings between conceptual domains work the same way in both modalities. Having the body and space as articulators, however, lets us represent far more types of imagery iconically, and many more concepts have visual, spatial, or kinesthetic images associated with them than have auditory images. The processes of iconicity and metaphor are modality-independent, yet their interactions with the two modalities of human language produce two distinct language types: the highly iconic signed varieties and the less-iconic (yet still highly motivated) spoken varieties.

Language, in any modality, is motivated – it draws on structures and associations in the language user's conceptual system. Iconicity, a feature of all languages, is based on our ability to associate sensory images with concepts, simplify those images, and create analogues of them using the resources of the language, all the while preserving the essential structure of the original image. Conceptual metaphor, another feature of all languages, creates associations between abstract and concrete conceptual domains. Although all languages have metaphor and iconicity, signed languages excel at putting the two together to create a vast range of iconic and metaphorical/iconic words, inflections, and syntactic structures. To give a real description and explanation of these phenomena, we must adopt a theory of linguistics that can also draw on the complexities of conceptual structure; we must not separate off semantics from syntax and phonology but must integrate them together in one linguistic representation. In short, we must adopt the cognitive linguistics point of view.

The field of linguistics owes a great debt to the world's Deaf communities for creating and sharing language in the signed modality. Signed languages are vital to our progress in figuring out the human language capacity, because their iconicity is too strong and pervasive and multifaceted to ignore. Truly taking signed languages seriously will cause a revolution in spoken-language linguistics: a new direction for all of us language scholars as we enter the third millennium.

Glossing Conventions

The glosses of ASL in this book consist of three lines plus an optional fourth. The top line, if present, shows the direction of the signer's gaze. The next three lines describe what the signer's hands are doing: The first, labeled *rh*, shows the right hand when it acts alone; the middle, labeled *both*, shows what the hands do together; and the bottom, labeled *lh*, shows what the left hand does on its own. A long dash following a gloss indicates that the sign is held by one hand while the other hand articulates another sign.

Lexical items are glossed by English words in SMALL CAPITAL letters (e.g., BETTER). A hyphen joining two English words indicates a multiword gloss of a lexical sign (e.g., LOOK-AT). A plus symbol joining two English words indicates that the sign is a compound (e.g., MOTHER+FATHER "parents"). A plus symbol following a sign indicates that the sign is repeated (e.g., LEARN++). A number symbol preceding a gloss indicates a finger-spelled loan sign (e.g., #ASL).

Pronouns are glossed using the form PRO-X, where X is a number giving the person of the pronoun. Three types of pronouns appear in this text: PRO, the general pronoun form; POSS-PRO, the possessive pronoun; and RESPECT-PRO, a special form indicating respect.

Classifiers' glosses consist of the letters *CL,* followed by an abbreviation for the classifier handshape, followed by a description of the classifier's meaning. For example,

CL: Flat-OO "hold flat object in front of self"

indicates a classifier that uses right and left flat-O handshapes to express the meaning "hold flat object in front of self." Classifier handshapes appearing in this book include O, flat-O, 5, S, C, B, H, F, open-8, and X.

Subscripts on glosses indicate several types of things. If the subscript consists of a direction (e.g., R, L, CTR, DOWN, UP), the direction indicates the region of space in which the sign is articulated or toward which it is oriented. If the subscript consists of a number (e.g, 1, 3), it indicates person agreement. Other subscripts notate specific inflections – in particular, IMPER indicates an imperative and TRILL indicates trilled movement.

Gestures are given an English gloss inside quotation marks (e.g., "what," "no, no").

The letters RS indicate a referential shift, in which the signer takes on a character's persona. The character's name is indicated within parentheses, and carets (< and >) show the beginning and end of the shift.

Translation of "The Treasure"

For a long time now, we Deaf
have been signing and signing,
telling our stories,
trading our experiences,
handing down what we know.
Yet what we know
has been covered up,
underground,
beneath notice.

I take a good hard look
and start to probe,
my shovel blade scrapes away the dirt,
and behold!
I pick it up, a sign
and then another sign.
Next to each other,
they look so much alike,
but their movements are different,
and they have different meanings!
How interesting!

I set them aside
and again I probe deeper,

(S. F. Taub, translator. All errors my own.)

the blade scrapes away the dirt,
my body leans into the strokes of the shovel,
and there!
I lift another one into view,
a sign with an English word pasted across its face.
I strip off that label and drop it,
look deep into the sign,
and see its profound meaning
out of our Deaf world.
How impressive!

Setting it aside,
again I probe,
my body leans into the strokes of the shovel,
the blade scrapes away the dirt,
and there!
I pick up another sign,
an English word pasted across its face;
I strip and drop the label.
And another sign
defaced with an English word
which I strip and drop.
I hold them next to each other,
look from first to second – no! –
the other way, I reverse their order –
that's better.
And the rise and fall of eyebrows,
wiggling over the first sign and the second,
how lovely!

Setting them both aside
again I probe into the matter,
the blade scrapes away the dirt,
my body leans into
the strokes of the shovel,
the blade scrapes away
more and more dirt, and
clunk! I've hit something!
Gently I uncover it, a box!
The lid opens easily,
and gleaming up at me,
the contents glitter and glow.

My spirits soar, exalted,
I look up out of my trench –
"Hey, you up there!
You! Look! Look down here!"

And one does look down and signs,
"Why in the world are you working on ASL?
I'm deaf, and I know all about signing.
Studying is for those hearing people!"
"No, no – all this down here
belongs to deaf people!
It is incredibly important for deaf people
to study and analyze it!
We'll be more proud,
and use our language more openly,
yes, we will!"
A long look. "Oh.
I'm busy; no time for this; catch you later."
And that one takes a shovel and heaves;
the dirt falls
and smears down my face
and body.

And another up there looks down, signing, "ASL?
Oh, signing is cool, it's so much fun!
We sign away, we leave so much out –
no 'a,' no 'is,'!
no 'be,' no '-ing,' no '-ment'!
But English sentences are precise and refined –
they're good for work, school, anything formal."
"Stop! ASL does not leave things out!
Look at all this!
It's lovely, incredible,
rich in so many things
that English doesn't have at all.
What's down here is just as refined as English!"
"Really?
I think you're just making it up."
And that one raises a shovel,
the dirt falls,
it smears down my face
and body.

And another looks down at me
and mouths in her monotone signs,
"Look, you haVe to accept
The Fact that It Is easy R for
Hear Ing Parent S of Deaf
Child reN to learn sign D English Ish
So hold off ASL to late R."
"No, no – if parents see what's down here,
they'll get so excited,
they'll learn ASL right away!"
"No, I Know better R
Be Cause I haVe A PhD."
Again the shovel is raised,
the dirt falls,
it smears down my face
and body.

And now the dirt comes falling from all sides,
again and again I am smeared,
it falls and falls
on our treasure.
The level rises,
and soon the dirt covers the box,
weighing it down once more,
buried under oppression.
Yet that treasure, those sweet glowing lights,
that treasure
still lives – it lives, my friend!
I leave it
in your hands.

References

Alpher, Barry. 1994. Yir-Yoront Ideophones. In Leanne Hinton, Johanna Nichols, & John J. Ohala, eds., *Sound Symbolism,* pp. 161–77. Cambridge: Cambridge University Press.

Armstrong, David F. 1983. Iconicity, Arbitrariness, and Duality of Patterning in Signed and Spoken Language: Perspectives on Language Evolution. *Sign Language Studies* 38: 51–69.

Armstrong, David F. 1988. Review Article: The World Turned Inside Out. *Sign Language Studies* 61: 419–28.

Baker, Charlotte, & Dennis Cokely. 1980. *American Sign Language: A Teacher's Resource Text on Grammar and Culture.* Silver Spring, MD: T. J. Publishers.

Battison, Robin. 1978. *Lexical Borrowing in American Sign Language.* Silver Spring, MD: Linstok Press.

Berlin, Brent, & Paul Kay. 1969. *Basic Color Terms: Their Universality and Evolution.* Berkeley: University of California Press.

Bickerton, Derek. 1981. *Roots of Language.* Ann Arbor, MI: Karoma Publishers.

Bickerton, Derek. 1984. The Language Bioprogram Hypothesis. *Behavioral and Brain Sciences,* 7:173–88.

Bloom, Ralph. 1979. Language Creation in the Manual Modality: A Preliminary Investigation. Unpublished bachelor's thesis, Department of Behavioral Sciences, University of Chicago.

Bolinger, Dwight. 1985. The Inherent Iconism of Intonation. In John Haiman, ed., *Iconicity in Syntax: Proceedings of a Symposium on Iconicity in Syntax, Stanford, June 24–6, 1983,* pp. 97–108. Amsterdam: John Benjamins.

Boyes-Braem, Penny. 1981. Features of the Handshape in American Sign Language. Unpublished doctoral dissertation, University of California, Berkeley.

Brennan, Mary. 1990. *Word Formation in British Sign Language.* Stockholm, Sweden: University of Stockholm.

Brennan, Mary. 1994. Pragmatics and Productivity. In Inger Ahlgren, Brita Bergman, & Mary Brennan, eds., *Perspectives on Sign Language Usage: Papers from the Fifth International Symposium on Sign Language Research,* Vol. 2, pp. 371–190. Durham, England: International Sign Linguistics Association.

Brentari, Diane. 1996. Trilled Movement: Phonetic Realization and Formal Representation. *Lingua* 98:43–71.

Buchler, Justus. 1940. *The Philosophy of Peirce: Selected Writings.* London: Rutledge & Keegan Paul.

Cameracanna, Emanuela, Serena Corazza, Elena Pizzuto, & Virginia Volterra. 1994. How Visual Spatial-Temporal Metaphors of Speech Become Visible in Sign. In Inger Ahlgren, Brita Bergman, & Mary Brennan, eds., *Perspectives on Sign Language Structure: Papers from the Fifth International Symposium on Sign Language Research,* Vol. 1, pp. 55–68. Durham, England: International Sign Linguistics Association.

Choi, Soonja, & Melissa Bowerman. 1991. Learning to Express Motion Events in English and Korean: The Influence of Language-Specific Lexicalization Patterns. *Cognition,* 41:83–121.

Chomsky, Noam. 1957. *Syntactic Structures.* The Hague: Mouton.

Chomsky, Noam. 1965. *Aspects of the Theory of Syntax.* Cambridge, MA: MIT Press.

Chomsky, Noam. 1981. *Lectures on Government and Binding.* Dordrecht: Foris.

Cienki, Alan. 1998. Metaphoric Gestures and Some of Their Relations to Verbal Metaphorical Expressions. In J. P. Koenig, ed., *Discourse and Cognition: Bridging the Gap.* Stanford, CA: CSLI.

Clark, Herbert. 1973. Space, Time, Semantics and the Child. In T. Moore, ed., *Cognitive Development and the Acquisition of Language,* pp. 27–63. New York: Academic Press.

Comrie, Bernard. 1985. *Tense.* Cambridge: Cambridge University Press.

Croft, William. 1990. *Typology and Universals.* Cambridge: Cambridge University Press.

Croft, William. 1991. *Syntactic Categories and Grammatical Relations: The Cognitive Organization of Information.* Chicago: University of Chicago Press.

DeMatteo, Asa. 1977. Visual Imagery and Visual Analogues in American Sign Language. In Lynn A. Friedman, ed., *On the Other Hand,* pp. 109–36. London: Academic Press.

DeLancey, Scott. 1981. An Interpretation of Split Ergativity and Related Phenomena. *Language* 57:626–57.

Dixon, R. M. W. 1986. Noun Classes and Noun Classification in Typological Perspective. In Colette Craig, ed., *Noun Classes and Categorization,* pp. 105–12. Amsterdam: John Benjamins.

Elman, Jeffrey L., & James L. McClelland. 1984. Speech Perception as a Cognitive Process: The Interactive Activation Model. In Norman Lass, ed., *Speech and Language, vol. 10,* pp. New York: Academic Press.

Elman, Jeffrey L., Elizabeth A. Bates, Mark H. Johnson, Annette Karmiloff-Smith, Domenico Parisi, and Kim Plunkett. 1997. *Rethinking Innateness: A Connectionist Perspective on Development.* Cambridge, MA: MIT Press.

Emanatian, Michele. 1992. Chagga 'Come' and 'Go': Metaphor and the Development of Tense-Aspect. *Studies in Language* 16(1):1–33.

Emmorey, Karen, & Judy S. Reilly. 1995. Theoretical Issues Relating Language, Gesture, and Space: An Overview. In K. Emmorey & J. S. Reilly, eds., *Language, Gesture, and Space,* pp. 1–16. Hillsdale, NJ: Lawrence Erlbaum.

Engberg-Pedersen, Elisabeth. 1993. *Space in Danish Sign Language: The Semantics and Morphosyntax of the Use of Space in a Visual Language.* Hamburg: SIGNUM-Verlag.

Fauconnier, Gilles. 1985. *Mental Spaces: Aspects of Meaning Construction in Natural Languages.* Cambridge: Cambridge University Press.

Fauconnier, Gilles, & Mark Turner. 1996. Blending as a Central Process of Grammar. In Adele Goldberg, ed., *Conceptual Structure, Discourse, and Language,* pp. 113–30. Stanford, CA: CSLI.

Ferrara, Kathleen Warden. 1994. *Therapeutic Ways with Words.* Oxford: Oxford University Press.

Fillmore, Charles. 1968. The Case for Case. In Emmon Bach & Robert T. Harms, eds., *Universals in Linguistic Theory.* New York: Holt.

Fillmore, Charles. 1982. Frame Semantics. In the Linguistic Society of Korea, ed., *Linguistics in the Morning Calm,* pp. 111–37. Seoul: Hanshin Publishing.

Fleischman, Suzanne. 1982a. The Past and the Future: Are They Coming or Going? In *Proceedings of the Eighth Annual Meeting of the Berkeley Linguistics Society.* Berkeley, CA: Berkeley Linguistics Society.

Fleischman, Suzanne. 1982b. *The Future in Thought and Language.* Cambridge: Cambridge University Press.

Fried, Mirjam. 1995. Grammatical Subject and Its Role in the Grammar of Case Languages. Unpublished doctoral dissertation, University of California, Berkeley.

Friedman, Lynn A. 1975. Space, Time, and Person Reference in American Sign Language. *Language,* 51:940–61.

Frishberg, Nancy. 1979. Historical Change: From Iconic to Arbitrary. In Edward Klima & Ursula Bellugi, eds., *The Signs of Language,* pp. 67–83. Cambridge, MA: Harvard University Press.

Frishberg, Nancy, & Bonnie Gough. 1973. Morphology in American Sign Language. Manuscript, Salk Institute, San Diego.

Gee, James P., & Judy A. Kegl. 1982. Semantic Perspicuity and the Locative Hypothesis: Implications for Acquisition. *Journal of Education* (Boston University) 164:185–209.

Gentner, Dedre, & Arthur Markman. 1996. Structure-Mapping in Analogy and Similarity: The Importance of Being Connected. Unpublished manuscript, Northwestern University, Chicago.

Givon, Talmy. 1979. *On Understanding Grammar.* New York: Academic Press.

Givon, Talmy. 1984. *Syntax: A Functional-Typological Introduction.* Vol. 1. Amsterdam: John Benjamins.

Goodman, Nelson. 1968. *Languages of Art: An Approach to a Theory of Symbols.* Indianapolis: Bobbs-Merrill.

Grady, Joseph. 1997. Foundations of Meaning: Primary Metaphors and Primary Scenes. Unpublished doctoral dissertation, University of California, Berkeley.

Grady, Joseph, & Christopher Johnson. In press. Converging Evidence for the Notions of "Subscene" and "Primary Scene." In *Proceedings of the Twenty-Third Annual Meeting of the Berkeley Linguistics Society.* Berkeley, CA: Berkeley Linguistics Society.

Grady, Joseph, Sarah Taub, & Pamela Morgan. 1996. Primitive and Compound Metaphors. In Adele Goldberg, ed., *Conceptual Structure, Discourse, and Language,* pp. 177–87. Stanford, CA: CSLI.

Greenberg, Joseph H. 1966a. Some Universals of Grammar with Particular Reference to the Order of Meaningful Elements. In Joseph H. Greenberg, ed., *Universals of Grammar*, 2nd ed. Cambridge, MA: MIT Press.

Greenberg, Joseph H. 1966b. *Language Universals, with Special Reference to Feature Hierarchies*. The Hague: Mouton.

Greene, Judith. 1975. *Thinking and Language*. New York: Methuen.

Grushkin, Donald A. 1998. Linguistic Aspects of Metaphorical Expressions of Anger in ASL. *Sign Language and Linguistics* 1:2, pp. 143–68.

Haiman, John, ed. 1985a. *Iconicity in Syntax: Proceedings of a Symposium on Iconicity in Syntax, Stanford, June 24–6, 1983*. Amsterdam: John Benjamins.

Haiman, John. 1985b. Symmetry. In John Haiman, ed., *Iconicity in Syntax: Proceedings of a Symposium on Iconicity in Syntax, Stanford, June 24–6, 1983*, pp. 73–96. Amsterdam: John Benjamins.

Hinton, Leanne, Johanna Nichols, & John J. Ohala, eds. 1994. *Sound Symbolism*. Cambridge: Cambridge University Press.

Hock, Hans Heinrich. 1986. *Principles of Historical Linguistics*. Berlin: Mouton de Gruyter.

van Hoek, Karen. 1996. Conceptual Locations for Reference in American Sign Language. In Gilles Fauconnier & Eve Sweetser, eds., *Spaces, Worlds, and Grammar*, pp. 334–50. Chicago: University of Chicago Press.

Hoemann, H. 1975. The Transparency of Meaning of Sign Language Gestures. *Sign Language Studies*, 7:151–61.

Holtemann, Derek. 1990. Metaphor in American Sign Language. Unpublished bachelors thesis, University of California, Berkeley.

Hopper, Paul J., & Sandra A. Thompson. 1980. Transitivity in Grammar and Discourse. *Language* 56:251–99.

Hopper, Paul J., & Sandra A. Thompson. 1985. The Iconicity of the Universal Categories "Noun" and "Verb." In John Haiman, ed., *Iconicity in Syntax: Proceedings of a Symposium on Iconicity in Syntax, Stanford, June 24–6, 1983*, pp. 151–185. Amsterdam: John Benjamins.

Jackendoff, Ray. 1990. *Semantic Structures*. Cambridge, MA: MIT Press.

Janis, Wynne D. 1995. A Crosslinguistic Perspective on ASL Verb Agreement. In Karen Emmorey & Judy Reilly, eds., *Language, Gesture, and Space*, pp. 195–223. Hillsdale, NJ: Lawrence Erlbaum.

Johnson, Mark. 1987. *The Body in the Mind*. Chicago: University of Chicago Press.

Kay, Paul, & Chad McDaniel. 1978. The Linguistic Significance of the Meanings of Basic Color Terms. *Language* 54(3):610–46.

Kegl, Judy, Ann Senghas, & Marie E. V. Coppola. 1995. Creation Through Contact: Sign Language Emergence and Sign Language Change in Nicaragua. In M. DeGraf, ed., *Comparative Grammatical Change: The Intersection of Language Acquisition, Creole Genesis, and Diachronic Syntax*. Cambridge, MA: MIT Press.

Kimura, Doreen. 1990. How Special Is Language? *Sign Language Studies* 66:79–84.

Kingston, John, & Mary E. Beckman. 1990. *Papers in Laboratory Phonology I: Between the Grammar and Physics of Speech*. Cambridge, MA: Cambridge University Press.

Klima, Edward, & Ursula Bellugi. 1979. *The Signs of Language.* Cambridge, MA: Harvard University Press.

Kövacecs, Zoltan, & Gunther Radden. 1998. Metonymy: Developing a Cognitive Linguistic View. *Cognitive Linguistics* 9(1):37–77.

Lakoff, George. 1987. *Women, Fire, and Dangerous Things: What Categories Reveal about the Mind.* Chicago: University of Chicago Press.

Lakoff, George. 1992. The Contemporary Theory of Metaphor. In Andrew Ortony, ed., *Metaphor and Thought,* 2nd ed. Cambridge, MA: Cambridge University Press.

Lakoff, George, Jane Espenson, and Alan Schwartz. 1991. Master Metaphor List, 2nd ed. Unpublished manuscript, University of California, Berkeley.

Lakoff, George, and Mark Johnson. 1980. *Metaphors We Live By.* Chicago: University of Chicago Press.

Lakoff, George, and Mark Turner. 1989. *More than Cool Reason: A Field Guide to Poetic Metaphor.* Chicago: University of Chicago Press.

Lane, Harlan. 1992. *The Mask of Benevolence: Disabling the Deaf Community.* New York: Knopf.

Lane, Harlan, Robert Hoffmeister, & Ben Bahan. 1996. *A Journey into the DEAF-WORLD.* San Diego, CA: DawnSignPress.

Langacker, Ronald. 1987. *Foundations of Cognitive Grammar: Volume I: Theoretical Prerequisites.* Stanford, CA: Stanford University Press.

Langacker, Ronald. 1991a. *Foundations of Cognitive Grammar: Volume II: Descriptive Application.* Stanford, CA: Stanford University Press.

Langacker, Ronald. 1991b. *Concept, Image, and Symbol: The Cognitive Basis of Grammar.* Berlin: Mouton de Gruyter.

Leite, Naomi. 1994. Master Metonymy List. Unpublished manuscript, University of California, Berkeley.

Liddell, Scott. 1990. Four Functions of a Locus: Reexamining the Structure of Space in ASL. In Ceil Lucas, ed., *Sign Language Research: Theoretical Issues,* pp. 176–98. Washington, DC: Gallaudet University Press.

Liddell, Scott. 1992. Paths to Lexical Imagery. Unpublished manuscript, Gallaudet University, Washington, DC.

Liddell, Scott. 1994. Conceptual and Linguistic Issues in Spatial Mapping: Comparing Spoken and Signed Language. Unpublished manuscript, Gallaudet University, Washington, DC.

Liddell, Scott. 1995. Real, Surrogate, and Token Space: Grammatical Consequences in ASL. In Karen Emmorey & Judy S. Reilly, eds., *Language, Gesture, and Space,* pp. 19–41. Hillsdale, NJ: Lawrence Erlbaum.

Liddell, Scott. 1996. Numeral Incorporating Roots and Non-Incorporating Prefixes in American Sign Language. *Sign Language Studies* 92:201–26.

Liddell, Scott K. 1998. Grounded Blends, Gestures, and Conceptual Shifts. *Cognitive Linguistics* 9(3):283–314.

Liddell, Scott K., & Robert E. Johnson. 1989. American Sign Language: The Phonological Base. *Sign Language Studies* 64:195–277.

Mandel, Mark. 1977. Iconic Devices in American Sign Language. In Lynn A. Friedman, ed., *On the Other Hand,* pp. 57–107. London: Academic Press.

Marr, David. 1982. *Vision: A Computational Investigation into the Human Representation and Processing of Visual Information.* San Francisco: W. H. Freeman.

McDonald, Betsy H. 1982. Aspects of the American Sign Language Predicate System. Unpublished doctoral dissertation, University of Buffalo, Buffalo, NY.

McNeill, David. 1992. *Hand and Mind: What Gestures Reveal About Thought.* Chicago: University of Chicago Press.

McWhorter, John. 1997. Identifying the Creole Prototype: Vindicating a Typological Class. Unpublished manuscript, University of California, Berkeley.

Meir, Irit. 1998. Thematic Structure and Verb Agreement in Israeli Sign Language. Unpublished doctoral dissertation, Hebrew University of Jerusalem.

Morford, Jill P., Jenny L. Singleton, & Susan Goldin-Meadow. 1995. The Genesis of Language: How Much Time Is Needed to Generate Arbitrary Symbols in a Sign System? In Karen Emmorey & Judy Reilly, eds., *Language, Gesture, and Space,* pp. 313–32. Hillsdale, NJ: Lawrence Erlbaum.

Morgan, Pamela. 1996. Metaphorical "Families," Unpublished manuscript, University of California, Berkeley.

Moy, Anthony. 1988. Metaphor in American Sign Language: Implications for Morphology and Saussure's Conception of the Sign. Unpublished manuscript, University of California, Berkeley.

Newport, Elissa. 1996. Sign Language Research in the Third Millenium. Paper presented at the Fifth International Conference on Theoretical Issues in Sign Language Research, September 19–22, Montreal, Quebec, Canada.

Ogawa, Yuko. 1999. Vertical Scale Metaphors in Japanese and Japanese Sign Language. Unpublished master's thesis, Gallaudet University, Washington, DC.

Ohala, John J. 1983. The Phonological End Justifies Any Means. In Shiro Hattori & Kazuko Inoue, eds., *Proceedings of the XIIIth International Congress of Linguists, Tokyo, 29 Aug.–4 Sept. 1982,* pp. 232–43. Tokyo: Sanseido Shoten.

Ohala, John J. 1990. There Is No Interface Between Phonology and Phonetics: A Personal View. *Journal of Phonetics* 18:153–71.

Ohala, John J. 1994. The Frequency Code Underlies the Sound-Symbolic Use of Voice Pitch. In Leanne Hinton, Johanna Nichols, & John J. Ohala, eds., *Sound Symbolism,* pp. 325–47. Cambridge: Cambridge University Press.

Ohala, John J., & Jeri J. Jaeger, eds. 1986. *Experimental Phonology.* Orlando, FL: Academic Press.

Oswalt, Robert L. 1994. Inanimate Imitatives in English. In Leanne Hinton, Johanna Nichols, & John J. Ohala, eds., *Sound Symbolism,* pp. 293–306. Cambridge: Cambridge University Press.

Padden, Carol. 1986. Verbs and Role-Shifting in ASL. In Carol A. Padden, ed., *Proceedings of the Fourth National Symposium on Sign Language Research and Teaching,* pp. 44–57. Silver Spring, MD: National Association of the Deaf.

Padden, Carol. 1988. *Interaction of Morphology and Syntax in American Sign Language.* New York: Garland Publishing.

Pizzuto, Elena, Penny Boyes-Braem, & Virginia Volterra. 1996. Seeing Through Signs' Iconicity: A Crosslinguistic-Crosscultural Study of Signers and Speakers. Paper presented to the Fifth International Conference on Theoretical Issues in Sign Language Research, September 19–22, Montreal, Quebec, Canada.

Poizner, Howard, Edward S. Klima, & Ursula Bellugi. 1987. *What the Hands Reveal About the Brain.* Cambridge, MA: MIT Press.

Reddy, Michael. 1979. The Conduit Metaphor – A Case of Frame Conflict in Our Language About Language. In A. Ortony, ed., *Metaphor and Thought,* pp. 284–324. Cambridge: Cambridge University Press.

Regier, Terry. 1996. *The Human Semantic Potential: Spatial Language and Constrained Connectionism.* Cambridge, MA: MIT Press.

Rhodes, Richard. 1994. Aural Images. In Leanne Hinton, Johanna Nichols, & John J. Ohala, eds., *Sound Symbolism,* pp. 276–92. Cambridge: Cambridge University Press.

Rosch, Eleanor. 1977. Human Categorization. In N. Warren, ed., *Studies in Cross-Cultural Psychology.* London: Academic Press.

Rosch, Eleanor. 1981. Prototype Classification and Logical Classification: The Two Systems. In E. Scholnick, ed., *New Trends in Cognitive Representation: Challenges to Piaget's Theory.* Hillsdale, NJ: Lawrence Erlbaum.

Rosch, Eleanor, & Carolyn Mervis. 1975. Family Resemblances: Studies in the Internal Structure of Categories. *Cognitive Psychology* 7:573–605.

Rumelhart, D. E., J. L. McClelland, & the PDP Research Group. 1986. *Parallel Distributed Processing: Explorations in the Microstructure of Cognition, vol. I: Foundations.* Cambridge, MA: Bradford Books, MIT Press.

de Saussure, Ferdinand. 1983 (1915). *Course in General Linguistics.* Roy Harris, trans. Charles Bally, Albert Sechehaye, and Albert Reidlinger, eds. London: G. Duckworth.

Schank, R. C., & R. P. Abelson. 1977. *Scripts, Plans, Goals, and Understanding.* Hillsdale, NJ: Lawrence Erlbaum.

Senghas, Ann. 1995. Children's Contribution to the Birth of Nicaraguan Sign Language. Unpublished doctoral dissertation, Cambridge, MA: MIT.

Shibatani, Masayoshi. 1990. Japanese. In Bernard Comrie, ed., *The World's Major Languages,* pp. 855–80. Oxford: Oxford University Press.

Silverstein, Michael. 1984. On the Pragmatic 'Poetry' of Prose: Parallelism, Repetition, and Cohesive Structure in the Time Course of Dyadic Conversation. In Deborah Schiffrin, ed., *Meaning, Form, and Use in Context: Linguistic Applications,* pp. 181–99. Washington, DC: Georgetown University Press.

Singleton, Jenny L., Susan Goldin-Meadow, & David McNeill. 1995. The Cataclysmic Break Between Gesticulation and Sign: Evidence Against a Unified Continuum of Gestural Communication. In Karen Emmorey & Judy Reilly, eds., *Language, Gesture, and Space,* pp. 287–311. Hillsdale, NJ: Lawrence Erlbaum.

Slobin, Dan I. 1996. From "Thought and Language" to "Thinking for Speaking." In J. J. Gumperz & S. C. Levinson, eds., *Rethinking Linguistic Relativity,* pp. 70–96. Cambridge, MA: Cambridge University Press.

Stokoe, William C. 1960. *Sign Language Structure.* Studies in Linguistics Occasional Papers 8. Buffalo, NY: University of Buffalo Press.

Stokoe, William C. 1986. Comment on Pulleyblank: Duality in Language Evolution. *Sign Language Studies* 51:135–44.

Supalla, S. J. 1991. Manually Coded English: The Modality Question in Signed Language Development. In Patricia Siple & Susan D. Fischer, eds., *Theoretical*

Issues in Sign Language Research. Vol. 2, *Psychology,* pp. 85–110. Chicago: University of Chicago Press.

Supalla, Ted. 1978. Morphology of Verbs of Motion and Location in American Sign Language. In Frank Caccamise and Doin Hicks, eds., *American Sign Language in a Bilingual, Bicultural Context: Proceedings of the Second National Symposium on Sign Language Research and Teaching,* pp. 27–45. Coronado, CA: National Association of the Deaf.

Supalla, Ted. 1986. The Classifier System in American Sign Language. In Colette Craig, ed., *Noun Classes and Categorization,* pp. 181–213. Amsterdam: John Benjamins.

Supalla, Ted. 1990. Serial Verbs of Motion in ASL. In Susan D. Fischer and Patricia Siple, eds., *Theoretical Issues in Sign Language Research, Vol. 1: Linguistics,* pp. 127–152. Chicago: University of Chicago Press.

Sweetser, Eve. 1980. Tagalog subjecthood revisited. In J. Kreiman & A. Ojeda, eds., *Papers from the Sixteenth Regional Meeting of the Chicago Linguistic Society,* pp. 323–41. Chicago: Chicago Linguistic Society.

Sweetser, Eve. 1987. Metaphorical Models of Thought and Speech: A Comparison of Historical Directions and Metaphorical Mappings in the Two Domains. In Jon Aske, Natasha Beery, Laura Michaelis, and Hana Filip, eds., *Proceedings of the Thirteenth Annual Meeting of the Berkeley Linguistics Society.* Berkeley, CA: Berkeley Linguistics Society.

Sweetser, Eve. 1990. *From Etymology to Pragmatics: Metaphorical and Cultural Aspects of Semantic Structure.* Cambridge: Cambridge University Press.

Sweetser, Eve. 1995. Coalignment in Metaphorical Systems. Paper presented at the International Cognitive Linguistics Association Conference, July 16–21, Albuquerque, NM.

Talmy, Leonard. 1985a. Lexicalization Patterns: Semantic Structure in Lexical Forms. In T. Shopen, ed., *Language Typology and Syntactic Description, Vol. 3: Grammatical Categories and the Lexicon,* pp. 57–149. Cambridge, MA: Cambridge University Press.

Talmy, Leonard. 1985b. Force Dynamics in Language and Thought. In *Parasession on Causatives and Agentivity, Chicago Linguistic Society, 21st Regional Meeting,* pp. 293–337. Chicago: Chicago Linguistic Society.

Talmy, Leonard. 1987. The Relation of Grammar to Cognition. In Brygida Rudzka-Ostyn, ed., *Topics in Cognitive Linguistics.* Amsterdam: John Benjamins.

Taub, Sarah F. 1997. Language in the Body: Iconicity and Metaphor in American Sign Language. Unpublished doctoral dissertation, University of California, Berkeley.

Taub, Sarah F. 1998. Multiple Metaphors in Single ASL Signs. Poster presented to the Fourth Conference on Conceptual Structure, Discourse, and Language, October 10–12, Atlanta, GA.

Taub, Sarah F. 1999. Path Directions in ASL Agreement Verbs Are Predictable on Semantic Grounds. In Shin Ja Hwang and Arle Lommel, eds., *LACUS Forum XXV,* pp. 73–86. Chapel Hill, NC: Linguistic Association of Canada and the United States.

Taub, Sarah F. 2001. Complex Superposition of Metaphors in an ASL Poem. In V. Dively, M. Metzger, S. Taub, & A. Baer, eds., *TISLR 6: The Sixth International*

Conference on Theoretical Issues in Sign Language Research. Washington, DC: Gallaudet University Press.

Tomasello, Michael. 1999. Children's Syntactic Development. Paper presented at the Sixth International Cognitive Linguistics Conference, July 10–16, Stockholm, Sweden.

Traugott, Elizabeth. 1975. Spatial Expressions of Tense and Temporal Sequencing: A Contribution to the Study of Semantic Fields. *Semiotica* 15(3):207–30.

Traugott, Elizabeth. 1978. On the Expression of Spatio-Temporal Relation in Language. In J. Greenberg, C. A. Ferguson, & E. A. Moravcik, *Universals of Human Language*, Vol. 3. Stanford, CA: Stanford University Press.

Washabaugh, William, James C. Woodward, & Susan DeSantis. 1978. Providence Island Sign Language: A Context-Dependent Language. *Anthropological Linguistics* 20:95–109.

Webb, Rebecca A. 1997. Linguistic Features of Metaphorical Gestures. Unpublished doctoral dissertation, University of Rochester, N.Y.

Wilbur, Ronnie Bring. 1987. *American Sign Language: Linguistic and Applied Dimensions*. Boston: Little, Brown.

Wilbur, Ronnie B., Mark E. Bernstein, & Rebecca Kantor. 1985. The Semantic Domain of Classifiers in American Sign Language. *Sign Language Studies* 46:1–38.

Wilcox, Phyllis Perrin. 1993. Metaphorical Mapping in American Sign Language. Unpublished doctoral dissertation, University of New Mexico, Albuquerque, NM.

Wilcox, Phyllis Perrin. 1995. Metaphor, Metonym and Synecdoche in American Sign Language: A Cognitive Intertropic Relationship. Paper presented at the International Cognitive Linguistics Association Conference, July 16–21, Albuquerque, NM.

Wilcox, Phyllis Perrin. 1998. GIVE: Acts of Giving in American Sign Language. In John Newman, ed., *The Linguistics of Giving*, pp. 175–207. Amsterdam: John Benjamins.

Wilcox, Phyllis Perrin. 2000. *Metaphor in American Sign Language*. Washington, DC: Gallaudet University Press.

Wilcox, Sherman. 1998. Cognitive Iconicity and Signed Language Universals. Paper presented at the Fourth Conference on Conceptual Structure, Discourse, and Language, October 10–12, Atlanta, GA.

Winitz, H., M. E. Scheib, & J. A. Reed. 1972. Identification of Stops and Vowels for the Burst Portion of /p, t, k/ Isolated from Conversational Speech. *Journal of the Acoustical Society of America* 51:1309–17.

Woodward, James. 1979. *Signs of Sexual Behavior: An Introduction to Some Sex-Related Vocabulary in American Sign Language*. Silver Spring, MD: T. J. Publishers.

Index

ASL examples are in SMALL CAPS. English examples are in *italics*.

249